A More Perfect Union
The Peculiar Predicament of American Democracy

A.M.N. Goldman

A MORE PERFECT UNTION

Copyright © 2014 by Angel Goldman

Illustrations and Design by La Lune Literary
Copyright © 2014 by La Lune Literary, LLC

All rights reserved.

First La Lune Literary Edition June 2014

Published by La Lune Literary, LLC
laluneliterary.com

No part of this book may be reproduced in any form or by any electronic or mechanical means, including information storage and retrieval systems, without written permission from the author, except for the use of brief quotations in a book review.

Includes bibliographical references and endnotes.
1. United States — History — Revolution, 1775-1783.
2. United States — Constitutional History.

Contents

Preface	ix
Introduction	xiii

1. **THE FOUNDING FATHERS: THE GOODLY GENTLEMEN** — 1
   - The Setting — 2
   - WASHINGTON — 3
   - JEFFERSON — 5
   - ADAMS — 7
   - MADISON — 9
   - HAMILTON — 11
   - FRANKLIN — 13
   - A GENERATION OF GREAT MEN — 15

2. **RADICAL THEORIES & MAJOR DEBATES** — 18
   - That 'Peculiar Institution' - On Slavery — 19
   - Separating God and Government – On Religious Freedom — 22
   - The Individual vs. the Community – On Unity — 26
   - A Republic or a Democracy – On Representation — 30
   - Federalist vs. Anti-Federalist – On Centralization — 33

3. **OUR FOUNDATION – THE CONSTITUTION** — 39
   - The Literal : What Our Constitution Really Says — 40
   - The Implied: What the Founders Meant — 46
   - Constitutional "Intent" — 49
   - By Finance: Pursuing the Dollar — 54

4. **CAPITALISM AND THE AMERICAN DREAM** — 57
   - Taxation without Representation — 58
   - Bring Me Your Poor — 61
   - A New Deal — 65
   - The Price of Freedom — 69

5. THE BIG BUSINESS BOOM AND BUST	71
The Cost of Doing Business: Corporate-Government Relations	73
Corporate Takeover: Co-Opting the American Dream	76
Networked: Connections among the Elite	80
6. IN PURSUIT OF HAPPINESS – AMERICAN FINANCIAL LIFE	85
The Lies We Tell Ourselves: Living in a Land of Make-Believe	86
Bad Habits: Choices that Undermine our own Wealth	91
Keep it Simple: Earning our Way to the Dream	95
By Society: Our White Picket Fence	99
7. THE PRESS OR THE BUSINESS OF INFORMING AMERICA	103
Freedoms from the Founders: An Unfettered Press	105
Yellow Journalism: Raking up the Muck	109
Selling Stories Instead of Telling Them	113
8. THE PREACHER- FINDING THE GOD OF FREEDOM	118
Faith of Our Fathers: Revolutionary Religion	120
Government under God: The Role of Religion in a Republic	124
Faithful Followers: Religion in Modern America	129
9. CULTURAL CONFORMITY: WEALTH AND POWER IN AMERICA	134
High Society- The Cult of Celebrity	136
Interested Parties – Factions in Society	142
Undue Influence- Greater Voices for "Greater" Citizens	147
By Politics: Buying Office	149
10. THE PRICE OF A VOTE – MOUTHS AND MEANS	153
The Great Lobby – The Perceptions of the Public	154
Money is the Root of all Evil – Campaign Finance	160
The Next Election...and the Next	164

11. WHO CAN YELL THE LOUDEST: THE TWO
    PARTY SYSTEM 169
    Partisanship 171
    The Perks of Power: Gerrymandering 176
    The Worth of Power: Pork-Barreling 180

12. MAINTAINING THE STATUS QUO 184
    Party Rule 186
    Political Stagnation 190
    Public Apathy 194
    By Us: Looking Towards the Future & Pursuing
    Permanence 198

13. ACQUIRING ECONOMIC STABILITY 202
    Slaves to the Dollar 204
    Savings and Solutions 208

14. REAL SOCIAL SECURITY 217
    Putting the Pieces Together 219
    Saving a Society 223

15. PERFECTING POLITICS 232
    Becoming an Eminent Citizen 233
    Speak Loudly… 239
    …And Carry a Big Stick 243

    Endnotes 249
    Acknowledgments 261
    About the Author 263
    Other Tomes from Our Hoard 265

For Isabella

"If I speak in human or even angelic tongues, but do not have love, I am a resounding gong or a clashing cymbal. And if I have the gift of prophecy and comprehend all mysteries and all knowledge; if I have all faith so as to move mountains, but do not have love, I am nothing...Love never fails."

Corinthians 13: 1-2, 8

PREFACE

We the People of the United States, in Order to form a more perfect Union, establish Justice, insure domestic Tranquility, provide for the common defense, promote the general Welfare, and secure the Blessings of Liberty to ourselves and our Posterity, do ordain and establish this Constitution for the United States of America.[1]

This book began as a conversation, a rather dispiriting conversation, with a group of fellow Naval Officers. Despite taking an oath and swearing to "support and defend the Constitution of the United States against all enemies, foreign and domestic" and to "bear true faith and allegiance to the same," many officers and many more enlisted service members that I encountered had no idea what exactly was in the Constitution, and much less what any of it meant. Even as a graduate student in History, the same scenario faced me over and over again. Most Americans, even highly educated Americans, had no idea what citizenry meant or what the nature of their own government was. The confusion that abounds among the general citizenry was dumbfounding to me, particularly as the scion of a highly political family (not that politicians particularly seem to know or care either). So despite my usual desire to pursue studies geared towards other facets of history, this book was born.

Primarily, this book sets out to clarify the uncertainty surrounding the basics of what citizenry in America is and how our government was designed to work. It is also an attempt to address our heading while we swim in a sea of confusion. Despite numerous political and historical works geared at our revolutionary origins, our founding fathers, our Constitution, and modern politics, no one book attempts to present this information coherently and in one place for citizens to truly understand and appreciate what it all means (much less to address any of this with some semblance of objectivity and historical perspective). My book interweaves history and current affairs in an attempt to rectify these oversights. My argument behind this presentation of information is surprisingly simple (and yet somehow so overlooked) – that our government and our place in it is about participation, perspective, and progress.

History is truly a fascinating subject (or at least it always has been for me). Contrary to popular opinion, it is more than mere dates and facts. Our history and our perceptions of that history set the tone of our entire culture and country. It defines us and our values as a people and a nation. History colors our views of not just the past, but also of our present and future. Through the lens of history, we can evaluate how we are doing and where we are going. And history's lessons can guide us, both as examples of what to avoid, as well as of what to follow.

To that end, this book is an analytical, philosophical history of our nation's government. Much has been made in politics about the need for change, about realizing the vision of our founders, and respecting our Constitution. Yet no one wants to talk about a cohesive idea of what this entails or how to accomplish it. How do we take our revolutionary past and bring its spirit into our present, using it to shape our future? Simply put, only by understanding our past can we hope to achieve a better future. And that is what this work is all about – using the past to illuminate the present and light a way forward.

In the past few years, it has been particularly evident (and fairly shocking) that most Americans do not really know the history or the very basics of our government. And therefore, we have no idea what is currently going on in our country or where we are heading. Many politicians and theorists have devoted a great deal of time and money to telling the public what our Constitution "really" means. But since there is always an agenda attached to their interpretations, they are very rarely historically accurate. In fact, now more than ever, ignorance governs the American citizenry.

In the pursuit of happiness, Americans have always been a particularly determined people. From our Revolution to our Constitution to today, we have always striven to provide for the happiness of our nation through good governance. Each generation has faced its own challenges and overcome them, thus continuing our country's tradition of greatness through perseverance. Our generation is only the latest in an illustrious lineage of American citizenry. So we must ask ourselves, will our actions now demonstrate the same commitment to country as those of our forefathers? When did the government as a system become more important than the individual citizens it is supposed to represent? And will the path we carve out now be one that can inspire and further the happiness of our posterity?

These questions that we face, as citizens in a democratic nation, will only grow more pressing with time. Only by arming ourselves with information that increases our knowledge of government can we hope to answer them. Now is the time that we must come together, once again, as a nation in order to form a more perfect union.

Introduction
By Design: For Us, By Us

"Just as an architect who puts up a large building first surveys and tests the ground to see if it can bear the weight, so the wise lawgiver begins not by laying down laws good in themselves, but by finding out whether the people for whom the laws are intended is able to support them. [1]*"*

-Jean Jacques Rousseau

As Americans, we have always been led to believe that our form of government, our Constitution, our way of life, is somehow inherently superior to those around us. After all, we are the proud owners of the world's first modern government controlled by the popular vote. The founding fathers of our revolutionary generation designed our democratic system, and, in theory, have passed it down "untarnished" and somehow unchanged to us. Everyone knows that our design works so well because it was created for us, by a group of men who were just like us. Or at least just like all the good and noble things we see in ourselves.

Yet, these notions that our design and its designers are the pinnacles of perfection present problems. If our democracy has always had flawless fundamentals, then why would change ever be necessary? Why would amendments ever even be needed? This is especially troublesome when one bears in mind that there have already been 27 articles added to the Constitution, the most recent of which was ratified in 1992. Not only that, but many of the modifications made by these 27 amendments contain principles we now consider absolutely essential in a modern democracy. Our Bill of Rights, including freedom of religion, press, and speech, as well as the right to bear arms, was actually established through the first 10 amendments. The 13th through 15th amendments, which abolished slavery and grant the right to vote regardless of race, were not enacted until the late 1860s (and not necessarily honored until the 1980s.) Women did not receive the right to vote until the 19th amendment, passed in 1920. And these laws had to be *added onto* our supposedly infallible Constitution, the very basis of our democratic design.

The most ironic part of the now almost mythological status of the Constitution, and its framers, is that the men who designed our government knew changes would need to be made along the way. (They also knew that they themselves were far from perfect.) They realized that change is both a difficult and complicated process. After beginning our government with a Revolution, the founders were so concerned by the prospect of internal chaos or even war over potential changes to our government's design that George Washington himself took the time in his *Farewell Address* to exhort the people that

> *"If in the opinion of the people, the distribution or modification of the constitutional powers be in any particular wrong, let it be corrected by an amendment in the way which the Constitution designates. But let there be no change by usurpation; for though this, in one instance, may be the instrument of good, it is the customary weapon by which free governments are destroyed."*[2]

The entire point of establishing the amendment process was so that the country would not descend into chaos and another revolution when new matters required the government to change. This principle and the founders' foresight in establishing this process are easily demonstrated by how quickly amendments went into use.

The very first amendments, the Bill of Rights represented the ideals of the revolutionary generation, but they were only added after the initial Constitutional ratification process. The reason the members of the Constitutional Convention did not originally include them was because the ideas expressed in the Bill of Rights were so much a part of Revolutionary rhetoric that they took their existence as part of the new government for granted. In fact, the general assumption was that if the Constitution did not specifically grant a power to the government, then it automatically belonged to the people. However, for some revolutionaries, this was not enough, and they insisted that these ideas be codified into law. Considering how often the first 10 amendments are cited in our era, it is fortunate a few stubborn and untrusting individuals and their home-states insisted on them being written down and written into the Constitution.

Stubbornness and the occasional delusions of grandeur aside, the Founding Fathers knew they were far from perfect. The sheer amount of heated post-Revolutionary in-fighting told them that. Even at the time, different people had different ideas of what the Revolution was supposed to have meant. And we have inherited these differences in opinion, which is why it's not all that shocking that people still have varying ideas of what our democracy entitles one to. The fact of the matter is, the founders were not flawless and neither is our Constitution or our government. They did not build a completely infallible and timeless system; they constructed something they knew the people of the time could live with. As Thomas Jefferson so aptly put it, *"On every question of construction [of the Constitution], let us carry ourselves back to the time when the Constitution was adopted, and recollect the spirit manifested in the debates."*[3] That spirit was not necessarily about all the issues and concerns that are present today; that is why the framers created amendments in the first place, because they knew change would eventually come.

So who were these men who built our nation? The answer may seem strange when we think about George Washington being raised on a "farm," but our founding fathers were actually the elite of the Revolutionary generation. Our government reflects their ideas, theories, and situations in life. Despite what is commonly implied, these men were not just like us today, and often, not very much like the people of their time either. Their theories were not always the prevalent ones of the day, and they did not even unanimously agree with one another very often. They debated, and fought, and eventually established a Constitution that most people could accept and live under. But the Constitution was not some grand universal consensus made by all the people for all the people. A few men created and designed it for everyone. That is what representational government entails. As Jefferson also explained, when interpreting the Constitution, *"instead of trying what meaning may be squeezed out of the text, or intended against it, conform to the probable one in which it was passed."*[4] And if the condition it was passed under no longer exists, they changed it, properly through the amendment process- the Constitution was not made to be manipulated to fit every possible circumstance presented by human history.

Yet whatever faults or good it may have originally possessed, our government has strayed further and further from the principles espoused by the Founding Fathers. Though the framers were not typical of their generation (the Constitution was never created "by the people"), they designed it with the common citizens of their day in mind. Representational government being what it is, the framers believed they represented the people and their desires, but the average man did not and could not typically hold political office. There are many myths like this surrounding the Constitution and its origins because, as a people, it pleases us to believe them. But, to unravel all the rhetoric surrounding the very basis of our government, we have to examine the founding fathers, their theories, and the Constitution they bequeathed to us. To discover what they truly intended for our government and how it applies to our governance today, only a real understanding, not the legends of the Revolution and its heroes, can aid us. We have to actually think about our union if we are ever going to make it a more perfect one.

The Founding Fathers: The Goodly Gentlemen

"Associate yourself with Men of good Quality if you Esteem your own Reputation; for 'tis better to be alone than in bad Company."[1]

This line was just one of one hundred and one lessons on gentlemanly behavior copied by a young schoolboy into his notebook. Yet, when one reads this line and its other companions, there can be no doubt that the schoolboy took their messages deeply to heart. What better company could there be than a nation's founding fathers? And who has ever enjoyed a better reputation than the great George Washington? The great general and gentleman, the ideal American, both during the Revolution and our own time, George Washington was the first among equals. To understand this prestigious group of men, we must know where they came from and how they thought. After all, what type of men could deserve such grand reputations and give so much for a country not even in existence when they began? In exploring the answer to this question, and the men it pertains to, we will draw one step closer to understanding the government they have given to us, and what has become of it.

The Setting

> "*Valour soars above What the world calls misfortune and affliction. These are not ills; else would they never fall On heaven's first favourites, and the best of men: The gods, in bounty, work up storms about us, That give mankind occasion to exert Their hidden strength, and throw out into practice Virtues*"[2]
>
> - Cato to Juba in Addison's play *Cato*

Unsurprisingly, the play in which Cato speaks the above lines was often staged throughout the colonial period, and was well known to be George Washington's personal favorite. Valor and virtue, both were the noblest qualities to the revolutionary generation, and both were part of the symphony of liberty which had echoed in the minds of the colonists from the days of the Mayflower all the way to the Revolution. These two ideals were conjoined in the minds of those who had settled in America, and Revolutionary era Americans believed that these twin values would guide the course of the colonies along a better path than the one they had left behind in Europe. Not that the colonials did not firmly believe themselves to be loyal British subjects; for they did. But they had all left the Old World for a reason, and they felt that they deserved a certain level of treatment from their government, that they were entitled to certain rights as free citizens. Addison's *Cato* spoke to these closely held beliefs, and perhaps they appreciated the play so much because *Cato* reflected not only their values, but eventually their lives as well.

Cato describes a time in ancient history when Rome's borders were at some of its largest, but also when Roman values and government were under siege. For many British-American colonists, old Rome was an apt comparison to the expanding British Empire and its ever-changing rules. A distant Caesar had gained control of Rome and turned Roman democracy into a dictatorship. In doing so, he began to strip the people of their rights and freedoms, and left the people without a voice in their own governance. He then used his vast armies to enforce his rule throughout his new Empire. While the play's messages on valor, virtue, and freedom are timeless, the specific scenario presented in the story was also particularly poignant during the years leading up to the Revolution.

Our founding fathers had grown up in a time of warfare on the American and European continents, but also a time of great expansion-geographically, economically, and socially. Following the French and Indian War, the distant British government began to change the rights the colonists had long enjoyed. The colonies joined together to protest what they saw as abuses by the British King and Parliament, and to demand a greater voice in their own governance. The British responded by quartering increasingly large numbers of troops in their quarrelsome colonies and enacting more restrictive regulation against them. Skirmishes began to break out, until finally, the situation developed into a full blown war of revolution.

In their minds, all the colonists wanted was the representation they felt entitled to as loyal British citizens. And the British government consistently refused to acknowledge their claims. All the revolutionaries could do was use their valor and virtue, and like Cato, hope to weather the storms heaven had set against them. And so change came to the American continent, through virtuous guidance and valorous actions by its own citizens. Our Constitution and government is as much a part of these men as it is anything else, and to truly understand it, we must first know the people who created it. Fortunately, they were in the right place in history, at the right time; and most importantly, they had the right cast of characters for the job.

Dramatis Personae

WASHINGTON

Every group, even one composed of strong-willed revolutionaries, needs a leader to rally behind. George Washington was that Leader.

> *"In executing the duties of my present important station, I can promise nothing but purity of intentions, and in carrying these into effect, fidelity, and diligence."*[3]
>
> – George Washington

> *"A degree of silence envelops Washington's actions; he moved slowly; one might say that he felt charged with future liberty, and that he feared to compromise it. It was not his own destiny that inspired this new species of hero: it was that of his country; he did not allow himself to enjoy what did not belong to him; but from profound humility what glory emerged!"*[4]
>
> – Francois-Rene de Chateaubriand on Washington

Bound by honesty, honor, and duty, George Washington did not merely lead an army or a nation; he headed the group of men who formed our very government. It was not so much that he was always in command, nor was he the smartest, cleverest, or even the best statesman. But, Washington was a leader of men - the leader, because his integrity was unquestionable and his judgment profound. He was not merely the ultimate gentleman, he was the consummate patriot. His influence on his peers was based on his renowned self-discipline and overwhelming sense of duty. He knew his behavior set the standard, and he constantly strove to master himself so that the example he gave, and the precedents he established, would be worthy examples for posterity.

Though a gentleman and member of the wealthy Virginia planter class, George Washington never received the level of education typical of his associates. Instead, he cultivated other, more physical talents; including hunting, dancing, and horseback riding (indeed, these final two were listed as some of his qualifications for being selected as the Commander-in-Chief of the Continental Army). He also developed his sense of duty and gentlemanly obligation; he always strived to be the ideal man. Every letter, every conversation, reflected his constant self-awareness. When writing an already dissatisfied Benedict Arnold in 1775, he reminded him that *"Every post is honorable in which a man can serve his country."*[5] And that was how Washington lived his life- dutifully accepting and applying himself to every service his country asked of him even as he grew *"not only grey, but also blind in the service of my country."*[6] Ever the leader, he never gave his country cause to regret its faith in him through word or deed.

Washington's consciousness of his actions and their effects, as well as his sense of obligation set him apart and above his colleagues. It also enabled him to play a unique role in the formation of our nation. Even at the time, his name and presence invoked reverence and awe. He stayed away from the political in-fighting that caught up the rest of the founding fathers. And instead, he deliberately chose to use his influence only in the moments where he had something important to say or in which he had carefully weighed the outcome. When the new nation was on shaky ground after the ratification of the Constitution, it was Washington's unanimous appeal that kept the country together. And it was through his example that our nation developed a stable system. Through his commitment to duty and restraint, he set the course for the presidency and his peers.

JEFFERSON

Each group needs a leader, but they also need a scholar; someone to create and support new ideas. For the framers, this was Thomas Jefferson, the Intellectual.

> *"I would rather be exposed to the inconveniences attending too much liberty than to those attending too small a degree of it."*[7]
>
> - *Thomas Jefferson*

> *"He possessed a genius of the first order. It was universal in its objects."*[8]
>
> – *Benjamin Rush on Jefferson*

Passionate, patriotic, and brilliant, Thomas Jefferson was the philosopher-statesman of the Revolutionary generation. He was obviously the most well-educated and well-traveled of his peers. His unparalleled knowledge of philosophy, history, and classical studies helped him to establish the moral and theoretical background for his famous revolutionary rhetoric. A prolific writer, he was one of the first to unite the historical and philosophical background of the colonies into a new, coherent ideology. His pamphlet, *A Summary View of the Rights of British America*, combined elements of Enlightenment theory, seventeenth century English history, traditional English law, and revolutionary era beliefs of British anti-Americanism into a radically new political theory. His memorable turns of phrase and active theorizing have made him the best-remembered and most oft-quoted framer. Jefferson's astounding intellect influenced the course of the Revolution from the very start, and he consistently endeavored to provide a strong academic background for the new America, even well after his retirement from political life.

Like many of the other founders, including Washington, Thomas Jefferson was born into the aristocracy of the Virginia planters. Though younger than some of his peers, he was thoroughly entrenched in Virginian and colonial politics by the time of the Revolution. He authored numerous important revolutionary tracts and notable documents, the crowning glory of which was the Declaration of Independence. And though he primarily wished to be remembered as *"The Author of the Declaration of American Independence, of the Statute of Virginia for Religious Freedom, and Father of the University of Virginia,"*[9] his revolutionary credentials included many political positions. He took his turn as an American diplomat, a Virginia legislator, anti-Federalist party leader, and even President. Yet, ever the *philosophe*, he desired and truly has been mostly remembered for his intellectual achievements.

As an academic idealist, Thomas Jefferson's immense acumen played an integral role in the birth of our nation. As fellow President John F. Kennedy once remarked to a group of Nobel laureates, *"I think this is the most extraordinary collection of talent, of human knowledge, that has ever been gathered together at the White House with the possible exception of when Thomas Jefferson dined alone."*[10] Jefferson's keen ideas and philosophical reasoning made him one of the top minds of his era.

Much of what we now heed and recall of our founding fathers comes directly from Thomas Jefferson. An ardent basic rights proponent, he used his influence to try and guarantee individual and state freedoms. In doing so, he faced off against Federalists like John Adams who believed in strong central government. Though his own presidency reflected many Federalist-like centralization trends, Jefferson, ever the intellectual, was never one to let practical issues or the possibility of self-contradiction get in the way of a good idea. In the end, his most lasting influence on our nation has been his ideas and words which drove his own deeds and those of the people around him.

ADAMS

The opposite of Thomas Jefferson's role was that played by John Adams. Where Jefferson was idealistic and academic, Adams was terminally rational, making him the ultimate Realist revolutionary.

> *"Now to what higher object, to what greater character, can any mortal aspire than to be possessed of all this knowledge, well digested and ready at command, to assist the feeble and friendless, to discountenance the haughty and lawless, to procure redress of wrongs, the advancement of right, to assert and maintain liberty and virtue, and to discourage and abolish tyranny and vice?"*[11]
>
> - John Adams

> *"Always an honest man, often a great one, but sometimes absolutely mad."*[12]
>
> - Thomas Jefferson on Adams

Devoted to legality, logic, and above all, liberty, John Adams was the most far-sighted of the founding fathers. He was the most logical and realistic of his peers, which greatly contributed to the accuracy of what he saw in America's future. His passion in these same opinions and beliefs also made his peers often think his notions quite 'mad'. Ironically, Adams' ideas would be so ahead of his time that they would only be vindicated in the course of history, especially in matters like the centralization of the federal government. And though he retired early upon his defeat in the presidential election of 1800, his principles were still strongly advocated in early America at all levels of governance. His ceaseless activism on behalf of a strong and free government, administered with justice and a reasonable mind, continues to leave a lasting impact on our nation.

Like Washington and Jefferson, Adams belonged to the wealthy colonial upper class, but unlike them, he called the other of the two major colonies home. A member of the Boston elite, Adams was descended from an original member of the Massachusetts Bay Colony (and his wife Abigail was loosely connected to British royalty). A lawyer by training, Adams' specialty quickly became constitutional law; his skill eventually reaching the point where he would author the entire Massachusetts Constitution on his own. Staunchly ethical, in keeping with the Puritanical heritage of Massachusetts, Adams often found himself taking and defending the unpopular position because it was the most logical, legal, and morally-correct choice. He was famous for defending the British soldiers in the Boston Massacre Trials of 1770, noting that *"Facts are stubborn things; and whatever may be our wishes, our inclinations, or the dictates of our passion, they cannot alter the state of facts and evidence."*[13] Though his stances were not always the public's preferred ones, his strong ethics saw him selected a Massachusetts legislator, Congressional representative, diplomat, and American president.

Both his greatest friend and fiercest opponent, Thomas Jefferson once referred to John Adams as the *"Colossus of Independence,"* and despite Adams' early retirement, this was a reality. Jefferson's description truly encapsulates Adams' character and his importance. His ability to take a strong moral stand, even an unpopular one, as well as his rational, legal mind were his greatest contributions to the revolution and the creation of America. In fact, Washington got along so well with him that he chose him over many others to serve as the first Vice President, no doubt, because Adams was very much a revolutionary Cato- full of valor and virtue. And like Cato, he left the political scene ahead of his time, relegated to the background as bigger forces gained control. Ultimately, it was his ability to obey the law and relinquish the presidency that helped to ensure the country's continuation, and set a tradition of peaceful transition between elected officials with opposing ideas (something that still causes many modern countries serious problems). His ability to shape government affairs and the minds of men through the reasoned positions he held and his skill with the law provided part of the framework on which our nation is built. Though not always appreciated at the time, through the hindsight of history, we can now see how invaluable his role truly was.

MADISON

But, still more was needed to round out these players. Someone had to help the differing founders like Adams and Jefferson meet in the middle. That man was James Madison, the great Compromiser.

> *"...I find in the presence of this respectable assembly an opportunity of publicly repeating my profound sense of so distinguished a confidence and of the responsibility united with it. The impressions on me are strengthened by such evidence that my faithful endeavors to discharge my arduous duties have been favorably estimated, and by a consideration of the momentous period at which the trust has been renewed."* [14]
>
> - James Madison

> *"...he acquired a habit of self-possession...Never wandering from his subject into vain declamation, but pursuing it closely...soothing always the feelings of his adversaries by civilities and softness of expression...with these consummate powers were united a pure and spotless virtue which no calumny has ever attempted to sully."* [15]
>
> – Thomas Jefferson on James Madison

Committed, eloquent, and persuasive, James Madison was the quintessential legislator. Known for his great oratorical skill and ability to argue his point even to his staunchest opponents, Madison orchestrated many of the compromises essential to our government's creation. His keen aptitude to sense what others wanted and how it worked into his own goals enabled him to fit multiple agendas into one legal framework. He was devoted to states' rights and to ensuring that the Constitution he helped create was respected. Adamantly refusing to go beyond the authority he was given, even as President, he respected his elected position. His obedience to the laws he developed, even while in power himself, and his unsurpassed negotiation skills made Madison an incredibly important part of the team of America's founding men.

A Virginian plantation owner like Washington and Jefferson, James Madison's appearance did not in any way reflect his gentlemanly origins nor his legendary legislative prowess. Once affectionately called *"but a withered little apple-John"* by Washington Irving, Madison was small, sickly, and very frail for most of his life. Yet beneath that weak shell was a vibrant, highly educated mind- well known from a young age for being a brilliant procedural man in both the state and colonial legislatures. Responsible for much of the Constitution and the compromises that made it, Madison continued to champion the document, co-authoring the *Federalist Papers* with Alexander Hamilton and John Jay. In doing so, he was extremely influential in getting his peers to pass the Constitution into law. Believing in a federal government strong enough to hold the states together, but unwilling to accept its encroachments on rights belonging to the same, Madison eventually broke with the Federalists and sided with longtime-friend Thomas Jefferson and his Democratic-Republicans. Not just a president, he served long terms in the Virginia State and federal legislatures as well as in other President's cabinets. Ultimately his greatest influence was his greatest talent – getting his peers to cooperate and come together on the laws that shaped our nation.

"The Father of the Constitution", James Madison championed the development of that famous manuscript. He helped to create the agreements, and bargain his contemporaries into a legal code they could accept. In

arguing for its creation, he once wrote that *"If men were angels, no government would be necessary...In framing a government which is to be administered by men over men, the great difficulty lies in this: you must first enable the government to control the governed; and in the next place oblige it to control itself."*[16] As the chief framer of the Constitution, and the arbiter among great gentlemen, Madison's sway over our form of government cannot be denied. It was him who helped the others come to a consensus, who promoted it, and who constantly defended its integrity even after leaving office. In doing so, Madison's efforts have earned him a place in our pantheon of national idols.

HAMILTON

But where would any of the founding fathers be without someone to carry their thoughts to the people and push passion for popular governance forward? It would be Alexander Hamilton that played the role of the first true Partisan.

> *"I have thought it my duty to exhibit things as they are, not as they ought to be."*[17]
>
> *- Alexander Hamilton*

> *"This I can venture to advance from a thorough knowledge of him, that there are few men to be found, of his age, who has a more general knowledge than he possesses, and none whose soul is more firmly engaged in the cause, or who exceeds him in probity and sterling virtue."*[18]
>
> *- George Washington on Alexander Hamilton*

Charismatic, clever, and strident, Alexander Hamilton was the consummate revolutionary politician. Famous for his often daring military service, impassioned politics, and business acumen, Hamilton helped to shape both the political and economic future of our nation. A staunch believer in strong central government and even stronger federal financial policies, he pursued his causes with an unsurpassed single-mindedness. Though cut down before his time, Hamilton's ideas and influence continued to affect the development of the early United States. His understanding of the passions which governed politics, and his ability to manipulate them, enabled him to play a key role in enacting legislation and crafting our government.

Unlike many of the other founding fathers, Alexander Hamilton did not come from wealthy origins or even the thirteen colonies. He was the bastard son of a semi-divorced French Caribbean beauty and a Scottish merchant. Despite this, Hamilton's intelligence and charisma did not go unnoticed by the local aristocracy, who sponsored Hamilton's education, taking up a fund to send him to King's College (now Columbia University). It was his immense talent and personal charm that saw him a wealthy businessman and prominent political writer by the start of the revolution despite his young age. Ever fervent in his ideals, when the war began, Hamilton chose military service over a political position, serving as Washington's chief of staff and one of his most trusted advisors. However, his true legacy would come from his time as a member of Washington's cabinet, his work on the *Federalist Papers*, and his place in the first political party wars. The first true partisan, Hamilton's role in the formation of the Federalist Party has had some of the most lasting effects on how we view politics today. Ever sure of his position, he died that day dueling with Aaron Burr defending both his honor as a gentleman and his belief that his ideas were the right ones.

Alexander Hamilton's firm, even stubborn, conviction in the truth of his principles, as well as his willingness to do anything to get them across, were both his most awesome attributes and his undoing. Despite his own lowly origins, he believed in the gentlemanly code and those who had gotten him to his high post, making him one of the staunchest centrists and most vehement opponents of complete democracy. During a speech in New York urging the ratification of the Constitution, he reminded his listeners that *"It has been observed that a pure democracy if it were practicable would be the most perfect government. Experience has proved that no position is more false than this. The ancient democracies in which the people themselves deliberated never possessed one good feature of government. Their very character was tyranny; their figure deformity.*"[19] Hamilton's utter faith in these principles led him to fund and found the Federalist Party, whose level of partisanship often provoked enmity from rival founders. Of all of them, he understood the passionate nature of the people and how they would react to different tugs on their political emotions. Thus, his most important contribution to our nation was his role in firmly establishing the two-party system. For Hamilton knew that without passion, popular politics would die. In creating a subsystem to ensure popular participation, Hamilton helped to set a political precedent which fundamentally controls our system of governance.

FRANKLIN

Finally, there was Hamilton's polar opposite. Whereas Hamilton divided and impassioned the people in politics, someone was needed to serve a role reminding his brethren of their common ground. This was Benjamin Franklin, the Unifier.

> *"We must all hang together, or assuredly we shall all hang separately."*[20]
>
> - Benjamin Franklin
>
> *"Eripuit caelo fulmen sceptrumque tyrannis (He seized the lightening from the Gods and the scepter from the Tyrants)."*[21]
>
> - Turgot on Benjamin Franklin

Experienced, practical, and sagacious, Benjamin Franklin was truly the glue that held the founding fathers together. Internationally famous by the time of the Revolution, both for his knowledge and wit, Franklin's renown lent much needed weight to the revolutionary proceedings. He was the one who kept his much younger colleagues on track and moving forward. As an original contributor to the ideals and writings that spurred the colonies towards revolution, Franklin was able to bring a true sense of cohesion to competing political theories. For Franklin, freedom had been his bread and butter for half a century prior to the signing of the Declaration of Independence. Liberty was his life, and his dedication to the cause challenged those around him to set their differences aside and come together with a unified plan that the new nation could support.

Of all his later associates, Benjamin Franklin had the only true middle class background. As the fifteenth of seventeen children born to a Boston tallow chandler[22], he was apprenticed early to his older brother, a printer. Though without any real formal schooling, he fueled his own education through voracious reading. Perhaps, it is these origins which would explain his sometimes folksy brand of wisdom and wit, as well as his devotion to the betterment of the common man. Eventually, Franklin ran away to Philadelphia after being caught publishing political tracts under the name 'Mrs. Silence Dogood." From there, he acquired both fame and fortune as an author, political theorist, activist, scientist, inventor, and printer. Through his numerous activities, Franklin's influence on the ideological foundation of the revolution was great, and his political position by the early 1770s was very prominent. Thus, during the war, it was Franklin who served as the colonies' key diplomat-securing the French alliance, and at the end, negotiating the Treaty of Paris with the British. When he returned to serve as a Constitutional Convention delegate, he was both aged and ill, but he would not allow infighting to cause the entire experiment to fail just as it began. Franklin's long lifetime of work convincing others to answer the call of freedom is what made him so important to the establishment and continuation of our government.

An ally to anyone who loved liberty, Franklin commanded great respect and had few political enemies (unlike nearly every other founder). For above all, he recognized that *"the Good particular Men may do separately...is small, compared with what they may do collectively, or by joint Endeavor and Interest."*[23] His ability to see beyond petty differences to the true objective allowed him to bring a sense of unity and purpose to all the dealings in which he participated. Throughout a lifetime of work, Franklin's true genius was not in his adherence to any particular agenda or party line, but rather the pure absence of dogma in his beliefs. His influence over our nation was his ability to moderate any discussion and to inspire others to bring their own talents and ideas onto the democratic scene. A champion of freedom, Franklin's importance in ideologically and politically establishing the very foundation of the United States cannot be underestimated.

A GENERATION OF GREAT MEN

Yet though these icons played the key roles in a cast whose drama shaped our nation, there is a voice still missing. For what of the mass of ordinary citizens who served in the militias and armies, and won the revolution with their bodies, hearts, and minds? These were the people our nation was built on and for, the Common Man- the Backbone of the entire American experiment.

> *"Happy, thrice happy shall they be pronounced hereafter who have contributed anything, who have performed the meanest office in erecting this stupendous fabrick of Freedom and Empire on the Broad Basis of Independency; who have assisted in protecting the rights of humane nature and establishing an asylum for the poor and oppressed of all nations and religions."* [24]
>
> - George Washington to the People

> *"Whenever the people are well informed, they can be trusted with their own government; that whenever things get to far wrong as to attract their notice, they may be relied on to set them to rights."* [25]
>
> - Thomas Jefferson on the People

Prosaic and conservative, but malleable, the Revolutionary common man formed the foundation upon which our government was built. Overwhelmingly rural in nature, revolutionary America was mostly small towns dispersed between farming communities, with a few small cities serving as regional centres. These were the men and women who bought the freedom of a nation, but who did not rise to the ranks of its leaders. Highly traditional and very spiritual, it was long-held core beliefs which led these people on the road to war. Though obvious regional differences existed and not all agreed, most people, even Loyalists, firmly thought they had rights that were "unalienable". Under the leadership and guidance of the founding fathers, they would give their lives to achieve a previously unthinkable goal – independence.

Unlike the founding fathers, the vast majority of colonial Americans lived a very mediocre existence. In comparison to the men who championed the development of our nation's government, the common man was significantly poorer, less educated, and more wrapped up in local concerns. Though part of the new nation was held in bondage, most Americans would be lucky to own even one slave unlike Washington, Jefferson, and Madison (who each had large, slave-labor, plantations). The peoples' lives were governed by the seasons that dictated farming schedules and local politics. Unlike the framers, few had the time or the resources to commit to any long-term revolutionary or constitutional activity. Instead, they relied on these gentlemen to act in their stead, and to represent them. And if a gentleman truly failed in this capacity, they would take steps to deal with him and remove him from his position. Though primarily concerned with local and personal interests, it was the common man's willingness to be roused to action, and to do something when things that mattered got out of hand, that created our country.

Commonplace revolutionary Americans formed the mold that our founding fathers used to produce our government. While not as prominently remembered as the founders, the average man's contribution to establishing and maintaining our government is undeniable (though often overlooked). Without the foot soldier, it does not matter how poor or great the general is - for he has no army with which to win the war. Without the rioters to make the crowds, it does not matter if one has the greatest oratorical skills of all time and even better ideas – for there is no one to incite. And if the people who serve these functions are unwilling, then there are no revolutions, no changes, and no popular governments. The willingness of the common man to answer the call of duty was paramount to the American Revolution's success. Though these average colonials did not sit down and create their own government, their elite built it for them and their sacrifices. The framers were good architects who designed our Constitution to fit inside the mold instead of around it. Thus our government was built by the few, for the many, in the hope that it would serve those dutiful new Americans well.

Radical Theories & Major Debates

"...freedom of men under government is to have a standing rule to live by, common to every one of that society, and made by the legislative power erected in it. A liberty to follow my own will in all things where that rule prescribes not, not to be subject to the inconstant, uncertain, unknown, arbitrary will of another man."[1]

- John Locke

A few good men and a revolution do not a working government make. It only takes a quick look around us to see how easily a revolution, democratic or otherwise, can fail. Throughout the world, in Asia, Africa, South America, and even Europe, the remnants and discord of shattered revolutionary dreams can be seen. This is the chaos that failed change brings. As Americans, we often wonder how others can fail where it seems we have succeeded so easily. Why do other nations have such a hard time building a society based on liberty for everyone to enjoy? Can change really be so difficult to institute and maintain? Can developing a common law really be all that hard?

The reality of constitutional creation is that commonality can be very hard to find. Two hundred plus years later it appears to us as if the founding fathers got together one day and settled everything then and there. But, in actuality, the problems began almost the second the revolution ended. It turned out that different revolutionaries had radically varying views on what the war had meant for the New America, or what sort of change the revolutionaries had died for. The debates were so extreme that the original Articles of Confederation were traded in for a new Constitution, and some issues (like slavery) were so divisive as to be put on hold for the time being (only to cause, among other things, a Civil War less than a century later). Just like today, major debates existed among the framers that had to be resolved or at least tabled in order to create a functioning government which the people could abide.

The debates and beliefs that separated the framers were as numerous as the ones that had brought them together in the first place. What was arbitrary in government to one man was often necessary for good governance to another. And ironically, many of these different interpretations of liberty still exist today, the same basic tug-of-war still playing out through our two-party system. Just like modern politicians, the framers took sides and bitterly battled political issues with one another. Though it is hard to believe today, the chaos of conflicting ideas in early America could easily have broken the nation apart. By understanding the major debates that began with our founding fathers, we will see how sheer determination and compromise balanced a system built to support these differing ideals.

That 'Peculiar Institution' - On Slavery

"Whenever I hear anyone arguing for slavery, I feel a strong impulse to see it tried on him personally."[2]

- Abraham Lincoln

Perhaps the most remembered early debate, when any is recalled at all, is that of slavery. There are several reasons it comes to mind- the first is the heinous nature of the American system of slavery; the second, its obvious contradiction to American notions of liberty; thirdly, the massive Civil War it took to see it abolished; and finally, the equally large civil rights movement it took to conclusively resolve the question of human equality in the American nation.

> *"We hold these truths to be self-evident, that all men are created equal, that they are endowed by their Creator with certain unalienable Rights, that among these are life, liberty, and the pursuit of Happiness."*[3]
>
> – The Declaration of Independence

> *"...we understand a very subtle and daring Attempt is made to dispossess us of a very important Part of our Property...To wrest from us our Slaves, by an Act of the legislature for a general emancipation of them. An Attempt unsupported by Scripture or Sound Policy."*[4]
>
> -Three Virginia Counties Defend Slavery

For modern Americans, the idea of slavery harkens back to a seemingly faraway time in our own history where other Americans were held in bondage and persecuted based solely on the color of their skin. Even during the Revolution, the contradiction between the 'peculiar institution' of chattel slavery and the cause of independence was obvious. At the heart of this hypocrisy lay the constant revolutionary references to the British "enslavement" of her American colonies and colonial rhetoric on being "set free". Notions of what exactly equality in citizenship meant had begun to transform not only the thirteen colonies, but the world. The legacy of these concepts has continued with us today- an argument at the very nucleus of our government's formation. What freedoms can a citizen expect under the laws of an <u>equal</u> nation? Where does tyranny end and chaos begin?

The meaning of "equality" has empowered and plagued us as Americans since the dawn of the Revolutionary War. It is difficult to identify as a unified thought, and even harder to decide what means greater liberty for all and what spells decay for us as a civilization. In this one word lays two centuries' worth of American debate on the nature of humanity and liberty.

The origins of this debate on equality start with chattel slavery, and the revolutionary oratory on the unrightful and unlawful "bondage" of the thirteen colonies to England. While this terminology might seem ironic today, it was most certainly logical to those who used it during the colonial era (despite the wide spread existence of actual slavery). It evoked a clear mental image that Americans of the time related to because slavery was commonplace. It was not until just prior to the Revolutionary War that abolitionism truly gained some traction and popularity among the colonists. Of course in hindsight, it is easy to see how the continuation of this debate led to the Civil War. But at the start of its contentious history, the necessity of war and civil unrest to eventually solve this fundamental question was not so obvious.

The founding fathers were torn both individually and en masse about how to handle the clear disconnect in ideology and actual policy presented by slavery. The pro-slavery versus abolitionist divide was not as clear then as it would be during the Civil War, nor was the heavy psychological significance of the words "all men are created equal" readily apparent to the framers. Within each of the two camps, there were still more differences, on how to enact legislation to fall in line with one's beliefs. Among the pro-slavery group, there were those who disliked slavery morally, but considered it impractical and inconvenient to end; those who thought slavery perfectly legitimate, and the idea of taking any property away from its owners, illegal; and those who believed it would eventually die out in a country like America, so there was really no need to force the issue. On the antislavery side, there were those who wanted a complete end to slavery immediately; those who considered a gradual phasing out of slavery to be the best; and those who thought that if the slave trade was outlawed, the death of slavery would soon follow. No one agreed, and many held more than one of these opinions (and still others) at one time. Few, if any at all, actually believed African slaves technically "equal" to their white masters, though this did not stop some from thinking it a moral and ideological abomination to American values to hold any people in bondage.

The question for us as modern Americans has therefore become how does a country founded on liberty end up with part of its population in chains and the near-continuous persecution of various groups in the quest for their equality as citizens? Simply put, by not being able to give an answer to such a divisive debate in the first place, the founding fathers permanently etched the question into the very heart of our government. Through their compromises, they ensured that the question of human equality would be asked over and over again throughout our history as a nation. At the time, it was the only way they could possibly see to keep a new nation together when faced with such an issue. Today, it keeps us on our toes, constantly having to make a choice on what constitutes oppression, and what rights full citizens should enjoy.

That the heritage of this debate did not merely end with slavery is obvious. Though the Civil War would eventually decide the fate of slavery in this nation, it, too, left questions unanswered. People of African descent became free, but would find no complete citizenship as Americans until after the Civil Rights Movement in the 1980s, more than one hundred years after the Civil War, and two hundred after the Revolution itself. Other groups as well, including women, have had to argue for the rights and privileges of citizenship equal to that of propertied white men. We ask this question today in our debates over sexual identity and whether citizenship entitles people of the same sex to marry. And now, just as then, we have to decide whether permitting these changes creates more equality or whether it destroys the values of our nation. It is probable that every generation of American will face this great discourse in its own way, for it comes to the very fabric of our existence as a civilization. And for us, like our founders, there is never one sure answer as to what it means to be equal.

Separating God and Government – On Religious Freedom

"The God who gave us life, gave us liberty at the same time."[5]

-*Thomas Jefferson*

The great American debate on religion in government also surfaced earlier than we commonly realize today. For a nation founded 'under God' by a set of mostly Deist men for a heavily religious and very Christian people (who often came from much-persecuted European religious groups), the question of religious freedom appeared both early and in earnest. By attempting to draw a line of demarcation between Church and State, the founding fathers were not rejecting religion or its role in Revolutionary fervor, but instead were struggling to define a government built on and by faith, but not to be ruled by it.

> *"While we are zealously performing the duties of good citizens and soldiers, we certainly ought not to be inattentive to the higher duties of religion. To the distinguished character of Patriot, it should be our highest glory to add the more distinguished character of Christian."*[6]
>
> - George Washington, Army General Orders

> *"Metaphysicians and politicians may dispute forever, but they will never find any other moral principle or foundation of rule or obedience, than the consent of governor and governed."*[7]
>
> - John Adams

Today, the question of religious freedom mostly occurs only when we try as a nation to remove or add references to God in our government. Our level of paranoia on this matter is certainly indicative of its strong role in our formation. For as long as Europeans have been on this Continent, religious freedom has been an essential part of the difference between us and the Old World. That is not to say that people have not experienced persecution in the Americas. After all, the Pilgrims who started the Massachusetts Bay Colony had left England primarily to escape religious persecution, but ironically, they ended up undertaking one of the most infamous religious persecutions in history during the Salem Witch Trials. But, for the most part, despite a wide variety of very faithful people, religious freedom has been the assumption we as Americans abide by. How then do we integrate our history as a fundamentally God-fearing nation with our role as a haven from religious persecution of any kind?

Our ideals as a moral country and 'City on a Hill' have long stood in contrast to the American desire to establish a nation based only on a contract binding the governors to the governed. The question of how to maintain ethics in a budding democracy without enforcing a specific ethical system has caused a great divide since well before the Revolution ever began. Religious freedom has always been the preferred American way, but for many that was never meant to include the absolute separation of God from government (nor was it meant to endorse religions the framers thought unsavory to democratic politics). Many founding fathers and revolutionaries believed God was necessary in government in order for the new American republic to succeed. They thought that without heavenly sanction, the revolutionary cause would surely fail. However, they considered certain faiths to be both counterproductive and dangerous to the cause of liberty – particularly Catholicism and Anglicanism during their day. These religions were state-supported both in some colonies and throughout Europe, and the framers found their manipulation of government affairs both insipid and perilous to the preservation of liberty. Over the course of American history, the debate has remained. How can a government promote morality in its citizenry without endorsing a specific religion, and without allowing any religion and its adherents to unduly influence politics?

Any real conversation on the role of religion in our republic begins with those who came here to escape religious persecution in Europe, and continues through the formation of our government, to today. Prior to the establishment of a national Constitution, many of the colonies did in fact sponsor certain sects of the Christian faith. As a result of the preceding Great Awakening period, the great majority of the population was very spiritual, if not necessarily religious. And in the experience of the founders, spiritual inquiry had actually tended to fuel religious freedom rather than erase it.

The founding fathers, themselves, while a moral group, were shockingly irreligious (Jefferson even created his own version of the New Testament, deleting and editing what he did not consider accurate or fit to be included in the Bible). Not one was either a staunch believer or strong supporter of any particular Christian group. By the standards of both their day and ours, their Deism and very general ethics would be considered an apathetic Christianity at best. Many of them were even antagonistic, especially in their personnel correspondence, to the strong Christian sentiments of their day. They worried about sectarian differences in religion that could potentially divide a new nation, and particularly feared the strong force religion could possess over its adherents' politics. The separation of Church and State started off as much a safeguard against potential abuses as it did a fundamental Constitutional design feature and public right.

As with any debate over the amount of liberty in a republic, the arguments over what religious freedom means for us as a nation have grown with us as a nation. To a man, every framer believed in a Supreme Being and held many moralistic and highly philosophical spiritual beliefs. The people of the revolutionary era were also heavily religious, staunchly adhering to their own Christian sects. When we argue over the Constitution today, this heritage cannot be overlooked in a desire to consider the document as permitting no mention of God in governance. Frankly, that was never the original intent in a God-fearing and faithful revolutionary nation, nor does it match the majority opinion still held in America today. Every day of the Constitutional Convention began with a prayer, at the request of Benjamin Franklin. He reminded his colleagues that their stand against the British had only been successful because of God, and that their new government could only come together under His good auspices. Basically, the line between Church and State was never so defined during our Founders' era that they considered universally absenting religion or morality from government. Yet, this once blurry line between Church and State has become much more demarcated over the course of our history.

The reasons for the continued divide are really quite simple. As a nation, we have always been strongly spiritual, throughout two centuries of history. Naturally, this has meant that religious inquiry is encouraged and the study of differing philosophies supported. As always, the freedom to ask these questions has been supported by a nation based on liberty. As time has gone on, the line between Church and State has become stronger as more abuses have needed to be corrected. But, it has often been morality that keeps us on a course of liberty and equality in our democracy, like with the slavery debate. It has also led us to ban and then un-ban alcohol in a Prohibition period that was sponsored and maintained by religious groups. As a nation, we have strived to stop forcing any religion on others. But we also concern ourselves with what price does our new government free of the word "God" come? As we continue to debate what level of mention we give faith in our governance, we should consider the spirit in which the Constitution was drawn. Ultimately, its goal has always been to maintain freedom without abridging it. As each generation moves forward, we will continue to debate the level of association the State can have with religion. In doing so, we will continue a debate on how to ensure the existence of morality without enforcing merely one kind of it.

The Individual vs. the Community – On Unity

> *"No man can suffer too much, and no man can fall too soon, if he suffer or if he fall, in the defense of the liberties and Constitution of his country."*[8]
>
> - Daniel Webster

As with our religious beliefs, the true 'spirit' of America has also had a long and dichotomic history. As a nation founded on equality and liberty, we have always possessed a strongly individual character, and yet, also a sacrificial, communal attitude. The split between these two ideals has always gone straight to the soul of what each citizen thinks "American" ought to mean. Through both the construction of our Constitution and civil life, the founding fathers strove to find a common ground between the extremities of individualism and communalism. In doing so, they created a nation torn between profound selfishness and a spirit of selflessness.

"It is not unfrequent to hear men declaim loudly upon liberty, who, if we may judge by the whole tenor of their actions, mean nothing else by it <u>but their own liberty</u>. - to oppress without control or the restraint of laws all who are poorer or weaker than themselves."[9]

- Samuel Adams

"The unity of government, which constitutes you one people, is also now dear to you. It is justly so; it is a main pillar in the edifice of your real independence, the support of your tranquility at home, your peace abroad; of your safety; of your prosperity; of that very liberty, which you so highly prize."[10]

- George Washington's Farewell Address

It is difficult to think of another culture that, as a whole, prides themselves so highly on their individualism. American society has always held that our uniqueness as persons should not be compromised by our government. And yet, there have also always been groups of people whose differences we reject as being opposed to 'American' nature. Majorities always tend to regard the opinions of the minority as somehow contrary to the good of the whole. Even in the United States, this has been true. In spite of a sense of personal distinctiveness, community permeates every facet of American life, and going against that spirit has always been frowned upon. Our great unity is disunity. That our society contains both a belief that government should not infringe upon the rights of anyone, but also that everyone should uplift the whole has constantly weighed heavily upon us as we struggle to define our system.

The Continental Congress took part in this great contest before the Constitution was ever written or the Revolution ever won. During the war, militias were easy enough to call up, but after the initial Revolutionary fervor died down, it grew increasingly difficult to keep soldiers in the Continental Army. Men would desert the battlefields in droves, especially during key agricultural times of the year. Washington constantly lamented the lack of a "regular" army that would keep to its duty. At its heart, the issue lay with the colonial sense of the relative importance of the individual to the nation as a whole. For revolutionary America, where people were often shamed into joining the majority, the lack of belief in "for the duration" military service can seem surprising. However, in the context of both the fear of standing armies and the vital importance one person could have for a farming family, it becomes more obvious why this was truly the norm. It was the strength of rugged individualism in America that had eked a living out of farmlands very distant from central support and defined a new world. The founders could hardly expect to enforce strong community discipline on an often unstructured, isolated, and distinctive population, so they did not force the issue.

During the development of the Constitution, the depth of this debate was delved from the beginning. One of the earliest testing grounds of the Constitution and country came during Washington's presidency, at a time when nearly all the founders were still serving the country in some capacity. The new federal government chose to impose a tax on distilled liquors, provoking border Western farmers who often used whiskey instead of cash for trade. With physical money in increasingly short supply, the Western border territories went into full-out insurrection, starting the Whiskey Rebellion. Their stance against the new federal government bore shocking similarities to the one the colonies had made after the British imposed similar duties on tea and stamps (and for similar reasons- namely, war debts). Just as they had during the Revolution, the farmers began to ostracize members of their communities and local governments who would not support their cause.

Ironically, the government at large chose to take a stand against them – in fact, many of the founders did not understand why the people were being so stubborn about helping get the new country on an even financial footing. The quarrel eventually resulted in Washington calling forth and leading the new American army against the rebelling farmers. At the end of the day, the act still proved futile (the western border counties still frequently refused to pay the tax and the government stopped trying to collect). However, this incident took on true importance because the government stretched its federal muscle, and won, at least on paper. The Whiskey Rebellion set a precedent contradicting the trend of individualism in America, showing that no matter how rugged the minority was, the will of the whole would not collapse under the pressure. This has helped to fuel the constant American debate over who is greater (and who the government is more designed to serve) – the individual or the community.

As we have aged as a nation, the rights of individuals have grown both stronger and weaker, a continuation of an old question. Minorities and small interest groups have become powerful with the advent of lobbyists who wield cash and influence to change government views. But, our government has also become more powerful. With increasing centralization at the federal level, it has become harder and harder for one person to oppose the will of the government. We have all seen the stand-offs between federal agents and people who refuse to pay what they view as illegal income tax, and the agents always win. The government can no longer afford to turn a blind eye to those who refuse their will. This is for two main reasons; one, it sows dissension in the remainder of the populace, and two, they no longer *have* to permit it. The federal government is no longer as weak as it was after the Revolution. Following the Civil War, and the increased drive to maintain a national standing army, America has become a place where the unruly are truly ruled by their government.

The acceptance of such staunch federal power still seems strange in a nation based on a tradition of individualism. The American sense of community has always faced its match in a country simultaneously proud of its rogue history. The balancing act between person and state continues to toss Americans between their feeling of self and their communal spirit. Ironically, the preservation of *individual* rights has weakened with the growth of *minority* rights through interest groups with big voices. The rise of government bureaucracy has not seen a rise in community though, for America as a whole has never been weaker. Self-imposed division and a lack of participation in one's own governance have only increased. That the contentious 2004 election only featured a 60.7 % turnout of the eligible voting population[11] particularly speaks to the decline in concern for the country as a community. The 2008 election faired roughly the same, with a 61.7% voter turnout.

With a final vote tally of 131.2 million votes cast, and an estimated eligible voting population of 212.7 million voters, that means 81.5 million people just did not vote. Even more ironically, we have never been so dissatisfied with our government. As the tug of war continues, it seems apathy on both sides is winning - a condition which would horrify every founder without exception. Of all the debates, that this one has waned in importance, sounds a dangerous tone for a still young nation.

A Republic or a Democracy – On Representation

> *"The republican is the only form of government which is not eternally at open or secret war with the rights of Mankind."*[12]
>
> -Thomas Jefferson

As Americans, we see our level of representation as an inherent right. Yet, the ability of adult-aged people to vote is both taken for-granted and all too infrequently used. We often forget that questions over political representation, in all aspects, have dominated our nation for over two and a half centuries.[13] Having been founded as a *republic*, it is ironic that we find ourselves more and more considered a *democracy*, both at home and abroad. The words have become interchangeable for us, and thus, we rarely realize they mean profoundly different things. By *democracy*, the founders meant a government where everyone participated directly on their own behalves; conversely, they understood a *republic* to be a government where people select representatives to act for them. For the founding fathers, this distinction lay at the heart of an essential political issue – who should be able to vote, and what can they be trusted to vote for?

> *"Remember, democracy never lasts long. It soon wastes, exhausts, and murders itself. There never was a democracy yet that did not commit suicide."*[14]
>
> -John Adams

> *"The preservation of the sacred fire of liberty, and the destiny of the republican model of government, are justly considered as deeply, perhaps as finally staked, on the experiment entrusted to the hands of the American people."*[15]
>
> - George Washington

For a historian, it seems rather humorous that we tout ourselves as a *democracy* in this day and age. For our founders, *democracy* was a dirty word, especially in the political arena. To be called a *democrat* in the Revolutionary era would be like calling someone a *communist* during the Cold War or a *fundamentalist* in today's heated political climate. For them, *democracy* indicated an undesirable, extremist view of popular government – one controlled and corrupted by the whims of the unenlightened, riotous masses. There were no *democrats* in their era (unless one counts slurs by rivals), only *republicans*. For earlier generations, a *democrat* was a demagogue, someone who manipulated the masses and public opinion for their own political ambition and personal gain. The preservation and sanctity of the *republic* kept amoral politics at bay, for it meant equality, liberty, and unity. The new American people wanted a *republic* that would guide them on a path of moderation and freedom. Only recently has the term *democracy* come into popular usage and acceptance; for centuries, *republic* was the preferred term for our nation. So how then do we find ourselves as a modern *democracy* despite our long history as a *republic*?

Representation has always been the rallying cry of our country. And yet, for a people passionately devoted to expanding their role in their own governance, Americans have always worried about poor representational choices causing the one voice to be drowned out by the many. For our founding fathers, balance in representation was a controversial problem that eventually resulted in our bicameral legislature. The best way to represent the varying interests of unique states and groups of people has always challenged a country based on fairness in governance. For this reason and this divide, the revolutionary generation almost unanimously rejected total *democracy* as a viable form of government. In the Greco-Roman era, one highly lauded by the revolutionaries, *democracies* had not done well, especially over bigger land areas. The founders firmly believed that the country was too large (at just 13 colonies!), and the general population too susceptible to political trickery and personal convenience for a *democratic* government to work. The *republican* form of government was selected because it enabled small interests to be balanced with large ones. In short, *republicanism* guaranteed vital stability in a tumultuous, changing period, and a place for everyone's ideas and needs.

The true irony of our "representative" form of government has been that its policies have not always been representative. With the creation of the Constitution, the founding fathers faced their first representational dilemma – how to apportion voting rights to a people used to monarchy? For them, the answer was simple, and so they only gave those with a vested interest in the republic and its success a voice. That is, white male property owners, all of whom had something to lose should the nation fail. The founders lacked faith in the masses, believing them too easily manipulated, especially for something as priceless (literally and figuratively) as a vote. After all, they had seen the people be bought before in town hall elections, or seen the crowd swayed by a powerful preacher. Since they could not trust a mostly ill-educated population, they built safeguards around the right to vote. Even the presidential election was not based on a purely popular vote, but instead on an electoral college whose members 'represented' each state's people. The founders established a republic by confining the electorate to those they felt could be most trusted to protect the liberty of all. Basically, they established layers of representation, in order to distill the will of the people into a reasonably coherent form.

The founding fathers' solution to worries over a tractable people has always stood at odds with the main principles they espoused. As we have aged as a nation, we have expanded our electorate as well as our other rights. African-Americans, women, and other traditional minorities have all gained the right to cast a vote. The powers of the electoral college members have become more limited as many states now legally restrict what votes they are permitted to cast as a "popular representative". Yet with all this progress, we still face the same issue that puzzled our first generation of Americans – where does true equal representation lie? While the founders may not have appreciated the judgment of women and African-Americans, they did foresee the issue of minority rights. In accommodating their desires (for even small states to have sway) and their fears (of true democracy breeding an eventual dictatorship) in the same fundamental law, they created a permanent schism in our system.

The founders had sincerely hoped and believed that a *republic* would be the answer to an infant nation's representational crisis. In modern times, it has often seemed like the wrong answer, especially as we gauge presidential elections where the popular vote has not been the same as the one in the electoral college. But our government and Constitution were designed the way they were for reasons deeper than the single one that has caused contentious presidential elections. Though inherently divided, the founding fathers sought to create a Constitution that could balance the needs of a whole nation – not merely its parts. That we would give that up now for an ideal *democracy* and complete popular control (which our founders would have despised) belies the issues losing our *republic* would create.

Democracies are subject to the whims of the majority; republics help maintain the rights of the minority. Without an even keel, a ship sinks. Our *republic* has enabled us to weather the storms of the world and nationhood while permitting us to grow and simultaneously retain our identity. Few other vessels of representational government can claim the same, and none has had the longevity the United States has been blessed with.

Federalist vs. Anti-Federalist – On Centralization

> *"The proposition, that the people are the best keepers of their own liberties, is not true; they are the worst conceivable; they are no keepers at all; they can neither judge, act, think, or will, as a political body."*[16]
>
> -John Adams

The most formalized of all the founders' debates is also the most forgotten. Upon answering the question of representation in their time and forging a Constitution, the founding fathers faced their most challenging and consuming debate – who did the Constitution grant the final, decisive authority to? Before the ink was dry on the new set of laws, the ramifications of attempting to build a "decentralized union" could already be seen. The irony that they did not realize it themselves until strong political in-fighting started may seem strange. However, the idea that so many different interpretations could be applied to the exact same set of words rarely becomes apparent until later. The disagreements over what part of the government is ultimately supreme according to our Constitution still take place today. Our founders' inability to settle this problem has become both a bane and a hallmark of our representational government.

> *"I consider the foundation of the Constitution as laid on this ground: that 'all powers not delegated to the United States, by the Constitution, nor prohibited by it to the States, are reserved to the States or the People.'"*[17]
>
> *- Thomas Jefferson*
>
> *"If the end be clearly comprehended within any of the specified powers, and if the measure have an obvious relation to that end, and is not forbidden by any particular provision of the Constitution, it may safely be deemed to come within the compass of the national authority."*[18]
>
> *- Alexander Hamilton*

The rise of the Constitution was also the downfall of the Articles of Confederation. With the advent of the Constitution, our national notions have tended towards greater centralization in government over time. This is in sharp contrast to the original Articles, which promulgated a strongly anti-federal government system. Not that this debate ended with the Constitution's creation, or is even closed now, but its character has significantly changed in the modern era. The dynamic of this contest has become about "big brother" government versus "downsizing" the bureaucracy, a discussion vastly different from the one that began with our predecessors. For them, this disagreement, which also began the two-party system, was about the federal government's very existence. Though they managed to turn the non-functioning Articles into a new, more federal Constitution, the founders could never truly agree over the scope that the new government should have. For them, at the heart of the issue lay a classic dilemma- how does one keep a republic from falling into a dictatorship? Does the federal government keep the people from becoming decadent and trampling on other citizens' freedoms or do the people keep the bureaucracy from becoming corrupt and removing these same liberties?

As we have discussed in the previous section on representation, none of the founding fathers particularly trusted the people *en masse* in either case. On the other hand, nearly all of them also believed that power corrupts. The new government's federal components frightened their republican sensibilities, and their experiences under both a monarchy and a tyrannical parliament had given them a sense of caution. The question of who should be the ultimate authority when federal government, state, and citizen came together- basically who the Constitution granted any "unstated" powers to- began as soon as the ratification process started.

The founding fathers suddenly found themselves seriously divided into two opposing camps. On one side were the Anti-Federalists, led by Thomas Jefferson, who firmly believed that the Constitution should be taken *literally*, word for word. Where it said that any powers not enumerated therein belonged to the states and the people that meant anything not in the Constitution could not become part of the federal government. In the other corner, the Federalists, led by Alexander Hamilton, held that the Constitution had certain *implications* relating to the original intentions of its authors. Basically, this side thought that the federal government could do as it needed to accomplish anything the Constitution had authorized it to do, and not specifically granted to the States or the people. The irony is that both sides had a hand in the composition of the Constitution to begin with, so one could have hoped that they all knew what it had meant. And while similar arguments are conducted today, none of us can claim to have been present at the original creation of the document, nor can we really know its 'intent'.

It can be difficult for us to comprehend how different this debate used to be from the tone it takes today. At its bitter, most simplified end, the issue at stake among the founding fathers was the very existence of a federal government at all capable of acting on its own. The switch from the Articles to the Constitution only occurred as a compromise to hold the 13 colonies together in some semblance of unity. This had been something that the completely toothless federal government under the rules of the Articles of Confederation had been unable to accomplish. In creating a Constitution with a slightly broader scope than the Articles had held, the founders hoped to turn a tide of disunity that threatened the very existence of the nation as a whole.

They were right to disagree over whether or not even the Constitution possessed enough federal muscle. As the debate raged on, it began to consume a country unable to settle other major dilemmas. At its core, the quickly approaching Civil War would not be mainly about slavery or equality, but about power. Did the southern states have the *constitutional* prerogative to withdraw from a Union they had voluntarily entered? Or was the federal government authorized by those same laws to hold the Union together at all costs and impose an overriding system on the individual states? The answers to these questions would be solved with blood, and a true Union created at the cost of more of its citizens' lives.

Government centralization came at even greater costs than one war, for the federal government had shown it held the true power. All of the states, not just the Southern ones, began to feel their strength and ability to force the federal government to change diminish. Following the civil war, the federal government's role in the nation was no longer in question, but rather the limits that could be imposed on the clear power it had gained. These limitations would see both rises and falls until the dawn of our modern bureaucracy. It would take another national crisis for our country to truly convert to a fully federal system.

In the event of unheard-of economic disaster, in the form of the Great Depression, the people ultimately looked to the federal government to solve their woes. In doing so, the final death knell for state and local power was sounded. For the founding fathers, even these dire straits would never have led them to the solutions created by the Depression-era administrations. Especially for the anti-Federalists, the modern bureaucratic welfare state would have been no solution at all. James Madison, the main author of the Constitution, was famous for his remarks in 1794 on the role of the US government in providing financial help to people after a natural disaster. In the *Annals of Congress*, it records that *"Mr. Madison wished to relieve the sufferers, but was afraid of establishing a dangerous precedent, which might hereafter be perverted to the countenance of purposes very different from those of charity. He acknowledged, for his own part, that he could not undertake to lay his finger on that article in the Federal Constitution which granted a right of Congress of expending, on objects of benevolence, the money of their constituents."*[19] That we have gotten so far away from the policies of even the broadest Constitutional powers espoused by our founding fathers is hardly shocking. They knew well that the tendency would always be toward more federal control because it simplifies the decision-making process. However, we are so far along now that any notion of citizen and national life without a significant bureaucracy is a thing of the past.

The shift in the dynamic of the federalist/anti-federalist divide has completely altered the course of our nation. As always, many still champion the causes of less government interference in peoples' lives. Few, however, mention that our nation was not always this way. Our written Constitution meant for many of our predecessors that government should not just be minimized where ever possible, but that legally it is really and truly limited in its role. The level of power and freedom the federal government now possesses would have been anathema to even the most Federalist of our founding fathers.

As a nation, we have fought and died for liberty, but given more and more of it up along the way because it made things easier, and the Union more secure. Through the Civil War and the systems created during the Depression, first States lost their rights and then more individual freedoms were abridged. National welfare and a sense of national unity are important. But the fact that we no longer worry over the cost these changes will have to the future of our republic is frightening. The founders where terrified over where this type of federal system could lead a free government. As Benjamin Franklin wrote, *"Those who would give up Essential Liberty to purchase a little Temporary Safety deserve neither Liberty nor Safety."*[20] We continuously face this question as a changing nation. Does the Constitution actually grant this level of federal authority, either implicitly or literally? Or instead, have we moved this debate and others beyond a scope ever intended by our forefathers?

Our Foundation – The Constitution

"If once they [the people] become inattentive to public affairs, you and I, and Congress and Assemblies, judges and governors shall all become wolves."[1]

-*Thomas Jefferson*

As long as we remain a nation, the question of whom and what can best preserve our freedoms will continue. Great debates have existed both before and after the Constitution's creation. But it is important to remember that the construction of this document marked all of the things the founding fathers *could* actually agree on (or at least agree to disagree on). Finding common ground even required building some of these very same debates into the very foundation of our government. That is why both the actual words and implications of the Constitution are so very important. The founding fathers' "original intentions" were not the results of one governing ideology on political life, but rather a middle ground that most people and politicians could accept during their time. By returning our attention to this starting point, we can discover the true basis of our republic.

The road to the Constitutional compromise was no short one, nor was it as obvious or inherent to the birth of our nation as many would lead us to believe. It was actually the failure of our first try at government, under the Articles of Confederation, that set us on the path. The Articles had been unable for nine years to effectively govern the economy, a cornerstone of any government; or control the states, which had kept any truly national interests from forming. The problem became big enough that something needed to be done or the infant United States risked total collapse. At first, the mandate of the Convention held in Philadelphia was to merely revise the existing laws. However, it readily became apparent that the structure was just too weak to ever properly function. Therefore, the delegates decided to scrap the Articles entirely and start over. By mid-September 1787, the Convention had adopted the new Constitution, and by March 1789, our government under it had begun. This marked a turning point in American history, a point where we decided, as a nation, that survival and compromise was more important than any individual or political group.

The momentous import of this change cannot be underestimated. By endorsing a new, more powerful, federal government, the states and the people chose to commit themselves to unity and compromise. In doing so, they attempted to give the new nation a fighting chance at continued existence during a tumultuous time. The strength of the new Constitution lay more in what it permitted than what it forbid, and its spirit signified the triumph of harmony over discord. The Constitution reflected a fresh resolve on the part of the former colonies – that what brought them together was more important than what tore them apart. The fundamental law, literally and implicitly, sought to protect this ideal. The Constitution did not create a new nation, but a new union, one based on a spirit of understanding rather than unbridled ideology.

THE LITERAL : WHAT OUR CONSTITUTION REALLY SAYS

"A government of laws, and not of men"[2]

- John Adams

The laws that form the basis of our government are permanently enshrined in the Constitution. Though we often cite its principles, its actual words are often forgotten. Yet the literal meaning the founding fathers imbued the Constitution with is extremely important. This is for two reasons; one, it contains the complete agreement reached by our predecessors (and they definitely argued vigorously over its wording); and two, it is modifiable, but only through an accord by a significant national majority (which basically means we can continue to change it to fit changing conditions-if most citizens can agree). These two grounds make our Constitution a "living" document, as it is often called, but not for the reasons we are often told. The foresight of the founding fathers was not in making perfect laws, but laws that fit their times well and could be changed again (to fit different times). Before we can understand what the Constitution means, we must analyze what it says and why it says it. In doing so, we embrace our government and the freedoms it espouses for all citizens and all beliefs, not just ourselves and our personal views.

> "We the People of the United States, in Order to form a more perfect Union, establish Justice, insure domestic Tranquility, provide for the common defence, promote the general Welfare, and secure the Blessings of Liberty to ourselves and our Posterity, do ordain and establish this Constitution for the United States of America."[3]
>
> - Opening to the United States Constitution

Our Constitution is, at its core, a legal contract binding both governors and governed to the same rule of law. The seven articles that compose the body of the document lay out the exact powers allocated to the federal, state, and local governments. It also establishes our well-known separation of executive, legislative, and judicial powers. But for the most part, the Constitution's initial form gives specifications of actual governance that vary from the highly specific and unquestionable, *"No person shall be a Representative who shall not have attained to the Age of twenty five Years, and have been seven years a Citizen"*[4], to the extremely vague and interpretable, *"To make all Laws which shall be necessary and proper for carrying into Execution the foregoing Powers, and all other Powers vested by this Constitution in the Government of the United States"*[5]. The basics laid down by the Constitution, as it was presented to the states for ratification in 1787, were mostly about actual governance and not political *rights*. Many of these original laws have since been modified through the Amendment process, but the government they put in place is essentially the same- a national bicameral legislature representing states' interests who work with an executive accountable to all of the people, both monitored by an independent judiciary.

The seven articles of the main Constitution are mired in revolutionary-era legal language, and occasionally difficult for a lay person to understand. However, the obligations they impose upon our government in return for the powers granted to it are very clear. As the introduction to the Constitution makes unmistakable, the government is bound to the continued welfare of its citizenry as a part of this exchange.

As this leads into Article 1, it is immediately of interest that the first Article of the Constitution is about the bicameral legislature and the powers accorded to it (and not about the executive). This was a reflection of the high importance that early Americans placed on the legislative portion of the federal government. For them, the senators and representatives were the people who held their local interests at heart and who actually made laws. The Congress was actually intended to be the mainstay and the soul of their federal government, and not the President.

Much of the authority we commonly think of today as executive in nature actually belongs to the legislature. This includes any and all *"Bills for raising Revenue,"*[6] which must *"originate in the House of Representatives"*[7]. It also gives Congress, **alone**, the powers of taxation, financial regulation both domestically and abroad, authority over naturalization of citizens, post offices, roads, patents, tribunals (courts inferior to the Supreme Court), rule over citizens' crimes at sea and abroad, the ability to declare war, maintain armies and navies, govern the armies and navies, call the militia, discipline the militia, govern the District and all places purchased by the federal government, and to make any laws to carry out the above. But while it gives to Congress the sole authority over these many objects, it also restricts them. Section 9 attempts to limit eventual slavery, prohibits the suspension of habeas corpus[8] (except in extreme cases), bans bills of attainder and ex post facto laws[9], taxation between states, federal preference to particular states, treasury withdraws except for appropriations made by laws, and the granting of titles of nobility. Section 10 goes one step further and bans the individual states from entering into foreign relations individually, usurping the powers granted to Congress, or allowing anything already banned to Congress. As is obvious, this first Article is both the most important and the lengthiest of the Constitution because Congress was granted the strongest role and responsibility in the federal government.

The rest of the physical government portion of the Constitution, found in Articles 2 and 3 features the rules governing the Presidency and the Judiciary. Article 2 details the method of electing and removing a President, and his oath of office. The only powers he is actually granted are the position of Commander in Chief, the ability to grant pardons, treaty-making (but only with the advice and consent of the Senate), and the appointment of federal officials (but again, only with Congressional permission). He is required under the same article to make a State of the Union address from *"time to time"*, convene or adjourn Congress when necessary, receive foreign dignitaries, commission military officers, and *"take Care that the Laws be faithfully executed"*. For what we often consider today the highest post in the world, it is not very much legally. In fact, much of what we consider 'presidential' duties is in fact the responsibility of Congress.

Article 3, on the Judiciary, is even slighter. It vests the judicial power in one Supreme Court, and grants Congress the power to appoint any lesser courts. It grants the judiciary power in all cases, *"in Law and Equity, arising under this Constitution, the Laws of the United States, and Treaties made"*, and in a series of specific legal scenarios. Other than that, it requires trials to be by jury and in the state where the crime was committed (except for the scenarios where the federal judiciary has precedence). It also defines treason, and requires at least two witnesses or an open confession in Court for someone to be convicted of it. And those are all the powers allotted to or responsibilities required of the

Federal Courts. Not quite the impressive amount of responsibility these positions have assumed during the present day.

That finally brings us to the close of the original Constitution, which was where the founding fathers attempted to insert all of their innovations in politics. These final sections were really their attempt to bring home the idea of a republic, truly joined together, where all the citizens and states were equal. In that vein, Article 4 deals with the states. It makes them equals under the eyes of the law and requires them to be equal with each other, by accepting the decisions of other states as binding in their own. It also contains provisions for the admittance of new states on the same footing as the old.

Article 5 is where the founders really stressed both unity and their new political ideas. This article establishes the legal methods by which Amendments can change the Constitution. In permitting this and ensuring there was a method for it, the founding fathers enabled the Constitution to change with the times. Both the ingenuity and importance of this particular article are easy to overlook, as well as its overwhelming significance.

Article 6 assumes, upon the nation as a whole, the debts of the states and the old Confederation. It also states that the Constitution and the laws in it are the *"supreme Law of the Land"*[10], and binds the Judiciaries of the states to uphold it. It requires government officials to take an oath of office, but expressly prohibits religion as a qualification for any office. This is interesting in that religion is not mentioned anywhere else in the Constitution, and it adheres to the non-religious principles espoused by the founding fathers without prohibiting religious expression in government.

Finally, Article 7 is very simple, and contains the requirements for ratification of the Constitution and the signatures of those at the Convention in approval (with the exception of Rhode Island, noticeably absenting). These articles proved to be both apt for the time and for the future by providing for the nation as a whole instead of just a particular group.

At last, we come to the amendments, the changes to our Constitution that both our founding fathers and later generations of America have found necessary at times. The Bill of Rights was passed by the founding fathers themselves as a series of amendments in 1789 and fully ratified by 1791. Many of the founding fathers felt that the rights were implied by the Constitution itself, however a few states made their ratification of the Constitution conditional upon the inclusion of a Bill of Rights. These states did not trust the government, and as it turns out they were not entirely off-base in their insistence that such amendments were needed. These first ten amendments safeguard the rights of the American citizenry- they give the right to free religious practice, freedom of speech, freedom of press, the rights to assembly and petition, to bear arms, to be secure in their property, to a speedy trial, a trial by jury, and to a grand jury for capitol offenses. They also ban the government from establishing a national religion, quartering troops in private homes, double-jeopardy, excessive bail, or cruel and unusual punishment. The final two amendments close by admonishing the reader that basically any rights not specifically given to the people do not necessarily belong to the government, and any powers not constitutionally given to the government **always** belong to the people.

The remaining 11th through 27th Amendments are mostly correctional or clarifying in nature. Some fix problems like the ways in which the Constitution's laws were originally written, such as changes to electoral laws, Congressional taxing ability, presidential terms, Washington DC's representation in Congress, presidential order of succession, and compensation for Congress. Those that further elucidate Constitutional principles have affected judicial power, abolished slavery, representational apportionment, citizenry requirements, public debt, voting rights regardless of color or sex after a specified age, and enacted and repealed Prohibition. Though it seems long and sometimes uses complicated wording, the Constitution is worth studying because it forms the basis of a nation created with the ability to always face the future.

The Implied: What the Founders Meant

> *"I have had an eye, my fellow citizens, to putting you upon your guard against all attempts, from whatever quarter, to influence your decision in a matter of the utmost moment to your welfare, by any impressions other than those which may result from the evidence of truth."*[11]
>
> *- Alexander Hamilton*

It is often remarked that 'beauty is in the eye of the beholder,' but even more so, "truth" can be incredibly subjective. It might seem that the afore-mentioned constitutional apportionment of federal, state, and individual powers would be unquestionable. After all, many of the Constitution's laws are incredibly specific. However, it has been the vagaries left by the founding fathers that have given the Constitution so much strength as well as caused so much disagreement. Not everyone finds the same "truths" in a certain set of words. This was especially true for the founding fathers and the implications they read into the Constitution's words. What they each thought was within the Constitution they had written did not always match. However, they did understand that their new government allowed them all to think something different- and that was what was important.

> *"No man is allowed to be a judge in his own cause, because his interest would certainly bias his judgment, and, not improbably, corrupt his integrity."*[12]
>
> *- James Madison*

Our Constitution contains many laws and enumerates many rights and duties. Many people from our founders on have differed about what exactly it entitles to each side in the agreement. In order to understand all the regulations and powers set forth in its pages, we must ask ourselves one simple question- why? Why did the revolutionary generation write and ratify a document, which even at the time, held different truths for different people? What inherent implications did the Constitution contain that permitted them all to more or less accept its contents? Was there one guiding political ideology that they all held before splitting over various issues? Or rather, was it that the Constitution encoded a kind of equality, one designed to protect each person from the imposition of another person's self-interested judgment?

The Constitution was by no means unanimous. Journals and letters of the founding fathers, particularly Madison's notes from the Convention, show the level of intense and often bitter struggle that led to its eventual creation. Ratification was also not a smooth process, and in many states came very close to failing (not to mention the few states that passed it after government under the Constitution had already taken effect).

The Federalist Papers, a collection of essays published in New York newspapers during the ratification period, demonstrate the variety of arguments both for and against the Constitution. While these letters to the newspaper took the side of the Constitution, they addressed many of the disagreements and ongoing conversations over its ratification. Written mostly by Alexander Hamilton and James Madison (with a few by John Jay), they represent the views of some of the most influential and intelligent founding fathers on the issues of the day. The Constitution's credibility as a set of laws that could truly work for the revolutionaries despite their disagreements can especially be grasped with the knowledge that Madison and Hamilton would later be on completely opposite sides when it came to Constitutional interpretation. What *The Federalist Papers* give us is a glimpse of how people who had such different views could agree. They saw something that others often did not, that unity was necessary for the continued survival of the county, or as Hamilton put it, *"A FIRM Union will be of the utmost moment to the peace and liberty of the States."*[13]

Due to the circumstances surrounding ratification, our two-party system pretty much came as a packaged deal with the Constitution itself (ironic considering that many of the founders warned of the dangers of partisan politics). Anti-Federalists took up arms against the Federalists who they feared were trying to impose a tyrannical federal government upon the states. In more than a few cases, there were founders who supported ratification as so-called Federalists (like Madison) who would later become members of the Anti-Federalist party, especially as the parties took on defining characteristics separate from notions of federal unity. However, we should not let the lack of unanimity in the Constitutional proceedings lead us to believe that the Federalist/Anti-Federalist split was about the existence of the Constitution itself.

These two parties represented something different- two distinct interpretations of what the Constitution actually meant. At the core, the Federalists believed in the supremacy of the federal government while the Anti-Federalists believed in the ultimate authority of the states. Both sides firmly believed that the Constitution supported the ideas they espoused. But it is truly revealing that though they debated the Constitution's implied meaning and each thought themselves right in how they viewed it, they never insinuated that the Constitution forbid the other side's way of thinking. That our founders considered it a valid argument to engage in at all indicates their fundamental belief that the document was open to opinion.

The new American republic definitely was not lacking in varied opinions that each person wanted to protect. Many historians have viewed the Election of 1800 where Thomas Jefferson defeated John Adams as a reversal of the Constitution and Federalism in general. At that time, people were still more affiliated with their states than with the nation as a whole, and Anti-Federalism was broadly appealing. However, the endorsement of *the* Anti-Federalist candidate over the Federalist Adams cannot be seen as post-ratification regret or an anti-Constitutional vote. Implying that the revolutionary generation merely had buyer's remorse over their new government is too simplistic. Instead, the election and presidency of Thomas Jefferson was a triumph of the new Constitution. The election of 1800 proved two very important things: one, that difference of opinion could be permitted and actively engaged under the new Constitution, and two, that its laws actually worked, as the transfer of power between the two sides was greeted without violence and with relative amicability. Jefferson's triumph demonstrated to the entire new nation that unity could work and that differences and shifts in opinion could be accounted for through the new Constitution. His election greeted a new era in politics and government, one where one could not be left out because of one's views.

The most valuable contribution of our founding fathers was the Constitution they created. By enabling the expression of differing ideas and making many positions valid under the eyes of the fundamental law, the founders gave us a document that could stand the test of time and intense public scrutiny. In allowing the Constitution to imply and back up more than one political ideology, the founders gave the Constitution a level of depth not seen before in governance. The reason we have been so successful as a nation, and at keeping our nation together has been the wide allowances the Constitution makes. The essential component to the Constitution was not a firm set of beliefs espoused by every single founding father and member of the revolutionary generation; instead, it was an unwavering devotion to equality and diversity of ideas under the eyes of the law. The Constitution was not meant to stifle, but to stimulate- within limits designed to keep corruption and self-interest at bay.

Constitutional "Intent"

> *"This country, with its institutions, belongs to the people who inhabit it. Whenever they shall grow weary of the existing Government, they can exercise their constitutional right of amending it or their revolutionary right to dismember or overthrow it."*[14]
>
> -Abraham Lincoln

The country belongs to the people, and so too, does the government, or at least it does according to our Constitution. The founding fathers created it with enough flexibility to fit varied views on its laws and the level of allowable governance. But room for opinions and innovation does not equal lawlessness. Just because the Constitution permits more than one interpretation does not mean it is entirely open for discussion.

A lot is made of the notion of the founding fathers' or the Constitution's true "intent". While they definitely had some specific intentions, they were also *intentionally* non-specific in some areas because even the founders could not agree. However, to attempt to ascribe *intentions* to the founding fathers from our future perspective on matters that they never addressed nor ever could have imagined is folly. The Constitution was made amendable for a reason- to oblige future generations to actually fix and come to agreements on the issues that faced a changing nation instead of avoiding them or inventing a basis for new rules into the classic Constitution. Usurping the Constitution by disobeying the laws it does specify or trying too hard to force *intentions* upon the less-specific portions does nothing but undermine our government. That the Constitution can legally change with us when required is a great thing; however, our history is full of attempts at shifting its composition improperly to suit ourselves.

> *"Let the end be legitimate, let it be within the scope of the constitution, and all means which are appropriate, which are plainly adapted to that end, which are not prohibited, but consist with the letter and spirit of the constitution, are constitutional."*[15]
>
> *- John Marshall, fourth Chief Justice of the United States*

The nature of our understanding of the Constitution and its laws has come far since the time of our revolutionary fore-bearers. The amendment process has been utilized to set into writing new understandings, as well as solidify old ones, as occasion has required throughout our national history. The Supreme Court has expounded upon its constitutionally-granted powers and taken on the process of judicial review throughout the same history, in order to determine the legality of laws under our Constitution. And though not explicitly granted by the Constitution, the foundation of judicial review is well-reflected by both the trends of prior colonial law and documents our founders wrote, like *The Federalist Papers*. Conspicuously absent from this record of Constitutional adjustments is any notion or legal basis for forcing a fixed set of ideals onto the Constitution. Our modern decision to pick and choose our portions of the Constitution like a cafeteria lunch has no true basis in history or legality. By examining the appropriate processes to modify our Constitution, we shall see how far away we have gotten politically from anything our founding fathers ever 'intended'.

The ability to amend our Constitution has been utilized throughout history to both add to and modify the original Constitution. Until recently, the level of reluctance associated with undertaking this path has never been so great. Every major period in American history has been associated with Constitutional change. This should not seem surprising given that the most trying times will always bring both the major features and flaws of any law to light. Ironically, the most effective demonstration of the versatility of the amendment process is also one of the strangest.

There has been only one notion that has prompted both the addition of an amendment and subsequent revocation of that amendment through another one, and that was Prohibition. When the 18th Amendment was ratified in 1919 banning the sale, manufacture, and transportation of alcoholic beverages, it followed the national trend towards forbidding liquor, which had already been made into law in several states and was actively promoted by large Protestant denominations. By 1933, the 21st amendment had repealed the 18th, once again allowing alcohol and its consumption in the United States. Many have seen this acceptance and then revocation as a failure of the Constitution, but it is really a victory. The Constitution demonstrated that it could change with shifting political views. By 1919, the Prohibition movement had been gaining traction in America for well over half a century, so it was only natural that something so important to a great portion of the country be codified in the Constitution. However, by the Roaring Twenties, violation of the amendment was so widespread that it became of no use to continue enforcing it federally. A decade changed a lot- the country had gone through a war, the great depression, and the suffrage movement. Social freedoms became more important than ever before. The Constitution's ability to accept both these time periods without compromising its own integrity speaks to the strength of its design and the importance of the amendment process to legal change.

The idea of Constitutional interpretation was also a source of legal strength created by our founding fathers. The ability of the Constitution to imply a basis for more than one idea was both intentional and helped get it ratified in the first place. However, it was the landmark Marbury v. Madison Supreme Court Case in 1803 that prompted full-scale judicial review from then onward. The Supreme Court under Chief Justice John Marshall took the position that judicial review was authorized by the Constitution under Article 3, and intended by his revolutionary-era peers. *The Federalist Papers* and many other documents left by the main founding fathers explicitly demonstrate agreement with the concept.

Judicial review has both upheld and clarified some of the most important legal points in Constitutional history. And its ability to shift with changing times has also showed the same strength present in both the Constitution itself and the amendment process. Judicial review by the Supreme Court has done and proved the same things that the Constitution did in creating and subsequently revoking Prohibition. When Brown v. Board of Education overturned the Plessy v. Ferguson doctrine of "separate but equal" and ended racial segregation, it changed an interpretation of the 14th Amendment that had been in place from 1896 until that day in 1954. The Constitution had not changed, the fourteenth amendment had not changed, but we had, as a people. Since the 14th amendment was still legally capable of reflecting our shift on racial equality, judicial review could be used to update an older interpretation.

Unfortunately, many people, especially politicians, have taken to using judicial review as a way to avoid the amendment process. This is mostly because the amendment process is much more intensive than judicial review, and requires a significant amount of citizen approval in order to ratify a new amendment. Getting enough people to agree to something as major as an amendment is not easy; so much so that taking a case to the Supreme Court has begun to seem mild in comparison. But the founding fathers did not ever *intend* judicial review to be a substitute for constitutional amendments. If anything, it was meant as a supplement, especially since they found the Constitution to be open to different opinions on its contents. It is easy to try and rationalize modern views by 'finding' them somewhere in our Constitution, but the fact is that the revolutionary era did not have some of the concerns that now occupy us. Imposing one's views onto the law does not make it magically function better. By trying to use the justice system and manipulate the selection of Supreme Court judges in order to get a certain ideology out of the Constitution, we destabilize the solid, but still flexible structure our founders built for us.

> *"The basis of our political systems is the right of the people to make and to alter their Constitutions of Government. But the Constitution which at any time exists, till changed by an explicit and authentic act of the whole people, is sacredly obligatory upon all."*[16]

- George Washington

At the end of the day, there is only one question we must ask ourselves about our government's foundation – is our Constitution worth keeping? By understanding its writers, its origins, and its true meaning, we give ourselves a way to honestly answer this issue. When we truly honor the basis of our Constitution, it works how it was intended. But when we undermine that basis by completely reinventing what it represents, we weaken the whole structure of our government to the point of collapse. Our Constitution was designed to possess infinite possibilities for the American people while still limiting the abilities of the government to oppress the same. When we actually utilize the stated and intended doctrine of constitutional amendment combined with a prudent practice of judicial review, we maintain the government built for us by our founding fathers.

There is no point in trying to make the Constitution so open that it could mean anything at all or so closed that it can never be adjusted. The founding fathers understood this give and take, that politics was not a one-way street. Thus, they created a system that could support multiple viewpoints, through the use of judicial review, while still making adjustments when ideas shifted so completely as to step entirely outside of anything the Constitution ever considered. The amendment process exists for a reason. Our government exists as it does for a reason. As citizens, we must either choose our Constitution and its laws or choose another system of governance; there is no middle ground. But when we decide to use our Constitution appropriately, we must be prepared to defend it against those who will not do the same. As Washington himself said, the Constitution in place at any moment in time is "sacredly obligatory upon all".

BY FINANCE: PURSUING THE DOLLAR

> *"All the perplexities, confusions, and distresses in America arise, not from defects in their constitution or confederation, nor from a want of honor or virtue, so much as from downright ignorance of the nature of coin, credit, and circulation."*[17]
>
> -*John Adams*

Americans have always enshrined the right to trade freely, own property, and in general, practice business as each individual sees fit. The Declaration of Independence itself states that one of a person's unalienable rights is "the pursuit of Happiness" (but in the original draft, it was actually written as the "pursuit of Property"). Our founding fathers did not just bestow on us a Constitution and laws defining merely the role of government in politics, but also in our economics. The modern concern for the economy is nothing new. In fact, many historians have viewed the Revolution as primarily economic in nature, rather than political.[18] The American dream of personal prosperity with political equality to match has always been a constant one. But how does that integrate itself with our Constitution and the everyday life of us as citizens?

A sound economy, which enriches all, regardless of personal origin, has long been a hallmark of our American republic. For our predecessors and ourselves, equality has above all meant the equivalent ability to earn a living. Immigrants have poured into America for centuries looking to go from "rags to riches". Coming to the United States has been just as much about finding wealth as it has been about finding freedom. As a nation whose rallying cry during the Revolution was "taxation without representation," it is easy to see that we have always looked at our economic freedoms as intimately joined with our political ones.

This outlook has produced many benefits; we only have to look around ourselves at an immensely prosperous nation to see that. However, the joining of the economy with politics in the American mind has also generated problems. The debate over how far or not the government should go in regulating the economy has been with us since the earliest post-Constitutional debates. Then, it was the existence and legality of establishing a national bank, really nationalizing financial matters at all, that troubled our founders. Today, it is trade restrictions and federal taxation that most absorb the American businesses and public. It has also brought on a welfare system that tries to ensure that everyone has the chance to "make it" by providing subsidies to those the government deems less fortunate or less able. But as we heard earlier from Madison, the founders made no provision for the federal government to provide social welfare from the Treasury paid for by American citizens, even to relieve the suffering of others. As Americans argue over what is the right way to govern the nation's financial affairs, the economy has become the number one issue for elected officials and the number one concern for citizens. Politics has come to be not just conjoined with economics in the United States, but overshadowed by it.

Consumerism in America has reached all time highs as people attempt to get the most for their money after they get all the money that they can. But as Adams put it, "downright ignorance" on the nature of economics plagues America as a whole. Few understand the connection between the government and the economy, and even fewer realize the intricate balance that is a nation's economy. It's not just cash in the bank or the highs and lows of the stock market that determine a nation's financial successes or failures, but rather, trading that occurs on every level. The job one takes and what one buys has an effect as well. Every transaction has a value to it, whether physical money has been exchanged or not.

The government cannot possibly assume responsibility for every last economic activity, but it also cannot ignore those that are large enough to affect the whole nation. Politicians play with a delicate balancing act by toying with the economy while still catering to their constituents who want lower taxes but more government benefits.

Thomas Jefferson remarked in his First Inaugural Address that *"a wise and frugal government, which shall restrain men from injuring one another, which shall leave them otherwise free to regulate their own pursuits of industry and improvement, and shall not take from the mouth of labor the bread it has earned. This is the sum of good government, and this is necessary to close the circle of our felicities."*[19] Our Constitution provides for exactly this, a government that interferes to keep citizens from oppressing one another, but that otherwise, leaves each person to their freedoms. Yet our government has grown stronger and more meddlesome on the back of economic disasters, as citizens have turned to it to solve their financial woes. Unfortunately, the Constitution was not designed for politicians to solve all the people's problems, but rather to ensure the people's liberties.

By manipulating the "intentions" of the Constitution, bureaucrats have justified their actions as "ensuring social welfare" for more than half a century. But if that is truly what we as a people desire, than certainly a Constitutional amendment could be ratified by the whole nation to that effect. After all, if the federal government can enact and maintain such effective policies, then there should be no problem gaining the votes for such an amendment to be passed. Perhaps citizens no longer desire to take personal responsibility for "regulating their own pursuits of industry and improvement".

Our economy is being eroded even as it assumes preeminence in every aspect of American political life. We can either choose to return to the founders' original design or to change it through amendment, but we cannot continue to ignore undisciplined, uneducated, and unfettered fiscal policy-making currently being practiced by our politicians. By examining our economy's foundations, its place in modern life, and its effects on government and society, we will see what our economic future has in store and if it is a future worth fighting for or against.

Capitalism and the American Dream

"Our new Constitution is now established, and has an appearance that promises permanency; but in this world nothing can be said to be certain, except death and taxes."[1]

- Benjamin Franklin

That our nation has always been consumed with economic affairs is no surprise. Many of the chief complaints of the colonists before the American Revolution centered around financial burdens imposed on them by the British. Taxation without the consent of the citizens and trade restrictions particularly troubled the merchant middle class. Their feelings on their rights developed as much from economic oppressions as civil ones. As our nation has aged, these feelings have not changed significantly. The ability to find economic stability and growth has even helped trigger high levels of immigration over time.

Ironically, questioning or criticizing complete capitalism and free-trade as a basis for a federally governed economy has never gone over particularly well in a "free nation" (consider all the uproar over potential Communists in America during the Cold War). Naturally, given this history, hot-button political issues still include over-taxation and free trade, but rarely our economic system as a whole. Now, we have even combined Franklin's classic 'death and taxes' scenario. One is certain to be taxed, one is also certain to die, and one's family is certain to pay a 'death tax' on their inheritance. In America, truly the desire of everyone, including the federal government, to make money knows no bounds.

Capitalism has long appeared to pose the perfect potential to launch Americans to their dreams. As a nation, we have used and abused the idea of pure capitalism to create federal taxation, conspicuous consumerism, a national debt, and nearly limitless global trade. That most of our founding fathers would have opposed such unrestrained capitalism hardly seems to enter the equation anymore. Thomas Jefferson even opposed banking as an institution, once remarking that *"The system of banking [I] have...ever reprobated. I contemplate it as a blot left in all our Constitutions, which if not covered, will end in their destruction."*[2] If they were to view the unplanned economic hodge-podge that now passes for "capitalism", the founders would be stunned. How could they have ever forseen a nation who would leave their entire financial future in the hands of the federal government and immense corporations? They could never have comprehended how vast, but insecure, our financial footing would become. As our nation has aged, unbridled capitalism has caused our economy to crumble at its very foundations. As our founders feared, the true American dream of economic security through social and political equality has been corrupted by greed.

Taxation without Representation

> *"...debts, and taxes are the known instruments for bringing the many under the domination of the few."*[3]
>
> *- James Madison*

For our founding fathers, economic freedom was not just a post-revolutionary government concern, it was a formative pre-revolutionary notion as well. The various taxes imposed by the British government on the colonies, as well as the duties on the colonies' trade, struck at privileges long-enjoyed in colonial America (as well as at their pocketbooks). As the classic revolutionary rallying cry "taxation without representation" demonstrates, ideas of civil freedom and rights were inexorably tied to economic conditions. Many of our most basic American debates on human rights and liberties can be firmly linked to co-current economic concerns; slavery presents one of the best examples of this connection. In the United States, economic prosperity and autonomy has always been seen as a precursor to continuing civil liberty.

> *"...true individual freedom cannot exist without economic security and independence. 'Necessitous men are not free men.' People who are hungry, people who are out of a job are the stuff of which dictatorships are made."*[4]
>
> - Franklin D. Roosevelt

Financial security has always had its place in the American Dream. The rights of citizens to consent to their level of taxation and the duties they pay on trade goods fueled a Revolution and helped to establish a nation. Property rights also featured just as prominently for a people burdened by laws that allowed an individual's property to be used at the State's whim for quartering soldiers. One of the most infamous pre-revolutionary actions is the ultimate economic protest – The Boston Tea Party – where Bostonians hurled tea into the water rather than pay duties on it. Boycotts of imported goods (which other heavy duties had been placed on) and refusal to pay taxes increased as the Revolution drew closer.

Britain responded by only increasing economic sanctions against the Americans. Frustrations over economic tensions mounted on both sides of the Atlantic. The corresponding civil issue at stake was that Parliament contained no representatives elected by the citizens of the colonies, and therefore, was imposing unlawful acts on them. Britain, however, considered the colonists "virtually represented" by parliament members who had been elected by "similar voters" and therefore had similar interests (in theory anyway). Strains on the American wallet and American financial ability to pursue the dream of property first roused the people to Revolution, and ever since, have continued to be able to rouse them to action.

The creation of the Constitution and the establishment of the new federal government caused similar arguments over economic issues. The Articles of Confederation were rejected precisely because they could not bring enough economic stability to the new nation, especially with the federal government completely unable to collect taxes or compel the states to do much of anything. The lack of a national economy was causing the new nation to flounder. In establishing the Constitution, the founders came to the conclusion that granting the government some moderated authority over the economy would lead to increased prosperity for the majority of citizens (at least as long as the federal government did not have the power to take over the economy as Britain had).

After the Constitution's ratification, the divide over the National Bank struck at the heart of the importance of economic power in the new union. That this was one of the first major anti-federalist/federalist issues that divided the country along party lines is no surprise. Economic interests had helped Americans clarify their position on liberty during the Revolution, why not on the new Constitution's authority as well? The ability of potential economic impact to help elucidate other matters has since been well-established. Every possible issue in America can be addressed from its financial side, and continues to trigger citizen's concerns.

Our nation's greatest test of fortitude and durability came with the Civil War, and the questions it raised about American society and liberty. However, slavery, over time, had become more an issue of property rather than equality. For many Americans, the idea of the government taking away someone else's property (even if that property happened to be a person) was frightening because of the precedents it set. The economic impact that outlawing slavery would have had on Southern slaveholders was obvious to them as well. Why discard an institution that had served American economic interests and provided financial security for several centuries? Even Lincoln declared that *"I have no purpose, directly or indirectly, to interfere with the institution of slavery in the states where it exists. I believe I have no lawful right to do so, and I* *have no inclination to do so."*⁵ Most people who opposed slavery were trying to ban it from states that it did not exist in yet, so that property and states' rights would be unaffected. The right to property featured prominently in politics throughout the era, and the economic concerns surrounding slavery were joined to those surrounding "liberty for all".

These historical precedents have not been the exception, but the standard throughout American history. We have wrapped economic and political concerns so tightly together in our minds and in our culture that they can hardly ever be separated. The American dream of prosperity and freedom are intertwined within the fabric of our Constitution and our very way of life. We cannot discard them without getting rid of the rest of the foundation of our government. In establishing our laws, our founding fathers recognized our tendency to unite these aspects of our governance. Thus, the founders attempted to give the government oversight without turning it into an overseer.

Bring Me Your Poor

*"I think the best way of doing good to the poor, is not making them easy in poverty, but leading or driving them out of it."*⁶

- Benjamin Franklin

In wrapping our political and economic concerns together, we have made it only natural for the federal government to play an ever-increasing role in our national financial affairs. As our country has aged and changed, social conditions and economic crises have taught the American people to hand their control over to the government so it can fix our problems for us. Our government was designed to protect the American dream, so what could possibly be wrong about having it help us get there too? People have journeyed from all over the world to come to the United States, hoping to improve their lives. America has promised freedom to all, and with it, an unfettered hope of prosperity. The federal government, under the Constitution, was built to watch over this nation and protect the people. Why would anyone ever believe that granting such a theoretically benevolent and beneficial authority more power might create more problems than it solves? We have chosen not to answer this question, and to simply act like the Constitution grants the government these powers. Nothing can be cured, however, until we actually decide whether the government improves social welfare or hinders it when it interferes.

> *"That some should be rich, shows that others may become rich, and hence is just encouragement to industry and enterprise. Let not him who is houseless pull down the house of another; but let him labor diligently and build one for himself, thus by example assuring that his own shall be safe from violence when built."[7]*
>
> *- Abraham Lincoln*

The United States has attracted newcomers through immigration since the days of Christopher Columbus. The 'land of opportunity' called to people in their oppressed and impoverished lives elsewhere and eventually led them to the shores of America. Equality inspired these men and women, but it was the potential for economic success that brought them in by the boatload. Under the Constitution, anyone who had the drive could thrive in the new nation, without regard to personal origin (at least under the law). Immigration became part of the economic and social building blocks of the nation.

One of the economic troubles that urged the founding fathers towards war against Britain was restrictive immigration laws imposed on the colonies. The Declaration of Independence remarked that *"He [George III] has endeavoured to prevent the population of these States; for that purpose obstructing the Laws for Naturalization of foreigners; refusing to pass others to encourage their migrations hither, and raising the conditions of new Appropriations of Lands."*[8] The founders realized that immigration was necessary for the physical and economic expansion of the states, and that by constraining it, the British were effectively trying to limit the growth of the colonies. By bringing in new citizens, the new America expanded its economic base and its dreams.

While the country experienced economic growth under the new Constitution, it also suffered hardship. More than one general crisis arose relating to the development of a national economy, including the issues pertaining to the National Bank, and later the silver/gold basis of paper money. Each incident gave the government a little bit more control over the state of the economy, as citizens turned to their federal system for answers. The government often characterized the issue as banks versus citizens. And frequently, the federal government was right.

Banks and new industry had indeed taken advantage of the American citizenry on multiple occasions, and the federal government was the only one powerful enough to stop them when they did. The most influential of these recessions was obviously the Great Depression, and Franklin D. Roosevelt himself placed the blame at the feet of the greedy industrialists, capitalists, and banks. Under his leadership, the federal government came to define one of four "essential" freedoms as "freedom from want."[9] As poverty deepened throughout the country during the Great Depression, the nation relied more and more heavily on government-created jobs and federal funding programs to help them survive. Roosevelt's administration attempted to base the jobs on the principle that *"All work undertaken should be useful — not just for a day, or a year, but useful in the sense that it affords permanent improvement in living conditions or that it creates future new wealth for the Nation."*[10]

By trying to improve the overall social welfare, the Roosevelt government hoped to stay somewhat within its Constitutional authority. In the same address, Roosevelt stated that *"We have undertaken a new order of things; yet we progress to it under the framework and in the spirit and intent of the American Constitution."*[11] However, the changes initiated by the New Deal helped to transform the federal government from a protector into a benefactor, and in doing so, undid the very minor economic role the Constitution had actually established for our federal government.

In exchange for increased social welfare and economic stability, the citizens of America ceded more of their constitutional prerogatives to the federal government. However, the issues with this "new order" of things have always centered around two problems. First, no amendment to the Constitution was ever ratified giving the federal government these powers over our economy, even if the majority of citizens would agree, there is as of yet no legal basis for it. Secondly, by not passing an amendment to legalize such powers on the part of the bureaucracy, we have undermined the basis of our government as given to us by the founding fathers and set a dangerous precedent for the future.

Our country was founded on principles of economic growth and safety. This required a federal government to protect our interests, but not one to tell us what those interests are in the first place. The founders almost universally believed that the best way to uplift the impoverished was to inspire them to work towards something, not just give them everything they desire. Can we honestly claim that the modern welfare system is motivating the majority of its recipients to better themselves? Or has social security and welfare subsidies drained an economy that used to be based on notions of self-reliance and self-sufficiency? If these programs are so helpful and popular among the American citizenry then it should be no problem getting them authorized by the people as a whole. But many would rather hear of dollars being spent on giving the American people better "things" instead of protecting them from the things that harm both their liberty and long-term economic potential.

Our American dream has been traded in. No longer do we base it on our founders, the Constitution they wrote, or our predecessors' struggles that extolled hard work and personal responsibility as the road to economic success in an equal, free nation. As Americans we believe our government owes us something; that thing used to be protection from any person or group who would try to take away our liberties, be they economic or civil. Today, many people think the government owes them a handout (in whatever form) instead. By not holding our federal government accountable under the Constitution for the things it does, in fact, "owe" us, based on the contract between governors and governed, we allow our nation to slide further and further away from its founding principles and from the economic security we are seeking in the first place.

A republic whose government's purpose is to defend its rights, but never usurp them, not even on projects of benevolence, has a chance to stand the test of time. In undoing the very things established for us to make us stronger as a whole, we have undone the very things which make our nation great for all its people. The economy is an important part of every person's life, and to protect the economy is the government's responsibility. But, we cannot expect the government to save it. There is a difference between protection and interference, and until we learn it, we permit our government to take on powers it should not. These powers place us on a dangerous road, one foreseen by our founders, leading away from a democratic republic and into a dictatorship.

It is not enough to have a Constitution, and a federal government established under it; we, as citizens, must hold that government to the rule of law, until we choose as a majority to change those laws. Our government is accountable only to us as a people. If we allow it to grow too much outside its legal limitations, it will eventually consume the very thing it was supposed to protect- our rights. Without our rights, our economy fails as well. The American dream has tied them together, for better or worse.

A New Deal

> *"The test of our progress is not whether we add more to the abundance of those who have much; it is whether we provide enough for those who have too little."*[12]
>
> Franklin D. Roosevelt

The economic catastrophe brought by the Great Depression fueled a new era in America, one with a New Deal for the American people. This deal proposed that the government was designed to defend social welfare, and thus, it was responsible for sustaining it as well. The idea that the government should provide for, as well as, protect the people required a re-imagining of the founders' principles and the Constitution. The Roosevelt administration relied on judicial review instead of Constitutional amendments as the basis for the adoption of this new political scheme. At the time, the Supreme Court often shot down various New Deal programs that just went too far beyond the legal Constitutional norm. But, in the panic of the moment, social and economic concerns became more closely bound in American society than ever before, and the New Deal agenda grew increasingly popular with an impoverished nation.

By the time the nation resumed normal life after World War II; American citizens had become dependent upon the federal government. What would have once been seen as federal interference in daily life had become the government's duty. Government benefits for the people required the government to exercise greater control in public affairs – generating social security numbers for identification, licensing people for jobs, or creating more bureaucracy to manage the work load (among many things). In accepting the "new deal" as the American standard, the old dream of unfettered liberty and prosperity has been eroded.

> *"Power always sincerely, conscientiously, **de très bon foi**, believes itself right. Power always thinks it has a great soul and vast views, beyond the comprehension of the weak."*[13]
>
> *- John Adams*

With the launch of New Deal American society, intended to solve tall he economic and social woes of the citizenry through government programs, taxation became more important than ever to the United States government. Extensive federal agendas coupled with increased federal employment of individuals required significantly enlarged funding. The most logical place for the government to obtain this money was through taxation, the classic solution for bureaucracies looking to build up the gold pot. The legality of the income tax had already been established by the ratification of the 16th amendment in 1913, which stated *"The Congress shall have power to lay and collect taxes on incomes, from whatever source derived, without apportionment among the several States, and without regard to any census or enumeration."*[14] The increase in federal programs had therefore increased the percentage of taxed income, rather than necessarily caused the existence of the income tax itself.

The problems with federal taxation are not due to its existence's unconstitutionality, but rather, it's facilitation of other unconstitutional actions. The Greek philosopher Plato once stated that *"when there is an income tax, the just man will pay more and the unjust man less on the same amount of income...mankind censures injustice, fearing that they may be the victims of it and not because they shrink for committing it...injustice is a man's own profit and interest."*[15] His point aptly illustrates our problem with modern federal taxation. As the final purpose of taxes becomes serving the government more than the people, inequality among citizens becomes the standard. The Constitution may allow an income tax, but it has certainly never taken away equal rights under the law. And the biggest problem with our taxation of income has been finding an "equal" way to tax people with different levels of income. In allowing a perversion of a legal amendment to continue, we permit the erosion of the true American dream – equality under the law (and therefore, equal economic opportunity).

With the advent of the new nation, we faced the beginning of another socio-economic concern, the national debt. In the beginning, the acceptance of a national federal debt was very important and served two purposes 1) to unite the colonies under the federal government through the economy and 2) to establish a basis for a national economy (and a plan to go with it). Alexander Hamilton advocated for these policies both as Secretary of the Treasury and Federalist Party head. As he pronounced in a letter to a fellow politician, *"A national debt, if it is not excessive, will be to us a national blessing."*[16]

For the early American republic, it was indeed a boon. The national debt allowed the states to come together and give the federal government enough power to set the economic agenda and properly maintain currency levels in an effort to gradually rebuild the previously war-driven economy. However, the plan was to pay off all the debts incurred by the Revolution and in construction of the new union as quickly as possible. The national debt was never meant to be a permanent piece of national finance, but rather a temporary tool to bring together the states under the federal authority by taking on debts that already existed. The national debt was designed to pay off revolutionary war debts, not take on new financial liabilities.

In accepting the direction the New Deal created, America increased the amount it was required to spend on federal programs. The federal income tax has not generated enough revenue to make up for the level of spending these programs have produced. Instead of protecting our country's economic future, we have used the national debt to mortgage that future. As Thomas Jefferson once put it, *"the principle of spending money to be paid by posterity, under the name of funding, is but swindling futurity on a large scale."*[17] We may save the economy in the short term through federal funding, but in bequeathing a large national debt onto each subsequent generation, we start their economic balance sheet in the negative.

The problem with the American Dream is that it is no longer about hope and opportunity for a better future for every citizen, because it has become no longer important to plan for that social and economic future. Thomas Jefferson once wrote that economy in the economy was *"among the first and most important republican virtues, and public debt, the greatest of the dangers to be feared."*[18] With the dawn of the New Deal, preparing initiatives to ensure American economic survival fifty years down the road has been supplanted by programs purely for the present. National public debt has been used to finance programs that American simply cannot afford at the moment. The justification for this lack of proper economic planning on the part of the federal government has been the refrain of "social welfare."

However, nowhere in the Constitution does "social welfare" ever take priority over the rule of law and protection of citizens' rights. James Madison had commented that *"With respect to the words, 'general welfare,' I have always regarded them as qualified by the details of power connected with them. To take them in a literal and unlimited sense would be a metamorphosis of the Constitution...[that] was not contemplated by the creators."*[19] Our Constitution was not designed to encompass a government welfare-based society, even one attempting to do as much as it can to provide for its people. By placing our future generations into insurmountable debt, we place their rights into jeopardy. If anything, our nation is meant to maintain these rights for our progeny, even if it means depriving the current generation of greater material wealth. In only trying to afford the present, we, as Americans, have bankrupted our future.

The American dream of economic stability and a chance for prosperity for every citizen has been a guiding principle for the United States since its inception under the Constitution. The founders realized that as a nation it is not enough just to live for the moment, we must also have hope, hope for a better tomorrow. The great genius of American society in incorporating this vision into law was not to create the perfect democracy or the best capitalist state – it was to create the most freedom. That freedom has meant the equality of everyone under the law, where the government plays no favorites, so that each and every citizen has the opportunity to succeed if they strive hard enough in the right direction.

Liberty and equality in the United States of America has meant economic growth over the long haul. Only when we alter the very basis of who we are and what we stand for does our economic spirit begin to waver. We should strive for the very thing that George Washington boasted of to an American minority group during the post-Revolution era: *"All possess alike liberty of conscience and immunities of citizenship... For happily the Government of the United States, which gives to bigotry no sanction, to persecution no assistance, requires only that they who live under its protection should demean themselves as good citizens in giving it on all occasions their effectual support."*[20] By supporting our founding principles and the rule of our Constitution, we enable our republic and our economy to function fully.

THE PRICE OF FREEDOM

> *"If it be asked, What is the most sacred duty and the greatest source of our security in a Republic? The answer would be, An inviolable respect for the Constitution and Laws — the first growing out of the last... A sacred respect for the constitutional law is the vital principle, the sustaining energy of a free government."*[21]
>
> - Alexander Hamilton

Freedom always comes at a cost. Securing that freedom can sometimes come at an even greater price. Personal sacrifice can be required of us in order to guarantee the same freedoms to our progeny that our predecessors bought for us. The price may come through war, or economic hardship. But by persevering under our legal system of governance, we bestow upon the America of tomorrow the same gift that was given to us – freedom. Our economic triumphs as a nation have not been due to any magical capitalist formula or even great luck; instead, the principles of hard work, initiative, and endurance in the face of adversity have allowed us to carve a living out of a huge nation. If we want to embrace the American dream and give it to our children, we have to accept the Constitution for what it is (and if it's really not fitting, properly modify it through amendment). We have to be willing to work on our economy through a truly common national plan instead of always expecting the government to produce a quick-fix. If we can make these changes in our outlook now, then we will continue to have the hope of future free days.

The Big Business Boom and Bust

"These capitalists generally act harmoniously and in concert to fleece the people, and now that they have got into a quarrel with themselves, we are called upon to appropriate the people's money to settle the quarrel."[1]

- Abraham Lincoln

Capitalism has long been represented as the economic system that truly enables the American Dream. Under this theory, the means of production are privately controlled and operated, and the Market Economy governs national finance. It is characterized by the belief that capital, or existing wealth can be used to create greater, future wealth, and it is this that holds the key to a sound economy, hence the term "capitalism". Businesses, corporations, and other financial institutions in the United States have been only too happy to accept this as our governing economic principle. And though capitalism has clearly provided for innovation and initiative in the marketplace, it has also heavily favored big businesses (and correspondingly bigger government to control them). Particularly since the advent of socialism, capitalism, in its most aggressive form, has become part of the essence of being "American".

There are several problems that arise, especially concerning our government, because of our economy's reliance on pure capitalism. Firstly, capitalism makes no allowances or opportunities for those who lack capital, namely the presently impoverished. Even in those very American "rags to riches" stories, inventors of fabulous new technology either have to secure investment from those who already have the capital or stow away savings for years, from a low-paying job, to accumulate enough capital to start their enterprise. This means that even though capitalism allows for significant economic potential, it is in no way inherently equal for the people living under the system, because those who inherit or already have capital have much better odds of success than those without it. Secondly, under capitalism, the capitalists are always seeking ever greater capital. Basically, there is never an end or a self-imposed limit on the reach of business. In order to thrive, a business can never, ever stop growing – to become stagnant, to have a steady clientele but no new customers, means eventual failure.

The problem presented by the requirement of constant growth is clear; a business must continue to do whatever is necessary for growth and success, even short change or use their own consumers. The end-line profit eventually becomes the only thing that matters. Most problematically, capitalism, (contrary to popular opinion) causes companies to possess significant concern about how our government functions. In fact, anything that could possibly affect a business' profit margins demands that company's attention. Because of this necessity, corporations must actively attempt to influence the government until it does what the corporation needs, regardless of the common national good. It also means that they typically rely on the government and its regulations to save them from their own financial mistakes, and hence, their own demise. Capitalism, after all, leaves little room for error; someone is always ready to step in and take the place of a lagging commercial enterprise. Since capitalism and democracy have become enshrined as "American" in citizens' minds, the potential dangers from this quarter have only increased.

The Cost of Doing Business: Corporate-Government Relations

> "The real truth of the matter is, as you and I know, that a financial element in the larger centers has owned the Government ever since the days of Andrew Jackson...The country is going through a repetition of Jackson's fight with the Bank of the United States – only on a far bigger and broader basis."[2]
>
> - Franklin D. Roosevelt

The corporations of America naturally have an interest in the functioning of our government. Our government imposes regulatory laws, defines corruption and monopoly, and controls national economic basics (from the tax rate to the minimum wage to international trade restrictions). Any one of these things can directly affect a business' performance; all of them, together, drastically govern the ways in which companies are allowed to do business in this country. Even since the days of our founding fathers, companies have strived to use the law in whatever manner best suited their financial positions. This has been through options as simple as convincing Congress to modify a particular law or has gone as far as flagrant violation of the same.

At the end of the day, most corporations have been willing to lie, cheat, and steal their way to higher profit margins regardless of what our laws say. Sometimes they have bought their way out of government reprisal, and sometimes they grease the government wheel (through gifts to influential Congressmen, Judges, or Law Enforcement Officials) just enough to avoid punishment entirely. That is not to say there have never been any honest businessmen in America, just no honest businesses. Capitalism does not allow a business to take a backseat to any federal authority or the rights of people when it comes to financial gain – to always do so would inevitably spell ruin. Because of this inherent interest, our founders attempted to build a Constitution that had enough power to look after only the people and not let people's rights be bought out by economic profits. They firmly believed that the cost of national economic prosperity through free enterprise should never involve a buyout of civil liberties.

> *"Certainly no nation ever before abandoned to the avarice and jugglings of private individuals, to regulate according to their own interests, the quantum of circulating medium for the nation."*[3]
>
> - *Thomas Jefferson*

The Constitution did not make capitalism America's economic system of choice; in fact, the Constitution does not even mention the term (never, not even through amendments). Despite a strong merchant presence amongst the colonies, the founding fathers did not trust entrenched financial institutions, be they businesses or banks. Thomas Jefferson also once noted that *"Merchants have no country. The mere spot they stand on does not constitute so strong an attachment as that from which they draw their gains."*[4] This statement aptly illustrates the founders' fundamental faith in the theory that those with wealth seek always to preserve and aggrandize that wealth, regardless of whether this wealth is physical or metaphorical in form. For the revolutionary generation, those individuals who strived for political or economic power without regard for its broader effects could not be trusted with either. The founding fathers knew how unbridled ambition in any aspect of the new nation could be a very dangerous prospect; for that was among the chief factors that had destroyed the ancient republics. The Constitution and our laws were therefore not designed to protect the economy or anyone's place in it, but to safeguard the *rights* of the citizenry.

The efforts of large, vested American financial institutions to maintain their own economic status throughout our history cannot be denied. Just as our government cannot be trusted to do anything besides its Constitutional role of protector, our predecessors knew businesses could not be trusted to do anything besides their economic role of accumulating wealth. Under our current economic system, there has simply been no other way for a financial institution to succeed besides continuous growth.

Our economic code of laws has effectively been lawyered away in an attempt to give corporations the same legal privileges as individuals while limiting their liability as a group, under a notion called "corporate personhood." This argument on behalf of big institutionalized business dates all the way back to the late 1800s, with a landmark Supreme court case[5] involving one of the giant railroad companies, now infamous in American history for their level of graft and corruption. While initially this concept may have seemed logical (or profitable for the officials who permitted it), it has effectively lessened government control over corporations by turning them into artificial citizens. In making a corporate entity an undying "person" of enormous wealth and influence, we have essentially allowed the creation of a corporate aristocrat (in a republican nation no less).

That capitalism, supposedly the most "democratic" and "American" of economic systems, has permitted the existence of these corporate aristocrats is unfortunately no mere ironic manipulation of words. Like a hereditary Duke or Prince, the corporation never truly dies, for its members can be replaced, thus maintaining its role in society and the economy. They continue to wield the power and the influence of its position and its inherent wealth, ad infinitum. Even bankruptcy, the utter financial failure of a corporation, does not mean its necessary end, for corporations have been permitted under Chapter 11 of the United States legal code to use bankruptcy as a tool to forgo their debts and continue operations. By perverting the laws of an "equal" nation, economic institutions have entrenched themselves and their own interests within those belonging to the people, claiming the people's needs and rights are identical to their own.

Instead of checking our reliance on the economy as a basis of American freedom, we have allowed our dependency on prosperity to grow. This has permitted businesses and banks to gain undue influence over our present and future as a nation, depending on their own financial interests at the time. They do not operate under any Constitutional obligation, as our government does, to maintain the rights of the citizenry. In his Second State of the Union Address in 1935, Franklin D. Roosevelt stated that the federal government had *"a clear mandate from the people, that Americans must forswear the conception of the acquisition of wealth, which, through excessive profits, creates undue private power over private affairs and, to our misfortune, over public affairs as well.*"[6] In three-quarters of a century, we still have not heeded this call as a nation.

We have effectively allowed businesses and banks to influence our level of rights, which ridiculously violates the very principles of the Constitution. In permitting interested parties to determine the course of our national economic future, we act incredibly irresponsibly with the liberties our predecessors fought and died to ensure. This in no way means that the ties between a free economy and a free nation will not always be close. However, it does mean that a free nation governs itself and does not allow its economy to govern for it.

In assuming that unadulterated capitalism is the only course for a democratic republic like our own, we have undermined the very values our Constitution attempted to guarantee. Businesses and banks have never operated under any legal requirement to preserve our liberties, and they frequently choose not to do so even when given the occasion. The President during our Great Depression once remarked that *"No business which depends for its existence on paying less than living wages to its workers has any right to continue in this country."*[7] That the minimum wage is still frequently paid to workers in this nation, and that it keeps these same workers below the national poverty line still speaks to a crisis that faced our nation in the 1930s. Citizens who have grown up dreaming the American Dream clearly do not believe in wages that they cannot live on or jobs that have no benefits. They do not want to be forced to rely on the federal government more and more to make up the shortfalls. The cost of doing business in America is high, and for the people of this nation, it has grown even higher.

Corporate Takeover: Co-Opting the American Dream

> *"It was natural and perhaps human that the privileged princes of these new economic dynasties, thirsting for power, reached out for control over government itself. They created a new despotism and wrapped it in the*

> robes of legal sanction. In its service new mercenaries sought to regiment the people, their labor, and their property."[8]
>
> - Franklin D. Roosevelt

The American government has consistently caved in the face of incredibly powerful business interest. Corporations have spent their time, influence, and money convincing the American people to hold the government accountable for the economy instead of them. Companies continuously tell us how they hold the very key to the American Dream; if we would only use their product or buy into a certain lifestyle, we could be prosperous American citizens. In the meantime, they are busy breaking business regulatory laws and fudging their accounting information in order to drive their stock prices higher. Businesses that claim to be the friend and ally of the average American are engaged in lowering employee benefits and reducing jobs in American industry to go along with the lower prices on the goods they sell.

When we pay the cheapest price for an item or invest in a stock that makes a suspiciously above average return, the businesses doing the selling and trading conveniently neglect to explicitly mention that in order to provide such "great" prices, they have taken the labor and customer service sections of their company overseas. Yet somehow, we in the United States have become more convinced than ever that the people who actually control many aspects of our economy are not liable for its problems, but totally responsible for its benefits.

> "Never spend your money before you have it. Never buy what you do not want, because it is cheap; it will be dear to you."[9]
>
> - Thomas Jefferson

The American life certainly does not come cheaply. It is no longer just the modest house (that one can actually afford) with the white picket fence; now it also includes the car, cell phone, high-definition TV, computer, and all the other high-end devices a "typical American" cannot live without. Not to mention, everyone is looking for a bigger, better house (up-selling their current home in the process, no matter what its true worth) because granite countertops are higher on the list of American priorities than actually being able to afford your mortgage payment.

Businesses in our country have only encouraged this rampant consumerism. The more people spend, the higher the profits of those doing the selling. The ability to turn to a large corporation for credit- basically money one does not currently have – has caused more and more citizens to fall under the sway of debt. The companies who have done this lending do not have to worry overly much about a consumer's debt-to-income ratio because they can simply heighten the interest rate as a precaution. Or when all else fails, cry for a government bailout or else the people might lose their things! Instead of earning money and saving it up for major purchases, the American public receives a message to "buy it now and pay later" (plus interest, of course).

Companies that extend credit do so on the basis of whether someone can eventually pay it back, and not on whether they can truly afford it. The longer someone is paying a debt, the higher the interest received. These same businesses advertise how "convenient" and "rewarding" their credit programs are, but they fail to mention that they provide this wonderful service because they get something out of the deal. Corporations do not extend credit to "reward" or "convenience" people; they do it to make money off the interest and fees.

The extension of credit and encouragement of purchasing power in the present is a pure business venture, not a charity. The issue with this new "American" way of life is not that credit is inherently bad or without its economic uses; it is the message that creditors and businesses propagate to the people. Basically, the refrain goes that the more goods one has (even if one goes into debt constantly to obtain them), the more truly "American" one becomes. But even for our founders, who understood the connections between political and economic freedom, possessions were not everything. As Franklin Roosevelt once stated, *"Happiness lives not in the mere possession of money...The joy and moral stimulation of work no longer must be forgotten in the mad chase of evanescent profit."*[10] In propagating the so-called "American" lifestyle and the material perception of success as contingent on rampant consumerism, businesses in our nation have placed earning profit over providing quality goods and services to the people.

The same disrespect for American origins and American laws in the supposed pursuit of the all-American life has inspired numerous legal violations by executives at the same large companies. Insider trading, graft, and "creative" financial accounting, among other "white-collar" crimes, continue to plague the business centers of this country. Activities like these, so-called "white-collar crimes" because they do not physically harm other people, have caused substantial financial problems throughout the country.

Thousands of laborers have faced lay-offs at work in corporate efforts to "improve efficiency"; but really to boost bottom line profits for its few elite trustees and shareholders. Pensions have disappeared for many retired workers (even when they have spent their whole working lives with the same company) due to manipulations of bankruptcy proceedings; while executives (who have been at the company for a few years) suffer little to no material losses from managing a business into the ground. It is a lot easier to take risks in business when you know your own personal bank account will rarely suffer any great losses. Violating regulatory laws is much easier when the pay-off is relatively high in comparison to the punishment one will receive.

The callous disposition of corporations to average wage-earners has come from both the ease of finding replacements and the level of gain involved from doing so. To begin a basic and brief example, the federal minimum wage[11] in the United States is $7.25 hourly, which amounts to about $15,080[12] annually before taxes; this is the lowest section of the reported, full-time working population. According to the CIA World Fact Book for 2011 and the Federal Labor Bureau, the American per capita GDP in the same year was $47, 400 per year (also before taxes); this means that a middle-income worker in this country theoretically make around this amount (the GDP is an average). In marked contrast to the above wages, the average CEO from a top 500 American company earns $10.9 million dollars[13] each year[14]. And they get to set the wage of those who earn so much less.

For better comparison purposes, the President of the United States[15] only earns $400,000 in yearly salary. The highest-paid military position, a four-star general or admiral serving on the Joint Chiefs of Staff, makes only $223,000 yearly (that would be for someone who is in charge of an entire branch of military service and has already spent at minimum, the last 30 years, if not more, serving that nation in the military), and many high-ranking officers make less than half that amount). Putting all those numbers further into perspective, that means that the average CEO (Chief Executive Officer of a company) earns 27 times more in salary than the President of the United States (the Chief Executive of our entire country). That, as a nation, we find this acceptable certainly sends a message to those same CEOs. They know they can get away with low wages for everyone else but themselves and their top executives, and that most people will think it's what an economy should look like.

When the pay-off is so large, how many people would not engage in insider trading in order to remain the CEO of a company that pays them over ten million dollars each year. After all, many corporations have made a concerted effort to let us know that their various legal violations are not a big deal, and that despite them, they are really sorry and business will continue as usual. In the business world, it is not too terrible to engage in any of these illicit practices, just bad to be caught. Since the stock market is now what determines a "good" company and whether or not the economy is doing well, most corporations and their leaders will sell out their workers and deceive their shareholders in order to drive their stock up half a percent by the closing bell. Until we as Americans realize that businesses have co-opted the American Dream, and manipulated it for their own ends, we will continue to demand the wrong things of our government and allow corporations to not live up to their potential or responsibilities.

Networked: Connections among the Elite

"There is danger from all men. The only maxim of a free government ought to be to trust no man living with power to endanger the public liberty."[16]

- John Adams

With great wealth also comes great influence in our nation. According to the new American lifestyle, it is money that defines success, and who would want their political or business leaders to not come from the ranks of the successful and prosperous? As citizens, we most greatly respect those who embody the American character and who seem to represent our needs and interests (or at least they tell us that they do). Knowing this, the corporate aristocrats spend their extra millions getting themselves or someone of like background elected to public office by telling each segment of the American people what the elite thinks they want to hear. And we believe them because many other people seem to, and we have gradually forgotten James Madison's warning that *"The man who is possessed of wealth, who lolls on his sofa or rolls in his carriage, cannot judge the wants or feelings of the day-laborer."*[17]

We have enabled our government to be run by an elite without ever actually ending our republic or even knowing that it is slowly dying. This elite aristocracy of the wealthy is marked by business and social ties that extend into political ones. Any good business would want to make sure the government acts in its favor on certain issues, to ensure continued profit. Networking is a business essential, and for the wealthiest of America, essential to business, politics and every aspect of life.

> *"It is to be regretted that the rich and powerful too often bend the acts of government to their selfish purposes. Distinctions in society will always exist under every just government...But there are no necessary evils in government. Its evils exist only in its abuses. If it would confine itself to equal protection, and, as Heaven does it rains, showers, its favors alike on the high and the low, the rich and the poor, it would be an unqualified blessing."*[18]
>
> *- Andrew Jackson*

The corporate aristocracy that forms the core of the elite in this nation has benefited greatly from laws that allow passed-down wealth and greater wealth to be subject to fewer tax penalties and restrictions. Trust funds and interest taxation laws have made collecting taxes from the already affluent virtually meaningless. If invested properly, money from 150 years ago can still be accruing more money in an account today, while allowing its beneficiaries to live off the interest. Basically, these rules have created a generation of trust fund elite: people who are very rich, but who did not originate the wealth they live off of nor do they contribute to the management of family assets in any way. And it is not even that this is necessarily a problem, but it is rather the ability of these elite to avoid any financial burdens via taxation that the rest of the population must pay.

This elite possesses great influence over American society and culture, not because they have done anything, but merely from being born into the ranks of the wealthy. These members of society are virtually identical in type and form to the formerly much-despised royal courts and nobility that democratic and republican societies have long eschewed as examples of corrupt and tyrannical governors. And just as during the height of aristocratic rule in Europe, the corporate aristocrats have become a permanent, self-propagating group in American society, passing down wealth and influence (be it social or political) to each subsequent generation.

But why should it matter to an average American if the benefits of prosperity give one benefits for oneself and one's children and allow one to become closely connected to the leaders in every aspect of society? The American Dream is property and happiness for all, why should it make any difference whether it stays around for generations or not, as long as everyone has an equal chance to break into that crowd? The problem is the odds have become less and less in favor of the average citizen's ability - to go from "rags to riches".

Congressional corruption, fueled by the dollars of business, has grown more and more rampant. Among a group of people who know each other very well, even less-illegal acts of favoritism occur each time our federal government meets. Contracts are awarded to established companies that have some connection with a politician (regardless of whether a startup company might have come in cheaper or with a better price for the product). Laws are established to "promote the economy" that mostly end up benefiting the pocket of the prosperous, and not the poor. Deals are made to save companies that have fallen on financial ruin because they provide "vital services" to the American people, even though the average American consumer is often maltreated by these same services (which now have absolutely no incentive to please their customers, a supposedly vital tenant of capitalism anyway). But for the elite who run the businesses and government of our nation, it's simply doing a friend or themselves a favor.

Politicians operate under no requirement to give up management of their financial wealth while in office, and since only the most blatant acts of preferential treatment and nepotism are picked up on or even truly illegal, how many people can honestly say that they would not line their own pockets at the expense of the broader government? And thus, the government becomes wasteful, spending more of the people's money than is within their authority, and liberties are abridged (ever so slightly) to convenience those with greater influence and assets.

> *"We find our population suffering from old inequalities, little changed by vast sporadic remedies. In spite of our efforts and in spite of our talk, we have not weeded out the over privileged and we have not effectively lifted up the underprivileged. Both of these manifestations of injustice have retarded happiness...we do not destroy ambition, nor do we seek to divide our wealth into equal shares on stated occasions. We continue to recognize the greater ability of some to earn more than others. But we do assert that the ambition of the individual to obtain for him and his a proper security, a reasonable leisure, and a decent living throughout life, is an ambition to be preferred to the appetite for great wealth and great power."*[19]
>
> *- Franklin D. Roosevelt*

Franklin D. Roosevelt made this speech over 70 years ago to a nation suffering under the most crippling economic crisis in its history. Today, these inequalities have only worsened under the same type of "sporadic remedies" Roosevelt deplored in his speech. In the place of a sound plan for the American dream and the American future, our federal government has dedicated itself to remedying problems only as they arise. This has not been necessarily because of incompetence, but rather, apathy. The business elite that have taken control of the American nation and changed the nature of the American dream have only devoted themselves to solving problems after the average citizens complain or suffer from them. For this interconnected group, the ability to weather the storms of the world has been bought with laws that give them separate protections from those afforded to the average person. The unity of economic, political, and social leaders and fortunes has begun to lead our nation down a road it was not ever designed to go- one where the voices of the ordinary citizens must scream ever louder to be heard.

In Pursuit of Happiness – American Financial Life

"Happy are the men, and happy the people who grow wise by the misfortunes of others."

- John Dickinson, American Revolutionary

History is full of examples of how nations rise and fall in every aspect of community life- social, political, and economic. In America, our civil liberties and freedoms have always been tied up with our financial prosperity. But when times are good and money comes in easily, we have tended to only loosely guard our laws. Even worse are the times when our financial situation declines, and then we have looked for someone to save us from our woes. We, as a nation, look to point our finger at *whom* the problem is instead of the underlying factors that have created the issue in the first place.

We are not the first nation in history to be complacent in wealth, but accusatory in hardship. In recent times, we have charged our government (most especially, the Presidency) with our financial success or failure as a nation. In doing so, we have given great powers, unoriginal to our Constitution, to our federal government. By allowing this, we have charged them with a duty that was supposed to be our own as citizens. The lack of responsible business practices in America can also be called to task for our fluctuating economic conditions, yet as citizens and consumers, we hold the key to their permitted behaviors.

If the financial misfortunes endured during the American Revolution have taught us anything, it is that the citizenry possesses the ultimate control over both government and business activities. The act of hurling tea into the Atlantic Ocean certainly contained a powerful message for both the politicians imposing the various Stamp Acts and the businesses not upholding the general American boycott on tea. As citizens of a nation, we must not only expect appropriate and legal behavior from our government and the companies who do business in our country, we must also be willing to step up and enforce it.

We must take personal responsibility for our futures and that of our posterity. A Revolutionary, John Dickinson wrote his *"dear countrymen"* that *"A people is traveling fast to destruction, when **individuals** consider **their** interests as distinct from **those of the public**. Such notions are fatal to their country, and to themselves."*[1] All our choices matter, from the smallest ones to the largest. When people refuse to consider the rest of their American brethren when they make their votes and engage in activities in society, then our nation slowly fails. If our government is to continue to succeed and our economy to prosper, we must accept our role in not just the fate that befalls ourselves, but all our fellow Americans as well. Our freedoms are always improved when we also respect the freedoms of others. In pursuing the happiness promised by the American Dream, we should remember that others pursue that dream as well.

The Lies We Tell Ourselves: Living in a Land of Make-Believe

> *"the great problem of legislation is, so to organize the civil government of a community...that in the operation of human institutions upon social action, self-love and social may be made the same."*[2]

-John Quincy Adams

Cohesive national sentiment has always been hard to come by, especially in a country like America. The problem is that not everyone agrees on what is best for the nation, and not agreeing is a grand part of the American tradition. This has especially been true when it comes to the economy; what may be financially good for one segment of the country can at the same time be ruinous for another. American government, with its checks and balances, was basically designed as a great equalizer for the needs and wants of the many, many different citizens.

But it is not really that simple, because the founding fathers also believed in a nation where people did not participate in the spirit of factions. As James Madison put it in *The Federalist Papers*, *"By faction, I understand a number of citizens, whether amounting to a majority or a minority of the whole, who are united and actuated by some common impulse of passion, or of interest, adversed to the rights of other citizens, or to the permanent and aggregate interests of the community."*[3] To bear the good of the whole in mind while still maintaining our own interests has become a lost art in American politics. A staunch faith that our republic means "majority rules" has become the norm in this country; something that the founders never considered to be true. In their minds, a good republic protected the rights of lesser groups as well as majority groups because the entire point of not living under a monarchy or dictatorship was that even the most unimportant individual still had a voice in his own governance.

Our economy, of all American institutions, aptly demonstrates this modern abstinence from the pursuit of national harmony. Companies are allowed to use policies that hurt the small-time worker, and they are still allowed to pay wages that do not allow a person to earn a living in this country. If anything, inequality in our society is once again on the rise as the government continues to spend as if money was going out of style; businesses seek to take advantage of political positions; and citizens continually vote their pocketbooks instead of their consciences.

> *"For too many of us the political equality we once had won was meaningless in the face of economic inequality. A small group had concentrated into their own hands an almost complete control over other people's property, other people's money, other people's labor – other people's lives. For too many of us life was no longer free; liberty no longer real; men could no longer follow the pursuit of happiness."*[4]
>
> - Franklin D. Roosevelt

It is easy to tell ourselves that our government owes us in some way; that other people are responsible for our woes and thus, also for fixing them. It is even easier to focus on all the fault others bear for our present circumstances without looking to see if we ourselves have gone wrong in any way. In the case of America's current state of financial affairs, the fact is that it is very easy to point the finger to the errors made by our government and the selfishness of business interests. But, at the end of the day, these institutions are led by people, by citizens, who have failed to fully consider the harm or good their actions might cause to fellow citizens.

The real problem is the lack of concern for other people's rights. We spend so much time worrying about the freedoms we want for ourselves that we often forget to pass onto others, those opportunities given to us. The great triumph of Franklin D. Roosevelt's Depression Administration was the re-taking of rights for the people, which corporations had consumed in the pursuit of profit. However, the many programs instituted during this same era have left many Americans with a sense of entitlement and dependency on the government to solve their problems, particularly economic ones. By understanding that the government's true role is not to assume total control over each citizen's future, but rather, that it is our job to ensure our own success – we place our rights and freedoms back where they belong, into our own hands.

While the government is responsible for enforcing our laws and protecting us from corruption in financial centres, we have a role as citizens and consumers in policing our nation's businesses as well. Even when we do realize the abuses of a particular company, we often fail to take action (or sometimes even consider what actions we could take).

And then sometimes we choose not to use the abilities in our power to hold businesses accountable because it is easier not to take a stand.

For the revolutionary generation, boycotts on both goods with unacceptable duties, and businesses with unacceptable practices, were commonplace. Even during the two world wars, the role of the boycott still existed in a powerful way. German goods went completely off the market as most Americans would not purchase anything from someone at war with the American nation. (And even products like hamburgers that were being made in America had their names changed to 'freedom burgers' to put distance between them and any German association). These previous generations of Americans endured great hardship in their standard of living between rationing and boycotts, but they did it anyways because they wanted to enforce standards on business practices in support of American interests. They knew that they had to personally ensure the victory of America at home and abroad through their actions as citizens and consumers.

Unions, too, used to play a major part in maintaining American interests in the decisions of large corporations. Unions helped to protect standards, wages, and pensions for citizens in the American workplace; they also ensured stable business ethics and workplace conditions. That is not to say that unions have no had their own issues, but their origins and true purpose as an accountability tool remains. The demonization and demise of major unions in this country has only led to further problems in the ability of the American consumer public to mobilize. The right of the citizenry and the working population to organize to fight injustice and campaign against violations to the American labor force has unquestionable origins in our national Constitution. To waive this right because some companies tell us that we do not want unions or some form of labor and consumer organization is simply ludicrous.

We as Americans now prefer to earn a dollar more an hour or to pay a dollar less for an item than support companies who do right by American workers and by the consumer public. We have allowed corporations to turn our financial stability into a numbers game instead of actually caring about what is going on in our economy. In not exercising our ability to punish an irresponsible company, we merely allow that company to continue violating our laws and standards. As Americans, we need to return to our roots, where a product's origins and the company behind it influenced our decision to purchase said product, and not just its end-line price.

> *"We reconsecrate our country to long-cherished ideals in a suddenly changed civilization. In every land there are always at work forces that drive men apart and forces that draw men together. In our personal ambitions we are individualists. But in our seeking for economic and political progress as a nation, we all go up, or else we all go down, as one people. To maintain a democracy of effort requires a vast amount of patience in dealing with differing methods, a vast amount of humility. But out of the confusion of many voices rises an understanding of dominant public need. Then political leadership can voice common ideals, and aid in their realization."*[5]
>
> *- Franklin D. Roosevelt*

Basically, we can change our own economy and the standards it exists by, but to do that we must be willing to take an active role in its governance. We can no longer depend on our federal government to solve all our financial woes or keep corporations totally in line. As Franklin D. Roosevelt also once stated, *"The lessons of history...show conclusively that continued dependence upon relief induces a spiritual and moral disintegration fundamentally destructive to the national fibre...It is in violation of the traditions of America."*[6] Though it might be easier to assign our duties as citizens to the government; in the long run, it does not help us excel as a nation in any fashion. By holding the federal government up to the Constitution, and our corporations up to our laws, we ensure the continuation of the American dream for our posterity. American businesses exist to make money and the power we possess over them when we realize that we are the keepers of that money can be awesome. We are supposed to be a nation where the people lead, and in exercising our duties as citizens that is what we become, true leaders in our republic.

Bad Habits: Choices that Undermine our own Wealth

> *"Have we not already seen enough of the fallacy and extravagance of those idle theories which have amused us with promises of an exemption from the imperfections, weaknesses and evils incident to society in every shape? Is it not time to awake from the deceitful dream of a golden age, and to adopt as a practical maxim for the direction of our political conduct that we, as well as the other inhabitants of the globe, are yet remote from the happy empire of perfect wisdom and perfect virtue?"*[7]
>
> -Alexander Hamilton

Our republic is not free from the fallacies and faults that have plagued other governments. As citizens, we too, are not perfect in our behaviors or in the performance of our duties as inhabitants of our nation. We have allowed ourselves to be lulled into complacency by institutions both government and commercial in origin. These groups have helped us to form bad habits, which have weakened our position as the true leaders in our own governance. Overspending, debt, and improper investing have cost us dearly both in our national economy and private lives. It is undeniable that our government and many businesses have also adopted these risky financial practices.

When we can no longer look to them for the right example, we must step up and set it ourselves. We cannot continue to permit ourselves to be misled by occasional prosperity- for these tendencies will eventually tank our economy, just as they did during the Great Depression. They have also allowed the creation of an increasingly powerful economic aristocracy in this nation that seeks to further entrench itself at other citizens' expense. In understanding that we as citizens create some of our own problems, we can reverse these errors before it is too late. Admitting one's own faults is never easy, but correcting the errors in judgment we have occasionally made will always lead us to a brighter future.

> *"Money is, with propriety, considered as the vital principle of the body politic; as that which sustains its life and motion, and enables it to perform its most essential functions...From a deficiency in this particular, one of two evils must ensue; either the people must be subjected to continued plunder, as a substitute for a more eligible mode of supplying the public wants, or the government must sink into a fatal atrophy, and in a short course of time, perish."*[8]
>
> - Alexander Hamilton

Current American deficiencies in the financial arena reflect the problems in business, politics, and society around us. The message that consumer, corporate, and government debt are alright, and that we can spend above and beyond what we earn, has undermined our financial structure. While the example is set by corporations and the federal government, change and accountability start with us as citizens. On a core level, we understand that our financial habits and priorities are not what they ought to be, and yet, the problems are very pervasive among us.

The chief issue is actually not debt in and of itself; it is living beyond our means. Somehow, the American Dream has gotten caught up with rampant consumerism, with our amount of material possessions. When we focus in on overspending, it quickly becomes obvious how debt and poor savings follow. We have forgotten how to sacrifice in the here and now in order to have a better future. Instead, we expect to have everything we want at the moment we want it. This is not the same American Dream followed by our forefathers, who worked hard and sacrificed greatly to earn a place in this country.

When times are rough, we no longer buy just what we need and put off what we want until later. Now we buy both and pay off the difference (and then some) once times get better again. We use debt to compensate for earning less than we would like, in order to live a lifestyle well beyond what we should on our present earnings. In the process, we hope to stretch the payments out long enough to make do and keep buying things. Debt has become a substitute for demanding higher wages, working harder, working more, or re-educating ourselves for a better profession. It is ironic that all of these things require effort on our part, as well as effort on the part of business and government. No wonder they wish to encourage us to give up on financial security. The ability to finance all our extra wants now and pay for them later has only given Americans greater ability to be lazy, complacent, and selfish.

As citizens are forced to find even greater sources of money to pay their bills and support their expenses, it is no great surprise that corruption has risen. On a very basic level, corruption and greed in business, government, and society can be chalked up to an inability to properly manage one's own finances. When a person resorts to illegal measures (be they as simple as lying on a tax form to get a higher rebate or as complex as deliberate false accounting in corporate logbooks) to put more money into their own pockets, something has gone seriously wrong. But our society now encourages this sort of quiet theft as long as the individual does not get caught at it; in fact, it is often smiled upon, as if getting away with taking money from others makes us all better off financially somehow.

Bribery is even more frequent because it is harder to catch, especially when it involves kickbacks that do not necessarily contain cash. If a person can make two million by paying out one hundred thousand in bribes, it is very difficult not to take the opportunity to do so (especially if one is already in bad financial straits). Even in an emergency, a well-prepared individual or business never has a reason to steal because they have savings at hand. Debt and high-spending lifestyles have eroded the value of savings in America, because even if an individual person endeavors to save, a business, bank, or the government has already spent that money too. It is not a huge shock that these institutions will lie, cheat, and steal in order to offset trillions of dollars in debt owed by our nation, as a whole (both from the public and private sectors), to other people. Change can only start from the bottom-up because now we cannot afford to start from the top-down; there is simply no money left in the debt-ridden government and businesses to introduce these types of change.

In the same area as overspending and corruption to keep it up, we have improper investing as another "new" American avenue to wealth.

Besides the obvious get-rich-quick schemes and cons that strive to deprive people of their money, there are also investment scams of subtler, but no less financially ruinous nature. The average American citizen absolutely does not possess the knowledge or the background necessary to properly analyze and invest independently in the stock market. That day trading and stock portfolios are even considered to be viable options for the under-educated investor is not just ludicrous, but dangerous to one's nest egg.

Buying stock in a company has turned into just as much of a game with just as long odds as playing blackjack at the casino. And when the market takes a downturn, it is the unexpecting, small-time shareholders who suffer, not the company heads with large sets of stock options (even though they own more of these stocks, they suffer less). This does not even include all of the businesses and people that have gone bankrupt on other people's dimes, as actually paying the debts we take on becomes too much of a hassle.

Defaulting on loans and credit cards is symptomatic of all of these problems. Even if a company is engaged in hurting the public in some fashion that does not give someone the right to not pay up on a valid contract. Permitting this type of behavior among private citizens only worsens the behaviors we consider allowable to public corporations. As Samuel Adams once wrote, *"He who is void of virtuous Attachments in private life, is, or very soon will be void of all Regard for his Country. There is seldom an Instance of a Man guilty of betraying his Country who had not before lost the Feeling of Moral Obligations in his private Connections."*[9] By allowing corrupt avenues and scams to continue to be broadcast as the secret to great wealth and the origin of the America Dream, we fuel our own overspending and debt-ridden culture. In even considering day trading as an option to regular savings because we might one day strike it big, we undermine our individual finances and even the broader American economy.

Bad financial practices now abound in this nation. However, it is not any one of these things taken at a minimum that is bad; occasionally, some practices such as debt can even be good. But the over-reliance on risky financial habits puts a huge strain on our economy and us as citizens. The use of these unsound endeavors only deepens the economic crises we have found ourselves in throughout our history. The American Dream has never meant that we do not have to work hard or take care of our affairs each day; rather, it was intended to provide an equal footing so that every member of society could have the opportunity to succeed (not just magically be wealthy and happy overnight). Benjamin Franklin's old maxim that *"Human felicity is produc'd not so much by great pieces of good fortune that seldom happen, as by little advantages that occur every day,"*[10] still rings true. In pursing prosperity in our country as a whole and individually, only daily hard work can form the true source of a sound future.

Keep it Simple: Earning our Way to the Dream

> *"The country needs, and unless I mistake its temper, the country demands bold, persistent experimentation. It is common sense to take a method and try it: if it fails, admit it frankly and try another. But above all, try something."*[11]
>
> - Franklin D. Roosevelt

For all of the issues facing our nation, there are an equally large number of solutions. No matter where a problem originates – with our own behavior, those of businesses, or that of the government, we must dedicate ourselves to correcting it, even if it requires multiple tries to get it right. Our form of government has often been called a great "experiment," and in order for that experiment to continue to progress, we can never stop working on it. If, as a nation, we strive to find ever-better formulas for a true republic, we can be confident in our success. A true scientist never gives up on his work merely because a possible answer to his question has been found; he keeps searching for better answers until the experiment is over. As long as we continue to play an active role in our governance and find solutions to the issues that face our country, our experiment will not die. Only in the face of complacency, in giving up the trials before the experiment is complete, will we fail. It is through hard work that we can earn our way to the American Dream and that ever-more perfect union.

> *"As a very important source of strength and security, cherish public credit. One method of preserving it is, to use it as sparingly as possible...avoiding likewise the accumulation of debt, not only by shunning occasions of expense, but by vigorous exertions in time of peace to discharge the debts...not ungenerously throwing upon posterity the burden, which we ourselves ought to bear."*[12]
>
> - George Washington

Security and strength, the American Dream, these things are not some unattainable goal – they are the heart and soul of our republic. The founding fathers did not create these goals on a whim; our country was built on them by a plan. To further our government and our economy, they knew that a cohesive approach was required. Our forefathers came at problems in this experiment with thought-out ideas and then they enacted them. When their theories failed to work, they developed new ones before they proceeded any further.

Enacting more legislation without a complete strategy first has never done any government or situation any good. Ill-considered quick fixes are like putting a band aid on a bullet wound. As a people, we have to hold our government to some sort of standard, we have to demand an actual strategy for our economic welfare, and not just a patch when things go wrong. Many actions can have unintended consequences, as the founders knew, especially in the case of our financial future. By not planning, we only increase the risk of worsening our condition.

Washington's sound advice has been forgotten in an age of massive federal spending, immense national debt, and negative savings. To truly maintain a dependable economy, we must be prepared to develop, and to force Congress to obey, a federal budget. If it is necessary, the possibility of laws or even an amendment that would require Congress to create and maintain an annual, non-deficit budget should be considered. We are the only citizens there are to hold our government accountable for how it manages our nation's finances, and we should never neglect our ability to do so.

That times have not changed so much since the era of the Great Depression, where negligence in monitoring businesses gravely hurt our economy, should seriously compel us to action. The numerous corporate regulatory laws and civil suits that have been enacted and prosecuted have not been enough to keep businesses from pursuing patently illegal activity. Franklin D. Roosevelt himself repeatedly condemned the business practices that had led to workers being paid wages too low to live on and banks misusing the funds they were supposed to save for their patrons. His cousin and fellow President, Teddy Roosevelt, once remarked that *"Our aim is not to do away with corporations; on the contrary...the effort to destroy them would be futile unless accomplished in ways that would work the utmost mischief to the entire body politic. We can do nothing of good in the way of regulating and supervising these corporations until we fix clearly in our minds that we are not attacking the corporations, but endeavoring to do away with any evil in them. We are not hostile to them; we are merely determined that they shall be so handled as to subserve the public good. We draw the line against misconduct, not against wealth."*[13]

How little modern times have changed from more than a century ago! The income of regular laborers is still well below what is required to subsist in this country. A full work week at minimum wage every week would still not pay a person enough to bring them above the national poverty line. Despite new regulations, many financial institutions still fail to appropriately utilize the funds of their investors and clients.

Our founding fathers did not bequeath to us a nation where the business interests dominate our economy, and the citizenry languishes under an economic system where wealth only trickles down to them slowly over time. The American Dream provides American citizens the opportunity to take control of their economic destiny in a meaningful way, by taking part in the government, which is supposed to control our financial system. It may be simple, and it may be obvious, but it is our participation in our national economy that can change the tide of these trends that weaken our fiscal infrastructure. If we could not allow this sort of business irresponsibility to continue during the early 1900s, we certainly cannot permit it to occur now, an entire century later.

Personal responsibility on the part of each citizen in politics, society, and business is the only solution to the trials we face as a nation. If every person took their American citizenship as a duty and responsibility instead of as an entitlement, the economy would see a rise in fortunes on every level. Teddy Roosevelt also once told his fellow Americans that *"The first requisite of a good citizen in this Republic of ours is that he shall be able and willing to pull his weight; that he shall not be a mere passenger, but shall do his share in the work that each generation of us finds ready to hand; and, furthermore, that in doing his work he shall show, not only the capacity for sturdy self-help, but also self-respecting regard for the rights of others."*[14] Being American is not just about our own inherent rights, but rather about regard for the rights of our fellow citizens. Concern for the broader community, responsibility for that community, and an obligation to participate in the national community life, are what was revolutionary about the American Dream and the republic established after the war that won it.

Perhaps it is strange to realize that despite what we often hear from either side, being truly "American" is not about wealth, privilege, and total selfishness or about hardship, conformity, and complete self-sacrifice. Rather, the fundamental beliefs of our country involve an obligation to both ourselves and everyone else around us, a grand balance between national unity and self-interest. But this works only when the citizenry recognizes and engages themselves in this attitude. John Adams once wrote a group of officers that *"We have no government armed with power capable of contending with human passions unbridled by morality...Avarice, ambition, revenge, or gallantry, would break the strongest cords of our Constitution as a whale goes through a net."*[15] Each citizen must be ready to contend with their own interests and that of an entire nation in order to allow our government to properly function.

In America, we as citizens, have the ultimate control over our own fates. Our economy has, and always will be, one of the most life-altering aspects of our country. The financial health of the country has the ability to illustrate how good a job our government is doing, whether our businesses are serving our nation, and whether we are paying more attention to the future of our pocketbooks or the future of our people. The American link between civil liberties and economic freedoms has proven to be both effective in providing prosperity and fueling corruption.

It is our choice whether we direct our nation on a road towards continued success or down the path of decadence and decay. Past generations have been able to step up and, at least temporarily, place America back on the train to a brighter tomorrow. We are a nation of corporations and laborers, government and citizens, the big and the small, it is our duty in this society to come together as members of these groups in a national discourse on what best serves us all (and not just any one person or interest group). In doing so, we follow the traditions set down by our founding fathers and hope to preserve a successful republic for our posterity.

By Society: Our White Picket Fence

> *"With public sentiment, nothing can fail; without it nothing can succeed. Consequently, he who moulds public sentiment goes deeper than he who enacts statutes or pronounces decisions. He makes statutes and decisions possible or impossible to be executed."*[16]
>
> *- Abraham Lincoln*

In America, our society and culture play an important role in our governance, our economy, and how we live our everyday lives. Public perceptions of people, places, and events help to shape our own attitudes on how our nation should proceed and function. As Abraham Lincoln remarked, public sentiment can overwhelmingly influence the success or failure of government and business actions. At the end of the day, the way in which our society as a whole views a particular matter can effectively alter our own individual views. From what we buy, to how we vote, the ideas of those around us profoundly impact our own unique judgment.

The question then of who and what molds our views is of the utmost importance. When a nation's rule is determined by popular opinion, then every effort is made by those in power (be it political, social, or economic in nature) to control that opinion. Control of public beliefs and values can come in many forms, from the highly negative to the very positive. For example, fear can be an exceptionally effective tool in shaping public perception. Many people will think what someone wants when they believe that something bad might happen to them or their families if they do not. On the other hand, charity can also inspire an audience to agree with certain ideals. Many people are motivated when they see good being done around them, and wish to help. Despite whichever of these tactics might seem "better" to us, both of these extremes work towards the same objective, namely manipulating public sentiment.

Playing on public emotions and desires is the only way for a few people to convince enough other people in a republic or democracy to accomplish anything (or receive enough support to even be able to do it themselves). Just because someone utilizes what seems like a negative tactic, does not mean that their intentions cannot also be noble or good. Likewise, using a seemingly positive tactic does not guarantee that that person's intentions are honorable.

Throughout history, entire countries of people have allowed fear to control their emotions and lead them to do unthinkable things, while firmly believing those things were for the good of their country (the most extreme example being the Holocaust in Nazi Germany). People have also been totally convinced that what they were doing was charitable and kind, while following the intentions of someone intent on ultimately doing harm (the example of missionaries converting people to save their souls, but also fueling the conquest of numerous native peoples comes to mind). Different interests, be they right or wrong, have to have some method of image control in order to succeed in any nation, especially one like ours.

That is not to say that image control is completely bad, or even an unnecessary aspect of society. After all, creating a public persona for the people around us is a very fundamentally human behavior. In order for anybody else to appreciate our point of view that view has to be structured in a way that another unique person can understand it. It does us no good to be full of great ideas or intentions if we cannot present those thoughts, and ourselves properly to those around us. In our country, this simply occurs on a much grander scale.

Politicians, businesses, and interest groups must all compete for the American people's attention and support. How the public perceives the desires and goals of any of these groups can radically affect the path of our nation. Politicians seek to put on an image that they believe their constituents share with them. They must not merely seem like a leader, but they also must appear to share the values and concerns of the citizens who elect them.

The entire fields of marketing and advertising are built on shaping the perceived image and worth of a particular good and the company that produces it. In order to sell something to as many people as possible, a product must seem either necessary to live life (hence the art of ads convincing people to buy things they "cannot live without") or possess an image of high value. Similarly, interest groups, small and large, attempt to promote interest in a particular faction or issue (hence the term "interest group"). They each try to make their issue seem like the most important or vital one at hand so that we will see their cause as our own and support it. Public interest is the means by which ends are accomplished in this country. Thus, public image is of vital importance to anyone seeking to operate in our society.

Therefore, the origins of an image or perception matter just as much as the image itself. The organizations and people who seek to control how the public views something have many reasons for doing so, as much for the general good as for themselves. Only in recognizing where our opinions come from and what the motivations of their orchestrators are, can we as American citizens make accurate judgments on what to believe.

These ideas and perceptions form the very society that exists around us and the culture that we accept as being "American". It is also one of the many reasons we have trouble all agreeing on what actually defines our society – images always leave room for interpretation in order to appeal to as many different types of people as possible. The shapers of public sentiment and societal control are numerous. They are politicians, businesses, interest groups, the press, and even the preachers who each have agendas for us and our nation. Sometimes they work in conjunction with one another when their ideas coincide. Other times, they work separately in an effort to enact policies that benefit only their particular faction. To oversimplify any image we see with the belief that it is the only image out there takes away from the variety of ideas our country provides us. In understanding how society can affect our views, we can see how they affect us and our lives as citizens in this country.

The Press or the Business of Informing America

"Our liberty depends on the freedom of the press, and that cannot be limited without being lost."

- Thomas Jefferson

The Press, a theoretically independent conduit for information, has long provided the news of current events and accompanying illustrative commentary, in our nation. The ability to freely express and publish this sort of information has never (before the American Constitution) been so unlimited. Newspapers and pamphlets had been a vital part of the road to revolution, which the founding fathers (all of whom had been published previously themselves on several occasions) appreciated. They had used this pathway to mobilize support for their ideas and beliefs, so it was only natural that they sought to protect it as best they could.

The very first amendment in the Bill of Rights expressly grants both the freedoms of speech and press, and absolutely prohibits Congress from making any laws to abridge these freedoms. This is an incredibly broad and powerful law, even for a country based on inherent rights. Ironically, the founders knew the Press' many evils and inaccuracies for themselves, for the revolutionary-era journalists were not ones to let much get by them.

The comments that preceded Jefferson's above quotation are about newspapers unfairly and completely falsely attacking and slandering the reputation of John Jay, a noted revolutionary-era statesman and ambassador (also one of three writers of the eventual Federalist Papers). The quote could even be better understood if it was prefaced with the word "unfortunately" because Jefferson too knew the bitter sting of accusations from that quarter. Though he knew that allowing the Press to say anything they thought up could gravely affect a person's reputation, he also realized forbidding anything could give a precedent where the Press could be silenced completely. Even during our founders' era, the media did not just provide the news, it created it for its audience.

Independent information, or news media accountable only to themselves and their viewers, has long been a staunch ally in the cause of liberty. After all, the Press suffers as well when the only stories that they can tell are state-sanctioned ones (since it cuts down on the number, content, and variety of articles and pieces, it effectively limits the growth of the media.) Yet even more so now than ever before, the origins of our media coverage are vital to understanding that coverage. The Press has grown from small, independent local papers to full-blown media corporations of immense scale with multiple venues - print, online, and television – all seeking to provide information for a price. They no longer tell the events of the day or the week, but rather seek to pre-package their coverage to sell more copies or bring in more viewers, as well as further their own particular agendas. The Press forms an essential component in how people perceive anything, and the images they present are carefully composed to do just that. To analyze the public perceptions of events and image control in action, we must start at the heart of where most Americans get their information, the Press.

Freedoms from the Founders: An Unfettered Press

> *"Some degree of abuse is inseparable from the proper use of everything; and in no instance is this more true than in that of the press. It has accordingly been decided, by the practice of the states, that it is better to leave a few of its noxious branches to their luxuriant growth, then, by pruning them away, to injure the vigor of those yielding the proper fruits. And can the wisdom of this policy be doubted by any one who reflects that to the press alone, checkered as it is with abuses, the world is indebted for all the triumphs which have been gained by reason and humanity over error and oppression."*[1]
>
> -James Madison

For our founding fathers, the press was instrumental not merely to the preservation of liberty, but also to its very establishment. During the formative years leading up to the American Revolution, the colonies were ripe with intellectual thought and political debate on the nature of government, the rights of man, and civil liberties under the law. The press of the time, in all its forms – newspaper, pamphlet, books, and lectures - played a vital part in not only providing news to the colonists, but also in giving commentary, producing editorials, and publishing the extensive debates.

One of the oldest and most influential founding fathers, Benjamin Franklin, not only got his start working in a printing press, but continued to be an influential press member, through his published articles (his first under the famous persona of "Mrs. Silence Do-good"), and later a printing house and newspaper of his own. Franklin's profession was both prestigious among his peers and also fueled many of their own political rises. Jefferson, Madison, Hamilton, and Adams had all participated in political writing, frequently for the express purpose of publication. Their ideas on republicanism and government helped to fuel an entire generation before, during, and after the Revolution.

Without the assistance and participation of the Press, the founders would never have been able to deliver their message and their cause to the ears of the people, who would help them to achieve their goals. The New America was more than deeply indebted to the Press for its assistance in the Revolution; the founders knew that the Press had been at the very core of the Revolutionary efforts.

For all of the Press' essential work during the Revolution, the founding fathers had also seen the potential problems posed by this sector. Even at this very early stage in our national history, newspapers frequently engaged in slander, sensationalism, and outright falsehood in the matters on which they wrote and reported. Objectivity faded in the wake of increased partisanship on all sides of the revolutionary and constitutional conflicts. Papers began to publish only the news and opinions their readership wanted to see, instead of their previous policy of printing everything.

The Boston Massacre and its subsequent depiction in the Press aptly illustrate this point. The Press' ability to capitalize on the issues at hand, playing on the tensions present among the populace, was obvious during those days in Boston. But despite his passion for independence, John Adams himself defended the very same soldiers accused by the public and the press of murdering civilians. He did not do this because he particularly desired to or even because he liked the British, but instead because he knew that the story had been blown incredibly out of proportion and that the soldiers were actually innocent of the charges. And above all, Adams believed in the rule of law.

Even the printer Revolutionary, Benjamin Franklin recognized these same abuses and qualities in his profession. In an *Apology for Printers*, Franklin reminded angry readers *"That the Business of Printing has chiefly to do with Men's Opinions; most things that are printed tending to promote some, or oppose others."*[2] For the time, this was an understatement. Things that even today would be considered slander and libel were freely printed with little regard for the damage they could do to a man's reputation or the truths they purported to present.

The great Revolutionary hero, George Washington, was not exempt from this treatment during his Presidency. Responding to frequently inaccurate news criticism of his tenure, and the even more ludicrous claim that he had some desire to be a monarch, he stated *"I had rather be in my grave than in my present situation, I had rather be on my farm than be emperor of the world; and yet they charge me with wanting to be a king."*[3] Abuses abounded, even in the time of our founders, and yet they left a general freedom of the press. So why did they think the role of the Press was so important as to leave them unchecked even though they often railed against the Founders themselves?

For men who both used and were abused by the Press of their day, it may seem odd that they then created a government that granted the same institution such unbridled freedom. In the context of the Press's role in the Revolution however, the reasoning becomes much clearer. The founders had seen first-hand how the Press shaped the images and perceptions held by the people; how it diffused information all over the new America. They understood that the role of the Press in ensuring continued freedom was of the utmost value. Especially in a period of much slower communication, the newspapers gave the people access to stories from around the states and the rest of the world that they might otherwise never hear.

The Revolutionary era press had helped to galvanize and fuel the war efforts, inciting passion and high emotion in its readership. When the creation of the Constitution was being debated, it was the newspapers that published the extensive and exhaustive debates between the Federalists and Anti-Federalists. Without the Press, many Americans would not have been able to take in all the various issues surrounding the Constitutional debate. Citizens would have been voting on their new Constitution without knowing the political discussion and climate that developed the document in the first place.

Similarly, the Press rose to the occasion when the first (and really the only) challenge to their Constitutional prerogative occurred. During Adam's presidency (that is, the second American presidency), the Alien and Sedition Acts were passed by a mostly Federalist Congress. These acts basically limited freedom of speech and press by making it illegal to publish any *"false, scandalous, and malicious writing"*[4] about the new federal government or its representatives. It probably seemed like a good idea in the context of the experiences with the often patently false accusations made by the Press at the time. However, the law was deemed broadly unconstitutional (on a variety of grounds) by both Anti-Federalists and Federalists, the Press itself, and most importantly, the people. As Madison had expressed, it was better to leave the Press alone, then to potentially give the government a power it could abuse. Why risk harming the role of the Press in the fledgling republic?

The Press gave the new American people a window into the politics and ideas of the day and how these politics affected their lives. The Founders realized that ultimately, in a republic, the leaders had to have a way of informing the people, and the people needed a way to get independent information about their government. They left the Press its total Freedom because the newspapers served the United States as the vital transmitter of information all over the republic. As Thomas Jefferson put it, *"The basis of our government being the opinion of the people, the very first object should be to keep that right; and were it left to me to decide whether we should have a government without newspapers, or newspapers without a government, I should not hesitate a moment to prefer the latter."*[5] At the end of the day, our founding fathers chose a government with the freedom of the press because it gave government a sense of transparency, an ability to be seen by all the people who had a right to participate in it. In permitting the Press to basically write as they wished, the founders gave the media their own role in checking and balancing our new government.

The special role of the Press in our system of governance conveys the true level of importance that a free news media has in a republic. As our founding fathers understood, the most vital asset of the people in ensuring that their government obeyed their will and respected their rights was information. Controlling information and the way it is projected gives great power to those that craft the information for public consumption. An independent and free press ensures that the government can never lie or trick the people into believing that their wishes are being honored when they actually are not. Unlike other nations of alternate government around us, whose presses are dictated by their government, our people can never literally be thrown in jail for publishing any ideas counter to our government's wishes.

In our country, this unofficial "fourth" branch of government is so completely separated from the other three that it can check on and criticize them all. In theory, the only interest that the media has is in its own continued existence as a broker of information throughout our nation. That is not to say that the history of the American Press has not been littered with scandals of their own. However, the role the Press plays in a republic such as ours has been too vital to ignore or dismiss. Despite the media's many faults and foibles, they serve the cause of continued freedom in our country. As Madison pointed out, we have to take the good parts with the bad, otherwise we risk accidentally excising something we might need. In understanding the continued presence of the news media and its role in our nation, we must acknowledge and accept its past contributions with its past errors, as well as its utmost importance to our future as a free people in a free nation.

YELLOW JOURNALISM: RAKING UP THE MUCK

> *"We live in the midst of alarms; anxiety beclouds the future; we expect some new disaster with each newspaper we read."*[6]
>
> *- Abraham Lincoln*

As the experiences of the founding fathers have shown us, the Press has had a major role in shaping our republic. Molding the public's perceptions and informing them on their government and national affairs has made the news media both incredibly influential and inherently vital to our nation. This business of informing America has become a lucrative and large-scale production. Controversy and passion have fueled the newspaper business since before the dawn of the revolutionary era. Yet, in our modern era, "good" news has become no news at all, and provocative or "bad" news has become the standard of the news industry. So the question remains, when did journalism in America become less about telling stories that people need to hear and more about selling the most copies to the most people? Basically, why has the business of bad news so overwhelmed the regular news we need? Instead of seeking the truth or presenting the views of a whole nation, we often find the media in the modern day continually trying to outdo one another in sensational or one-sided coverage.

> *"It is not yet forgotten that well-grounded apprehensions of imminent danger induced the people of America to form the memorable Congress of 1774. That body recommended certain measures to their constituents, and the event proved their wisdom; yet it is fresh in our memories how soon the press began to teem with pamphlets and weekly papers against those very measures. Not only many of the officers of government, who obeyed the dictates of personal interest, but others, from a mistaken estimate of consequences, or the undue influence of former attachments, or whose ambition aimed at objects which did not correspond with the public good, were indefatigable in their efforts to persuade the people to reject the advice of that patriotic Congress."*[7]
>
> *- John Jay*

Our founding fathers had experienced first hand the ability of newspapers to manipulate the truth to their own ends. Yet, they also still insisted on the freedom of the press, despite its faults. In stark contrast to the ability of the press to do great service to the public, it has still maintained and even grown in some of its evils. If the American Revolution was the most important era in terms of freedom of the press, the Gilded Age was the most important era in terms of its character. And this page in American history has left a lasting stamp on the methods that the news media still utilizes to this day.

The Gilded Age was the period following the Civil War. It was exemplified by significant growth in American population, industry, and wealth. However, it was also typified by the problems this growth caused- rampant government and business corruption, intense polarization between the wealthy and the poor, and lavish lifestyles among the very small upper class. The so-called "robber barons" dominated government, business, and society. These were also the days of Rockefellers,

Carnegies, and Vanderbilts with their great wealth, immense influence, and lavish lifestyles.

Party politics and their political machines, such as the infamous Tammany Hall, dominated the government stage, sometimes turning out as many as ninety percent of all eligible voters. This system was of course based on the principles of "spoils" or patronage, where a winning candidate repaid supporters and political machines with government positions, contracts, and jobs. In this arena, the press played a significant roll in mudslinging and political competition; it also served to increasingly "out" the worst of the scandal and corruption plaguing the nation (as long as it served that particular paper's interests). In this climate of negative politics and exploitation, yellow journalism, with its sensational and emotive stories, overtook the old journalistic tactics of relatively fact-based news with complementary commentaries.

The most infamous and illustrative instances of the increased role of the press in society, as well as their increasingly incendiary tactics to attract readers occurred with the drive up to the Spanish-American War. Readership battles among competing newspapers, especially that between the *New York World* and *New York Journal*, had caused journalists to be busy in the field of investigative work, that is, in actively seeking out stories on scandal, corruption, and crime, or "muckraking" as it would come to be called. The term yellow journalism would eventually come to describe the ever-worsening and salacious depictions that these newspapers used to sell copies. Deliberately provocative headlines were used to grab readers' attention and interest; such examples include "How Babies Are Baked", "Screaming for Mercy", and "Burning Babies Fall From the Roof" courtesy of the *New York World*. While these attention-grabbing tactics did partially fuel reform, they also helped to transform the nature of the press.

The outright partiality of the great majority of the press in this period while covering an increasingly poor situation in Cuba, (which was then a Spanish territory undergoing a Revolution) inspired much of the American public to call for war. The culminating incident was the 15 February 1898 explosion of the *USS Maine (ACR-1)*, which sunk, in port, to the bottom of Havana Harbor, Cuba. The Press headlined the episode, making the situation out to be a deliberate act of war on the part of the Spanish; Americans grew increasingly irate. By April of the same year the Spanish-American War had started. The *New York Journal* placed "How do you like the *Journal's* war?" on the front page of its papers, taking credit for helping to incite the conflict. The Press had just aptly demonstrated their ability to galvanize and instigate the public's opinion in matters even as serious as going to war.

The irony is, the accusations towards Spain about the sinking of the *Maine* were inconclusive and ambiguous even at the time. The Naval Court of Inquiry held in 1898 had been unable to determine who was ultimately responsible for the sinking- a fact that most newspapers neglected to mention.[8] In fact, Spain and Spanish Naval officers immediately sent their regrets over the incident and repeated denials that they had acted in the matter, something else which often failed to appear in print. After the war, following the 1900 election, the *Journal* published two columns (at different times) that called for the assassination of President William McKinley. President McKinley was shot on the 6th of September 1901, and died a few days later. The Press now knew the full range of its influence and power. Though for a time, they retreated from such sensational positions due to regret[9] by the publishers of the yellow papers.

These American journalistic experiences have not only re-enforced the role of the press in our society, but empowered it- demonstrating to those who own these media companies the incredible influence their trade can have. It is not so much that the press engages in investigations of government and business, or even that it publishes opinions and editorial pieces. The real issue lies in the misrepresentation of opinions or even downright falsehoods as facts. Our modern media has taken the era of the yellow journalist and learned nothing but the power of their word in society from it. The self-imposed standards of the journalistic profession in this nation do not reflect trends of truth in reporting, broad representation of views, or even the desire to discover the truth in national affairs. Instead, many in this field have chosen to sell stories instead of tell them, relying on ratings numbers and the amount of copies sold to be their guide in journalistic integrity.

Content has come to matter little in a nation where more money earned can buy a business, even a news business, the impression of veracity and reliability. Perhaps it is a reflection on the American character that negative news sells so well, but it is most definitely a reflection on the character of our news organizations that they engage in these practices. How can the American people reliably obtain vital information on the state of the nation if the press does not play the role intended for it by the founding fathers?

Selling Stories Instead of Telling Them

> *"To your request of my opinion of the manner in which a newspaper should be conducted, so as to be most useful, I should answer, 'by restraining it to true facts and sound principles only.' Yet I fear such a paper would find few subscribers. It is a melancholy truth, that a suppression of the press could not more completely deprive the nation of its benefits, than is done by it's abandoned prostitution to falsehood."*[10]
>
> - Thomas Jefferson

The news business in America is just that, a business. Since the days of our forefathers, it has only grown in its coverage and scope. Following the yellow journalism of the Gilded Age, publishers of news began to expand their areas of operation. Newspapers went from smaller, local publications to broader, regional ones. A handful of companies began to own the majority of printing houses. Today, the major broadcast corporations own large chunks of the paper, television, and internet news sources, using them to make a point and a living. This shift has only encouraged continued sensationalist tactics, in order to drive up ratings and sales. Instead of catering to the needs of the citizenry, these corporations cater to their wants.

The public now demands news that interests them personally instead of the news that they require as citizens in a republic. The media corporations have been only too happy to provide people with the news that they want to hear about, versus the news they need to hear about. It is a small wonder that "bad news sells" in a society obsessed with everyone else's issues (to the detriment of the troubles that plague themselves). It is only natural that the press, a business, seeks to attract the most customers possible, and to do so they willingly choose news that sells. However, no other business has the unlimited freedom that the press enjoys, and this freedom imposes on our Press a duty in return (that they have not been doing) - to inform the citizens accurately on the state of the union.

> *"Nothing can now be believed which is seen in a newspaper. Truth itself becomes suspicious by being put into that polluted vehicle."*[11]
>
> - *Thomas Jefferson*

Truth in news has become less and less frequently a requirement of reporting and coverage by the Press. Even in the case of outright, proven fabrications, news outlets have suffered very few consequences for failing to tell the truth in what they publish. Real journalistic integrity requires not just the relating of facts, but the verification of these facts as well. The audience of any particular media corporation should not need to double-check the facts presented by these companies. Why pay someone to keep you informed if they are going to do a poor job of it, ultimately forcing you to research the issue for yourself if you want an accurate answer?

The Press has an obligation to be accurate in its coverage, not just because of consumer support, but also because of the freedom they possess. If the Press was not expected to play a reliable third-party role as a broker of information, then why bother granting it unlimited freedom in the first place? This does not mean that opinions and commentary have no place in an accurate news media, quite the opposite. The ability of the Press to elucidate and distill facts into a coherent image for the public to view is a large part of their true purpose. A line must be drawn, however, between opinion and misrepresentation. There is no room in a public press for opinions based on falsehoods or commentaries based on representing fiction as fact. An editorial piece is only as good as the documentation used to back up the opinions it presents.

Slander, libel, and fiction have no place in journalistic expression. Abraham Lincoln once wrote, *"I believe it is an established maxim in morals that he who makes an assertion without knowing whether it is true of false, is guilty of falsehood; and the accidental truth of the assertion does not justify or excuse him."*[12] In analyzing our media, we must remember that it is also their established purpose to accurately provide the public with information. We cannot justify or excuse ignorance of the facts and poor documentation because the occasional slander happens to be true. Without the highest standards of integrity, the role of a free press in our American republic becomes meaningless.

If we only seek to read newspapers that already agree with our views and watch news programs that already back up all of our beliefs, why bother with journalism at all? The ability of the news media to sell back to us our own opinions as "fact" hardly lends credulity to the industry. In the place of information, we receive so-called "infotainment" – information designed to entertain and please the audience rather than actually inform it. The advent of the massive tabloid news industry in this country directly evidences this growing trend. *"Defamation is becoming a necessary of life; in so much, that a dish of tea in the morning or evening cannot be digested without this stimulant. Even those who do not believe these abominations, still read them with complaisance to their auditors, and instead of the abhorrence and indignation which should fill a virtuous mind, betray a secret pleasure in the possibility that some may believe them, though they do not themselves."*[13]

The desire of people to read these kinds of stories cannot be denied; after all, the Press would not publish such tales in news or tabloid form if they did not sell well. As Jefferson's quote pointed out, even people who do not believe the inflammatory things they read still buy the paper to read them, and even repeat them to friends. Our Press now caters to these rumors and gossip instead of sticking to facts that can reasonably be verified. Our media industry has basically taken its freedom of speech and freedom of the press well beyond any bounds thought possible by our fore-fathers. In accepting the transition in the purpose of the news from mainly informative to primarily entertaining (and entertaining the beliefs we already accept), we have allowed the press to undermine its own role in our country as a guardian of liberty.

The Press' issues go beyond entertainment and falsehood, however, to downright manipulation of even factual reporting. Through deliberate editing and emphasis, certain facts can be downplayed, while others are highlighted. Thus the Press does not just relate a story, it creates its own context. This has made the news media incredibly powerful in their ability to influence public perceptions. Since most people believe (or choose to believe) the news they read and see, the Press can drastically alter and remold public opinion.

The afore-mentioned *USS Maine* story is a prime example of how effective this practice can be in producing sensational and image-shaping news. The *Maine* was, in fact, destroyed by a great explosion, and many American sailors lost their lives. It is also true that this incident took place in Havana Harbor, Cuba, which was under Spain's rule at the time. The rest of the story, as told by the Press at the time, was either made-up or manipulated to support the image they wanted to create of the evil colonial power Spain. And their news was designed to fuel the war they wanted to garner enough support to begin. The Press faulted Spain publicly without proof (and contrary to an American Naval Board of Inquiry's findings of the time), and suggested that Spain wanted war with the American states. These tactics succeeded in helping to launch the Spanish-American War. They also illustrate the issues we still face about truth in news and potential media bias.

It is hard sometimes to tell the difference between opinion and bias, especially as it relates to the news media. However, there is a relatively easy litmus test- if a news organization only covers certain topics while expressing a certain opinion, and lies or manipulates facts to support those opinions, then it is clearly biased. *"I really look with commiseration over the great body of my fellow citizens, who, reading newspapers, live and die in the belief that they have known something of what has been passing in the world in their time...General facts may indeed be collected from them...but no details can be relied on. I will add, that the man who never looks into a newspaper is better informed than he who reads them; inasmuch as he who knows nothing is nearer to truth than he whose mind if filled with falsehoods and errors."*[14] Stories that raise ratings and present a particular viewpoint are now considered more vital in the news business than stories that present the facts and the truth of our times. If the media is going to manipulate every bit of information they relate, why even bother with a free press at all?

The same problems with the free press that the founding fathers had, as well as subsequent generations, still plague us as Americans today. The importance of a free press is still paramount to a free society, even though that press has been in the habit of failing us in their duty. The answer has never been to get rid of the press, but to enforce a standard in their conduct by only purchasing from those news media who actually have some standard of news. Jefferson once wrote that any paper which dealt in possibilities and lies on its pages *"should be professedly for those readers who would rather have lies for their money than the blank paper they would occupy;"*[15] in the same letter, he reminded his compatriot that *"it seems to escape them, that it is not he who prints, but he who pays for printing a slander, who is it's real author."*[16]

As citizens, it falls once more to us to police the press, just as we must keep a watchful eye on our government and our businesses. It is us who gave the Press its unfettered freedom, and it is us who must hold them accountable for using it properly. The value of a free press providing the people with accurate information cannot be underestimated, but only when the citizens who pay for the news do not allow the press to be undermined in their role because they want more money. Information is very valuable; falsehoods are worth nothing. A free people who know and understand the matters that occupy their nation and the facts behind them have all the power to dictate their fate. By requiring of the press the same responsibility we should demand of ourselves as citizens (in return for all the freedoms we and they have), we ensure the continuation of the America created by our founders and protected by our forbearers for our future generations.

THE PREACHER-
FINDING THE
GOD OF FREEDOM

"Twenty times in the course of my late reading have I been on the point of breaking out, 'This would be the best of all possible worlds, if these were no religion in it!!!' But in this exclamation I would have been as fanatical as Bryant of Cleverly. Without religion, this world would be something not fit to be mentioned in polite company, I mean Hell."[1]

- John Adams

Religion has always been a part of the American experience. From the very beginning it has dictated to and been governed by a people devoted to freedom in every aspect of life, especially faith. Religious freedom has been championed as well as challenged by the free citizens of this nation. Because of its fundamental role in shaping our views on everything related to life, liberty, and the pursuit of happiness, the preachers, philosophers, and pious persons of all creeds greatly influence public perception.

Our founders easily recognized this age-old ability of faith to both support and undermine liberty, and so built our Constitution on the idea of equal protection for all believers of every type. In doing so, they hoped to bring the benefits of faith to the American citizenry without permitting its banes. Understanding the role of religion in a republic like ours has never been an easy task, and the founders themselves extensively struggled with the nature of relations between the various Churches and the State. The divide they placed between faith and federal government was not designed to erase religion or its influence (especially its moral one) from our republic. In fact, the best summary of this matter would be to say that the separation of Church and State was meant to work both ways.

> *"Of all the dispositions and habits, which lead to political prosperity, Religion and Morality are indispensable supports. In vain would that man claim the tribute of Patriotism, who should labor to subvert these great pillars of human happiness, these firmest props of the duties of Men and Citizens."*[2]
>
> - George Washington

For Americans, freedom and faith are inexorably intertwined. What we believe fundamentally governs our actions and how we perceive what goes on around us. Thus, philosophers and preachers can significantly shape our outlook on our governance. The importance of various dogmas to us as individuals can lead us to both good and bad behaviors as citizens. People have been known to preach defiance of the government and condemnation of any who disagree with their own views, even in a nation such as America. It is ironic that their staunch faith and that of their followers can lead them to believe that overturning the very freedoms that allow them to think these things is an idea for the good (and salvation) of all.

Likewise, history is full of those who have intimately linked obedience to faith, to the detriment of everyone involved. In our country, we face the dilemma of promoting all faiths while simultaneously imposing upon no one's beliefs in particular. Unfortunately, powerful preachers and religious interests in America do not always see their civil duty this way. To deny the role that faith plays in our continued freedom demonstrates a shallow understanding of our national history. But to deny the influence faith and its leaders can have over us and our responsibilities as American citizens is equally fallacious.

Faith of Our Fathers: Revolutionary Religion

> *"Statesmen, my dear Sir, may plan and speculate for liberty, but it is Religion and Morality alone, which can establish the Principles upon which Freedom can securely stand. The only foundation of a free Constitution is pure Virtue, and if this cannot be inspired into our People in a greater Measure than they have it now, they may change their Rulers and their Forms of Government, but they will not obtain a lasting Liberty. They will only exchange Tyrants and Tyrannies."*[3]

-*John Adams*

The religion of the Revolutionary generation was full of the same fervor and passion that the eventual War for Independence would possess. Both the Age of Enlightenment and the First Great Awakening preceded the American Revolution, and inspired the people of the colonies. Eloquent reasoning and powerful preaching (in oratorical and written form) characterized both of these movements. Despite the theological differences between the Enlightenment Deists and the Awakening Christians, both groups would be motivated by their movements' leaders to profoundly take their existence, individual and communal, into their own hands.

Philosophers on both sides of the aisle advocated responsibility and duty as the only means to achieve one's salvation (be it in heaven or on earth). The people possessed the ability to change their own state in life, and no one else could do it for them. Fiery rhetoric shaped the perceptions of this Revolutionary public and molded its sentiments. Neither the logical reasoning of the Deists nor the obedient devotion of the Christians changed this communal demand among the Revolutionary generation for persuasion and enthusiasm on the part of their philosophical champions.

Two of the most classic examples of this type of powerfully persuasive argument and oratory come from two radically different figures. Jonathan Edwards, one of the leading ministers of the First Awakening, gave a famous sermon throughout the 1740s entitled "Sinners in the Hands of an Angry God". The influence of this infamous speech on its audiences is well-known; congregants fainted, cried out to God, underwent convulsions, and many reportedly had intensely heart-felt conversions. In one section, Edwards said *"There is no want of **power** in God to cast wicked men into hell at any moment. Men's hands cannot be strong when God rises up...There is no fortress that is any defense from the power of God."* [4] The sermon's exhortations to the Christian community to take accountability for its actions and to realize God's powerful judgment and ability to condemn any person at any time played to the hopes and fears of people and their belief in an afterlife (one which condemned or rewarded each person for their actions in their life on earth). This dual message of obedience and responsibility was persuasive and effective, as colonists embraced their duties to God and country.

Similarly, the very Deist (and extremely anti-church) Thomas Paine used philosophical reasoning and intense rhetoric to shape the minds of his peers prior to the Revolution. His pamphlet, *Common Sense*, contained one of the most well-known and effective calls to the colonies to challenge the impositions and abuses of Britain. His argument was built out of powerful rhetoric such as, *"Interested men, who are not to be trusted; weak men who cannot see; prejudiced men who will not see; and a certain moderate set of men who think better of the European world than it deserves; and this last class by an ill-judged deliberation, will be the cause of more calamities to this continent than all other three. It is the good fortune of many to live distant from the scene of sorrow; the evil is not sufficiently brought to their doors to make them feel the precariousness with which all American property is possessed."*[5] For Paine, the point of his pamphlet was obvious, but he argued it with expression and energy to sway his fellow colonists to his side.

Speakers and writers like Paine and Edwards changed the outlook and nature of their entire community. The philosophers of the twin

Awakening and Enlightenment movements reshaped an entire nation's basic beliefs on their own heritage, their rights, and their duties to themselves and their posterity. Their impact on Revolutionary society through their ability to convert their fellow colonists to their way of thinking cannot be denied.

These religious and moral appeals to the colonists did not go unheeded. Heaven's call to arms to save the people from tyranny and oppression was felt throughout the colonies on a political and philosophical level. *"Self-preservation is an instinct God implanted in our nature. Therefore we sin against God and nature, when we tamely resign our rights to tyrants, or quietly submit to public oppressors, if it be in our power to defend ourselves."*[6] Sermons like this one by Nathaniel Whitaker were heard and reprinted in every colony as Revolutionary fervor grew. Ministers and philosophers reminded and called upon their peers and audiences to embrace their God-given liberties and heaven-demanded roles as soldiers for that liberty.

The public, inspired by its moral leaders, firmly believed that the American Revolution was heavenly ordained and guided by the hand of God. As another preacher reminded his congregants, *"The Cause of AMERICA...is the cause of GOD, never did man struggle in a greater, or more glorious CAUSE."*[7] Preachers did not just confine themselves to their parishes during the war; many instead went with the Continental Army and the state militias and exhorted them to do their duty on and off the battlefield. Ministers, with the ability to inspire and incite the troops to excellence were highly regarded and prized by the citizen-soldiers and their leaders. Revolutionaries did not just want to know that what they were doing was right; they wanted to hear it and feel united with their peers in the cause as well.

Thus, the passionate revolutionary zeal was not just political in nature, but highly religious as well. Ministers, preachers, and philosophers played a significant role in not only maintaining public morale and support for the war, but also enlisting society as a whole in the broader cause of liberty and revolution. Appeals to the public's faith and their perceptions of the divine were just as important to the revolution as their desire for political liberty and financial freedom (particularly in the form of property). On the eve of the Declaration of Independence, John Adams wrote his wife in the same vein, telling her, *"I am surprised at the suddenness as well as the greatness of this revolution...It is the will of Heaven that these two countries should be sundered forever. It may be the will of Heaven that America shall suffer calamities more wasting, and distresses yet more dreadful. If this is to be the case it will have this good effect at least. It will inspire us with many virtues...The furnace of affliction produces refinement in states as well as individuals."*[8]

That American revolutionaries firmly believed in the righteousness and the eventual outcome of their cause immeasurably helped to keep public perception of the war positive. The idea that virtue and morality made America different, and destined it for a better future greatly impacted the image of the war held by the people. The same philosophical rhetoric that helped to fuel revolutionary fervor also played its part in keeping the colonists-turned-revolutionaries upbeat and on track. Revolutionary faith in a God of freedom maintained and encouraged a people at war. This was so much so that membership in the leadership and governance of the Revolutionary generation came to hang upon the perception of virtue and morality possessed by that figure.

In the wake of the Revolution and its joint message of valor and virtue, our forefathers turned to the idea and advocacy of not merely a republic, but a moral republic- one in which the regular citizens and leaders valued duty, responsibility, and morality, and were guided by it. As George Washington reminded the country on the eve of his departure from the Presidency, *"It is substantially true, that virtue or morality is a necessary sprig of popular government. The rule, indeed, extends with more or less force to every species of free government."*[9] The new Americans firmly believed that without a firm moral basis, free government was impossible.

They had staked the Revolution and their liberties on a belief that virtue in governance was what they possessed and what Britain ultimately lacked, it was only natural to follow up with a Constitution predicated on that foundation. The founding fathers and the first generation of free Americans were convinced that ethics and morals were needed among the governors and the governed in order for the new nation to succeed where Britain had failed. A people who were not devoted to these principles could never hope to maintain a free republic because with the failure of virtue in the populace and government, corruption and greed by individuals would override the preservation of the public good.

The founders' greatest fear was not that the people could not establish their own liberty, but that they could not maintain it. The Constitution, with its many checks, balances, and regulations on voting and government, was meant to safeguard the new country against the potential of people to lose their way. The founders also believed that even these safeguards would be woefully inadequate if the citizenry lost its sense of virtue for any extended period of time. The revolutionary rhetoric and the faith of our fathers solidified the role and importance of preachers and philosophers to the preservation of the new moral republic.

Government under God: The Role of Religion in a Republic

> *"Whereas Almighty God hath created the mind free; that all attempts to influence it by temporal punishments...or by civil incapacitations, tend only to beget habits of hypocrisy...and are a departure from the plan of the Holy Author of our religion, who being Lord both of body and mind, yet chose not to propagate it by coercions on either...no man shall be compelled to frequent or support any religious worship, place, or ministry...but that all men shall be free to profess...their opinion in matters of religion, and that the same shall in no wise diminish, enlarge, or affect their civil capacities."*[10]
>
> - *The Virginia Statute of Religious Liberty by Thomas Jefferson*

The government established under the new American republic tended to its roots of morality and liberty. As the religious freedom statute from Virginia above demonstrates, the states and their leaders found it necessary and simple to have a government under God, but not ruled by his earthly agents. To us in the present day, it might seem strange that a text about religious freedom has its very basis in the notion that the same freedom was a God-given right, but for the founders' generation, it went straight to the heart of their moral republic. Basically, as the Jefferson-authored law points out, since God did not force any one to believe in him or any particular religion, how could man ever think it acceptable to do the same? It is often hard to understand how our forefathers could consider religion and virtue so vital to our republic, and yet proceed to grant so much freedom in faith and worship. But, in the context of the preceding revolutionary philosophies, and the constitutional debates that followed, it becomes much clearer how our country became such a jointly faithful and faithless place.

"Let them revere nothing but religion, morality, and liberty."[11]

- John Adams

The Revolutionary generation was firmly convinced that faith was the key to true freedom, and freedom the key to true faith. As contradictory as this seems, it basically meant that the founders were for faith in some philosophy, some basis of moral grounding, but did not think any one in particular was the best for everybody to follow. Our government has never been for any specific creed or against any individual one either (at least in theory). This was not a rejection of the role of religion in the Revolution and its aftermath, but rather an affirmation of its importance and influence.

Preachers and philosophers had been responsible for inspiring the populace to take part in a war for liberty and American salvation. Irregardless of inter-religious rivalries, the pastors of the colonies had lent their support and voices to the cause (even the pacifist Quakers who would not physically take part in the fighting helped to support the Independence movement in other ways). It was only natural for the new government and its laws to protect and preserve the rights of all of these different groups; keeping them from overriding or being oppressed by each other, the new government, and even themselves. As Jefferson, one of the most vocal advocates of religious freedom, put it, *"Nothing but free argument, raillery, and even ridicule will preserve the purity of religion."*[12] In trusting in freedom to keep morals pure and morals to maintain that same freedom, the revolutionary generation created a system they hoped could stand up to the trials that had plagued the republics of the past.

> *"Believing with you that religion is a matter which lies solely between a man and his God, that he owes account to none other for his faith or his worship, that the legislative powers of government reach actions only, and not opinions, I contemplate with sovereign reverence that act of the whole American people which declared that their legislature should 'make no law respecting an establishment of religion, or prohibiting the free exercise thereof,' thus building a wall of separation between church and State."*[13]
>
> - *Thomas Jefferson*

"Separation of Church and State" is the rallying cry upon which modern moral leaders, on both sides, have made their stand and staked their claims involving the role of religion in our government. As we have discussed earlier in this book, the notion of separation between church and state has permitted many interested parties to push the government to support one view or another relating to the freedom of religious expression in this country. However, for the founders, the separation of Church and State was more complex than the mere removal of religion from the federal government. Instead, the notion encompassed a much broader view of how faith should function within a moral republic.

The revolutionary generation had embraced the idea that America was a "city on the hill," and that her virtue and that of her citizens was what made her different from the decadent and corrupt courts of Europe. This same virtue was also what would prevent the new American republic from falling into the same decay that had destroyed the Greek and Roman republics. Revolutionary-era thoughts on what "virtue" really entailed and required were suitably broad, especially for a new nation whose size spanned thirteen colonies composed of vastly differing faiths and traditions.

George Washington, for example, was often noted and highly regarded for his "virtue", despite the fact that his personal religious beliefs were rarely on display, and that he almost never spoke of God in public except in the most general way. Like many of his peers, his devotion to God or to any particular faith was a highly personal and private affair. What mattered was his public persona and behavior. That determined whether or not he would be considered "virtuous" by his fellows- in short, one's actions and not one's ardent avowals of a specific faith determined how the public perceived one's morality and virtue. Or as Jefferson put it, *"It is in our lives, and not from our words, that our religion must be read."*[14] The separation of Church and State, the Constitutional amendment that forbid the abridgment of religion, these designs were not about banning God from the American nation, but about keeping faith within the private realm, for the continued purity of both liberty and morality.

By understanding that the founders intended for religion to be kept personal, a matter between each man and his God (or lack thereof), we can see what freedom of religion truly meant for the new republic. James Madison once wrote that *"Religion and Govt. will both exist in greater purity, the less they are mixed together."*[15] The ability to practice one's faith anytime, anywhere, under any circumstances in America was of the utmost importance to the revolutionaries who built our nation. The non-interference of the government in this same practice was equally vital. The new American law granted equality to everyone of every denomination, making their faith a matter for their own Churches and homes, and not for public consumption or condemnation.

The government was built on all gods and none, preferring to leave religion and clerical governance to the religious. This was in marked contrast to the rule of law as it had occurred in past centuries, and continued to occur in Europe. While still colonies to Great Britain, Americans had been under the charge of the British monarch, the head of the Anglican religion, which was both state-supported and state-maintained. Similarly, in many of the colonies prior to the revolution and in places like France and Italy, the official national religion dominated all aspects of public life and could even preclude one from holding public office. It was also financed by the taxes levied in those nations, irregardless of one's own beliefs. In nations with these religious requirements, dissenters from the official state creed frequently faced punishment and harsh regulations above and beyond that imposed on conforming citizens. The most dramatic examples of this in European history involved the prolonged Catholic-Protestant battles (even within single nations), which involved mass killing of religious rivals by both sides.

The new moral republic hoped to attain morality while still maintaining religious freedom and civil stability. Perhaps George Washington addressed this matter best:

> *"Of all the animosities which have existed among mankind, those which are caused by difference of sentiments in religion appear to be the most inveterate and distressing, and ought most to be deprecated. I was in hopes that the enlightened and liberal policy, which has marked the present age, would at least have reconciled Christians of every denomination so far that we should never again see the religious disputes carried to such a pitch as to endanger the peace of society."*[16]

By separating the Church and the State from one another, the founders hoped to achieve what had never happened before in European history-keeping religious disputes out of the public arena, thus preventing them from destroying government stability. The new America was created with the Old World's failures in mind, in a concerted effort to correct its faults and foibles, both in freedom and in faith. As Jefferson once wrote, *"I never will, by any word or act, bow to the shrine of intolerance, or admit a right of inquiry into the religious opinions of others."*[17] The new nation followed the founders in this belief, establishing laws that made all faiths equal. Knowing the importance and value of morals to a republic as a whole, the founders and the revolutionary generation of citizens left the role of religion in America to each private person, and not to the government, so that a higher reverence for both could be attained.

Faithful Followers: Religion in Modern America

> "The truth is, that the greatest enemies of the doctrine of Jesus are those, calling themselves the expositors of them, who have perverted them to the structure of a system of fancy absolutely incomprehensible, and without any foundation in his genuine words...But may we hope that the dawn of reason and freedom of thought in these United States will do away with this artificial scaffolding, and restore to us the primitive and genuine doctrines of this most venerated reformer of human errors."[18]
>
> - Thomas Jefferson

Unfortunately, the role of religion in modern America is not what our founding fathers might have wished it, free of error and persecution and not infringing upon the liberties of any citizen. The powerful influence of faith over our other civil and governmental institutions still remains strong. However, it is not the maintenance of our morality that is problematic, but rather, the increased persuasive tactics of religious groups in the United States. The desire of many different denominations, Christian and otherwise, to have laws established relating to religion is troubling. Traditional religious faiths have been no more at fault for this than other, more modern, creeds, such as atheism and nihilism (imposing a belief in no God is just as philosophically-motivated as imposing a belief in God; neither of which belongs in a country about equality under the law).

The real issue is that the ideas, which many of these ardent believers present to the public, can fundamentally alter the tone and content of political debate, and even the course of elections. The fact is, not everyone is as good as the founding fathers were at separating their personal faiths from their decisions as members of the public. As Americans, we rarely consider in modern times, how our choices can affect the whole community, particularly when it comes to religion. We no longer judge our ministers by the strict standards that our forefathers used to evaluate them; instead, we follow them blindly, full of faith, without stopping to analyze the origins and motivations of their ideas and positions. By understanding how our preachers affect our politics, we come one step closer to better performing our duties as citizens, and reclaiming our government for ourselves and our posterity.

> *"I am really mortified to be told that, in the United States of America...this can become a subject of inquiry, and of criminal inquiry too, as an offence against religion...Is this then our freedom of religion?... And who is thus to dogmatize religious opinions for our citizens? Whose foot is to be the measure to which ours are all to be cut or stretched? Is a priest to be our inquisitor, or shall a layman, simple as ourselves, set up his reason as the rule for what we are to read, and what we must believe? It is an insult to our citizens to question whether they are rational beings or not, and blasphemy against religion to suppose it cannot stand the test of truth and reason."*[19]
>
> *- Thomas Jefferson*

The religious freedom established by our Constitution was well-planned and thought out. As Jefferson pointed out above, even if we wanted to subject our beliefs to the whims of another person, whose opinions could possibly judge rightly for all? This is the reason that such freedom in faith was allowed in America, for even the founders could not decide amongst themselves whose creed was the most correct. Yet today, many philosophers and religious leaders, with great influence, have taken to judging what is right and what is wrong for all of America, not just their own adherents. They advocate for and against particular politicians, political agendas, and cultural activities. That religious figures have engaged themselves on the political battlegrounds of our country only speaks further to the desertion of their real role in our republic. By seeking to alter public perception, and in doing so, effect certain political outcomes, they undermine the very freedom that protects their practice of faith.

That is not to say that one's religion, morals, and values should not affect how we judge and act as citizens in our country. Rather, it means that religious authorities should stay above the fray and not attempt to manipulate politics through other means by galvanizing their congregations. It is the right of citizens, through their own individual judgment, to come to an opinion on matters of politics without interference from outside influences. Religious leaders have been given every right to provide moral leadership, but not to pollute the political process of our nation. Biblical and anti-biblical bureaucracy only corrupts a free and equal political system in seeking to influence otherwise independent citizens to impose their faith or faithlessness on others.

> *"Whenever...preachers, instead of a lesson in religion put off with a discourse on the Copernican system, on chemical affinities, on the construction of government, or the characters or conduct of those administering it, it is a breach of contract, depriving their audience of the kind of service for which they are salaried, and giving them, instead of it, what they did not want, or, if wanted, would rather seek from better sources in that particular art of science."*[20]

If the authority of leading believers and non-believers was based merely on moral judgment and firm faith, perhaps it would not pose so many problems to our nation. It would then be nothing more than an endless debate on whose beliefs are the right ones; a discussion that could not be solved with any surety in this existence in any event. However, piety has also made religious figures incredibly powerful and become increasingly profitable. The business of belief is booming in America, and the benefits, such as tax-exempt status, are not bad. (And even if such benefits are equally awarded under the law, the government has no right to interfere in the business of a religious institution even to grant a boon, just as that institution has no right to interfere with the work of the government, even if the matter its done in is positive.) Faith has become not just a moral interest in the condition of our nation's governance, but a business interest as well.

Madison wrote, *"Besides the danger of direct mixture of religion and civil government, there is an evil which ought to be guarded against in the indefinite accumulation of property from the capacity of holding it in perpetuity by ecclesiastical corporations...The danger of silent accumulations and encroachments by ecclesiastical bodies has not sufficiently engaged attention in the U.S."*[21] Various faith-based interest groups, filled with contributions from congregants and adherents, have continued to strive to convince the rest of the citizenry of America to be for or against certain candidates and political acts as a means to religious, political, and social salvation. However, the only basis of our religious freedom is our political liberty, and the basis of our political liberty is religious freedom. Allowing our religious organizations in this country to spend thousands of dollars to alter the perceptions of the public only does harm to our government institutions. Only in allowing free-thinking citizens to judge for themselves, instead of under the threat of eternal damnation or in-house condemnation, can we hope to have a government equal and equally fair to all citizens in their political and religious beliefs.

The power of faith to motivate and guide us has never been denied by our founding fathers or the government they bequeathed to us. Instead, it has been codified and granted the most freedom possible in order to allow for the most free-thinking possible, a chance for every citizen to contemplate, without fear or oppression, what he believes of the universe and country in which we live. As Jefferson wrote, *"From the dissensions among Sects themselves arise necessarily a right of choosing and necessity of deliberating to which we will conform. But if we choose for ourselves, we must allow others to choose also, and so reciprocally, this establishes religious liberty."*[22] The faith of our fathers and our own families is incredibly important to the maintenance of the type of nation we have grown into, a moral republic, a city on the hill. But to succeed, we must acknowledge the abuses and corruptions that faith has visited on past societies and continues to visit upon us.

Our moral leaders can easily mold the perceptions and opinions we have on those around us in society. Sometimes they are right, and sometimes they are wrong, and sometimes they are acting in their own self-interest, to their own ends. As Alexander Hamilton pointed out in the *Federalist Papers*, *"In politics, as in religion, it is equally absurd to aim at making proselytes by fire and sword. Heresies in either can rarely be cured by persecution."*[23] Basically, the fundamental idea of America is that forcing people to believe in anything does not really work in the long run, and only leads to more social and political instability. Thus, a moral republic only works when we think our faith through for ourselves instead of relying on preachers and philosophers to do our thinking for us. Just as with our economic and political ideas, the final determination of how to vote and how to govern our nation is up to us as citizens. Even though it can be difficult to stand up to conformity, freedom entails responsibility both in political and religious beliefs, and responsibility on the part of any citizen who wants to remain free.

Cultural Conformity: Wealth and Power in America

"In fact, each individual, as a man, may have a particular will contrary or dissimilar to the general will which he has as a citizen. His particular interest may speak to him quite differently from the common interest: his absolute and naturally independent existence may make him look upon what he owes to the common cause as a gratuitous contribution, the loss of which will do less harm to others than the payment of it is burdensome to himself; and, regarding the moral person which constitutes the State as a persona ficta, because not a man, he may wish to enjoy the rights of citizenship without being ready to fulfill the duties of a subject. The continuance of such an injustice could not but prove the undoing of the body politic."[1]

- Jean-Jacques Rousseau

Our religion is not the only thing that influences our decisions as citizens. Far from it, society and culture as a whole also affect how we perceive what occurs around us, and our obligations to the rest of society. In fact, society-at-large is the place that we receive the great majority of our public perceptions from, and that our faiths preach to us about. The urge to conform, to be like our fellow citizens, has always been a strong driving force in human society. As Rousseau pointed out, in a founding father favorite on the nature of government, individuals can have wills that naturally run quite counter to the will that is best for society.

When individual wills come together as a driving force, but not one that is necessarily about the public good, and rather about combined personal goods, it has classically been called *interest*. These guiding currents of individual will, interested will, and public will dramatically affect how we see what goes on around us, particularly when one will is more vocal than another. It is, after all, only when we come together in some semblance of unity and agreement that it is even possible to form a government, of any type, at all. Thus, the things that unite us can be just as important as that which makes us different.

Despite the good that cultural conformity can bring to a society, just like too much of any one thing, it can bring evil as well. History is full of examples of an interested majority imposing its will on the minority, in spite of whatever view is the best one for the overall public good. The religious wars between Protestants and Catholics that sparked internal and external chaos all over Europe, and even in colonial America, are probably the best example of an interested or powerful majority forcing its will upon a minority and ruining the state as a whole. Entire nations have been consumed in the fire of this type of struggle, which the founding fathers knew well, especially considering the inclusion of Britain herself (on multiple occasions) on this list. When one person or a few people's voices become so powerful that they can drown out the public good and the will of other citizens simply because of prevailing sentiment, then a society will face problems in its governance.

> *"There is often a great deal of difference between the will of all and the general will; the latter considers only the common interest, while the former takes private interest into account, and is no more than a sum of particular wills: but take away from these same wills the pluses and minuses that cancel one another, and the general will remains as the sum of the differences."*[2]
>
> *-Jean-Jacques Rousseau*

High Society- The Cult of Celebrity

Private interest does not necessarily have all the power in every government; in fact, more important are the private interests that attract the most attention and fellows in agreement to their own ends. In that regard, especially in America, the private interests with the most influence and power tend to also have the wealth or celebrity to campaign for their causes in the most public fashion. In our country, celebrity status in politics, high society, or the mass media pretty much guarantees both the money and the microphone needed to publicly plead for one's interests. This, too, is not always an inherent problem; after all, activists, especially famous ones, can definitely bring much-needed attention to matters the public at least ought to be aware of, even if they are not solely generating awareness just for the public good itself. The real problem lies in the ability of those people with wealth and fame to unduly influence how the public perceives its own will. When the voices of a few people become so important that the rest of a nation's people can no longer be heard without their own celebrated activist, than we are treading on dangerous grounds.

The cult of celebrity in this country has become such that famous figures are almost a requirement now for any interests – general, private, or those for the public good – to be heard at all. Citizens change their ideas and own interests, as well as their perceptions of the public good, based on what more famous citizens talk about on the national stage. As Rousseau pointed out, the general will, the common interest of a society, is about the balance of all the vast interests in a nation, not merely the sum of a certain set of interests. In modern America, increasingly only certain causes, with celebrated advocates, are the ones taken into account by our government or heard by our public.

As responsible citizens, the only way to turn this tide is to take our public duty to the general good seriously, and to ensure that the broadest possible discussion of ideas is shared throughout our republic. We do not need just the sum of particular private interests if our country is to function *for the people*, but rather all the interests and beliefs should be represented, as our founders intended. As James

Madison wrote, "*Liberty is to faction what air is to fire, an ailment without which it instantly expires. But it could not be less folly to abolish liberty, which is essential to political life, because it nourishes faction, than it would be to wish the annihilation of air, which is essential to animal life, because it imparts to fire its destructive agency.*"[3] We can no more take away private interests, or factions as many founders also called them, than we can take away liberty and hope to have a free republic based on the good of the whole. However, we can hope to use our government to control these factions, these often overwhelming private interests, from drowning out the voice of the general will. In recognizing the role celebrity and high society play in the formation and maintenance of powerful private interests, we can once again gain control over our public domain and the images that compose it.

The media plays a vital role in dispersing and providing information to the public for consumption; however, this media coverage has shrunk considerably in its depth and breadth while becoming more sensational in its nature. This poses an inherent problem for the American citizenry, who rely on accurate news to make informed decisions. When media coverage only includes those with the biggest, wealthiest, and most famous voices, the public easily becomes lost in a swarm of images that are full of power and influence over everyday life.

Average Americans have always looked up to the leaders who have inspired and galvanized our nation. It is only natural to follow and emulate those with the best ideas for all of us or those who can unite us in common purpose. But a new breed of conspicuous leadership has emerged as the wealthy and powerful in our society frequently work hard to demonstrate how important and right *their* ideas are to the public. The result has been that instead of having leaders of equal citizens, we now often see rulers of unequal ones.

These high-influence citizens have taken the opportunity to manipulate public perceptions so that many regular citizens now believe that the opinions, behaviors, and lifestyles of more famous citizens matter more than one's own. Being rich or celebrated now can make one citizen's interests greater than the average and more important than another's when we tally the sums of what makes the general will. For right or for wrong, in their own self-interest or even the interest of what *they think* to be the public good, wealthy and famous figures in American now dominate the social and cultural views of our nation.

Average Americans have embraced these factional leaders, not in a spirit of public good but of private interest. And these leaders have in turn used their influence frequently for the goal of personal gain (for both themselves and their followers). Ironically, the founding fathers frequently worried about the potential for this problem, even in a republic such as ours. The lessons of the old Greek and Roman demagogues, who had so factionalized their own societies that they destroyed themselves internally, were a constant source of concern during the framing of our Constitution (and one of the motivations behind not having a complete democracy).

As *The Federalist Papers* put it, *"The aim of every political constitution is, or ought to be, first to obtain for rulers men who possess most wisdom to discern, and most virtue to pursue, the common good of society; and in the next place, to take the most effectual precautions for keeping them virtuous whilst they continue to hold their public trust."*[4] While this clearly applies to elected political leaders, we can also see it in the context of economic and social leadership as well, especially those who affect politics and national interests by wielding public opinion. This enables these leaders, without checks, balances, or any sort of regulation, to influence politics, economics, culture, and even faith in America. In the midst of these competing private interests, how can our public possibly expect to discern what is best for society as a whole?

Competing interests and factions use public perception to advance their own agendas, whether they are political, economic, or social in nature. In fact, many interests can have a variety of objectives that touch each of these public realms (and in a republic, everything can become political at any time.) In a nation where capitalism is the established economic system, money plays a huge role in how far interest groups and people can get in their goal of persuading other citizens.

Thus, the objectives of these factions in finances are frequently twofold. Firstly, money is what funds the activism and causes of interest groups in the first place. One needs a great deal of money to even start an interest group, not to mention maintain it afterwards. This means that already, most interested parties have to begin with wealthy backers and thus typically have some goal in mind which primarily benefits these backers. It also means that without the constant limelight and public attention and funding, interest groups cannot stay in business (unless financed by obscenely wealthy benefactors, in which case, the odds go up considerably that these backers have some sort of personal interest in the matter at hand). Which brings us to our second observation on interest group finance, that is, since they must constantly bring in revenue to continue to crusade for their cause, many times they are just as concerned with selling their views to the public as they are with actually accomplishing whatever their supposed end is. After all, if they end their crusading campaigns, the cash stops coming in, and they have to find a new cause or a new job (not to mention the business of "non-profit" organizations and "idealistic" interest groups is not exactly unprofitable for their administrators and organizers).

Even purely for financial reasons, it can obviously be in the interest of an interest group to maintain its own existence, even if that means they never quite achieve their entire goal. As James Madison aptly and accurately reminded his peers:

> *"As long as the reason of man continues fallible, and he is at liberty to exercise it, different opinions will be formed. As long as the connection subsists between his reason and his self-love, his opinions and his passions will have a reciprocal influence on each other; and the former will be objects to which the latter will attach themselves. The diversity in the faculties of men, from which the rights of property originate, is not less an insuperable obstacle to a uniformity of interests. The protection of these faculties is the first object of government. From the protection of different and unequal faculties of acquiring property, the possession of different degrees and kinds of property immediately results; and from the influence of these on the sentiments and views of the respective proprietors, ensues a division of the society into different interests and parties. The latent causes of faction are thus sown in the nature of man; and we see*

> *them everywhere brought into different degrees of activity, according to the different circumstances of civil society.*"[5]

Basically, men are self-interested creatures even while they are dutiful ones, and society, particularly American society, is designed to take in and mesh all their different views and their different motivations for the end of the public good. The government in our country has been designed specifically in an attempt to compensate for this, but the ability to profit both first and second-hand from interested politics cannot be denied. That does not mean that every private-interest-gone-public has managed to or even wanted to do so, but many have, and the potential for abuse and corruption is obvious. Whenever a group actively solicits donations for its continuance in pursuing a particular cause, there is reason enough to look carefully upon its objectives, credentials, and most especially, its spending habits. Grabbing the attention of enough of the public to accomplish anything to a certain end is certainly not a cheap affair. Products, politicians, and interests all have to be effectively marketed in order to sell them to the American public. Advertisements and news coverage do not come without some sort of price tag. Shaping public perception is an art, a cause, and a business endeavor wrapped into one, always with the ultimate goal of influencing citizens and their political beliefs.

This combination of self-interest and political interest is only natural; after all, what we perceive in the world will always be wrapped up in how that world affects us personally. Having both the public good and a private interest in mind while advocating for that good, is completely normal for any citizen in any country pursuing a certain cause. Feeling the effects of an issue personally is usually the fastest way for someone to want to get involved in the same issue publicly. And, the ability to receive some benefit from tireless activism and continuous work towards a cause can often keep passionate people involved who otherwise would not have the time or resources to continue crusading indefinitely.

Passion and passionate interests are one of the things that makes our American republic great; one where people can get involved and constantly want to as well. However, these passions can also incapacitate our government and create party spirit in our nation; as George Washington reminded the new American people on the eve of his retirement from the Presidency, passionate interest *"serves always to distract the public councils and enfeeble the public administration. It agitates the community with ill-founded jealousies and false alarms, kindles the animosity of one part against another, and foments occasionally riot and insurrection."*[6]

Emotion and factional spirit have done more than their share in further dividing the American public from within. Attacking opposing interest groups or contrary government decisions has become part and parcel of the private interest phenomena. Even regular citizens who have opted not to participate in these concerts of cultural conformity can often find themselves publicly ridiculed and criticized by interest group leaders and their faithful followers. Nothing serves to attract public interest in a private cause more than lots of dissent and discord. Many wealthy interest groups have not been above using their public influence and financial strength to slap down challengers who had legitimate questions and concerns.

It is in the interest of interest groups to continue their own existence. So how can interest groups possibly hope to maintain their own existence if critical analysis can be allowed to strike down their platform? The only solution is for these private-interests-turned-public to use their resources to quiet these critics, especially by generating public backlash against any who seek to critique them. Money does not just buy private interest groups influence and publicity for their causes; it also can be used to silence their opposition – a bitterly dangerous practice in a country based on hearing out the opinions of everyone (something which ironically, interest groups need to ensure their own freedom of expression in the first place).

Those with the loudest voices in our society use their microphones to drown out the rest, and the more money one has, the bigger a microphone one can purchase. As James Madison explained, *"the public good is disregarded in the conflicts of rival parties, and that measures are too often decided, not according to the rules of justice and the rights of the minor party, but by the superior force of an interested and overbearing majority."*[7] In short, by becoming so wrapped up in their own conflicts and finances, interest-based groups often forget or choose to disregard the very public good that they were advocating their view of in the first place. Instead of *seeking* change for a better future, they start to try and *force* that change upon the rest of society. They give up their crusading roots, and become full-fledged factions in the process, constantly using their interests to demand by right and privilege the change they once sought to simply convince their fellow citizens was needed.

Interested Parties – Factions in Society

> *"Wherever the real power in a Government lies, there is the danger of oppression. In our Governments, the real power lies in the majority of the Community, and the invasion of private rights is chiefly to be apprehended, not from the acts of Government contrary to the sense of its constituents, but from acts in which the Government is the mere instrument of the major number of the constituents."*[8]
>
> - James Madison

It is easy to explain away the problems often generated by powerful interests in America with the cliché notion that wealth and money inevitably cause some sort of corruption. Unfortunately, this situation, especially in a republic, is not so easily resolved by just evaluating financial motives behind major societal factions. Just as interested parties can become dominated by the need for more money and resources to the point where it takes over precedence from their original objective, so too can the pursuit of power purely for the sake of more power become a new driving goal. As John Adams wrote, *"No man is entirely free from weakness and imperfection in his life. Men of the most exalted genius and active minds are generally most perfect slaves to the love of fame. They sometimes descend to as mean tricks and artifices in pursuit of honor or reputation as the miser descents to in pursuit of gold."*[9]

Especially amongst those already possessed of great fortunes, the desire for control and fame in our society can often become their motivation after the initial passion for a particular cause dies off. In fact, sometimes those citizens with great means begin to pursue a cause purely so it can bring them power and sway over society, and not even ever for the stated goal itself. Those who desire power in a republic and over its people are almost universally more dangerous than those merely pursuing personal financial gain through their crusading (though a combination of the two can also prove significantly hazardous to public welfare). The term faction most aptly describes those interest groups and their leaders which use their cause to gain personal glory and public power.

Perhaps it is important to explain why factions in a democratic or republican society can prove so problematic in the first place. Why did the founder's generation so dread the spirit of faction and interest when our government is based on the notion of differing interests and ideas having a place in our country, even when held only by a minority? On initial consideration, one could even say that interest groups are merely a vehicle for like-minded citizens to come forward with a joint cause.

And sometimes, interest groups are really and truly that, or at least they start out that way – as citizens with similar ideas. But the real reason the founders warned against such permanent, interest-based groups was that their influence over society can become far from benign activism (or even the pursuit of financial gain through said activism). When factionalism becomes ingrained in a society based on popular control, the propensity of a faction to seek to impose their views on everyone else by manipulating the public's perceptions only grows. After all, it is a great deal easier to accomplish one's goals when it is possible to incite one's fellows into unthinking action.

A republic's success depends greatly on the moderated will of its citizens. The ability of faction to reshape this will into an unreasoned and malignant public force is the true issue at hand. As Jefferson reminded his supporters during his First Inaugural Address, *"All, too, will bear in mind this sacred principle, that though the will of the majority is in all cases to prevail, that will, to be rightful, must be reasonable; that the minority possess their equal rights, which equal law must protect, and to violate which would be oppression."*[10] The problem with factions is their belief that the prevailing part of majority rule comprises the essence of

American government, instead of the notion of the rights of the minority. Heavy-handed factionalism which engages in oppression instead of equal treatment under the law was what the founders truly dreaded about interest groups and parties.

Between their wealth and influence, many of these factions have achieved a much greater place in our society and governance than the average citizen can ever hope to achieve at this point in time. Often, now, regular citizens must join with already-existing interest groups in order to have their real interests incorporated into the political process. Without merging with an established faction, smaller interests can have an extraordinarily difficult time trying to navigate the arena of incredibly wealthy interest-based politics. Money is used by these factions to purchase positive public opinion, political power, and even the votes of elected politicians.

The very point of the Constitution was *"to secure the public good and private rights against the danger of such a faction, and at the same time to preserve the spirit and form of popular government."*[11] But the idea of a popular government based on the public good is not the same thing as a national popularity contest for issues, candidates, and interests; just as the rule of the majority does not give that majority a right to oppress the liberties of any minority. Somehow, factions have convinced the American populace that a simple show of hands, with the greatest number raised prevailing, is how our government is supposed to function. That the founding fathers explicitly opposed this political style in favor of respecting minority rights (thus the reason for having certain "unalienable" rights) rarely seems to merit a mention any longer. The ability of factions to provide powerful and wealthy interests with increased political control was always a prime fear of our founding fathers.

But why is it such a problem if those few with the money and the power to change minds use it to do so? Our society is founded on a right to different opinions and the discussion of those personal interests. Yet there is more to factions than just the desire to propagate the reasoning behind their ideas. Factions always seek to prevail, and they are willing to use their financial resources and public influence without regard for the true will and good of the public, to achieve victory. We have only to look to the numerous examples of interest-based government scandal throughout our nation's history to see this sort of behavior in action. Even officials who do not want to cater to these interests often find themselves forced to do so, because factions frequently play a role in keeping politicians in office through direct and indirect campaign contributions.

Since they have more money engaged in the political process, interest groups can basically buy themselves a greater say in our government. Factionalism is then allowed to run uncontrolled over the rights and desires of the public because they allow no rivals to their own interests. As John Adams wrote, *"The essence of a free government consists in an effectual control of rivalries...the weaker will ever be the lamb in the paws of the wolf. The nation which will not adopt an equilibrium of power must adopt despotism. There is no other alternative. Rivalries must be controlled, or they will throw all things into confusion; and there is nothing but despotism or a balance of power which can control them."*[12] When we allow interest groups to effectively govern our nation because we cannot control their influence, we risk our republic decaying into a dictatorship.

The founders knew that the cause of Greek and Roman political failures had been the social factions that they could not find a way to adequately control. The citizens of these old-world republics had turned in desperation to popular heroes, like Julius Caesar, to save them from the corrupted, interested politics rampant in their societies (because interest groups eventually started to collude with politicians to defraud the people). In establishing a republic under our Constitution, our founders had hoped to combat these perversions of genuine public interest by instilling in Americans a belief in inherent rights and a general public will that ought to be followed. Their level of forethought in creating our government clearly demonstrates their concern about controlling these types of factions and rivalries that had frequently caused ruin to old republics and classic governments.

The nefarious and aggressive tactics employed by factions in their constant pursuit of more resources and greater public power serve to illustrate the disconnect in their stated interests and their actual ones.

The biggest and loudest claim interest groups make is that they are only around to serve the needs of the citizens who support them, and that they have a right to be heard. And in America, at least, this is true; every citizen most certainly does have the right to freedom of expression and demonstration. However, that right does not grant *some* citizens the right to speak for *all* citizens; nor does it grant a *few* citizens the right to manipulate the rest of the people and the government to their own ends in the name of public good.

The use of wealth and power to intimidate and influence the political process was never part of any bill of rights in our nation. John Adams, himself, once exhorted his peers not to *"suffer yourselves to be wheedled out of your liberties by any pretenses of politeness, delicacy, or decency. These, as they are often used, are but three different names for hypocrisy, chicanery, and cowardice."*[13] In permitting factions to convince us that we do not need to actually think about what our liberties mean for ourselves and our fellow citizens, we step ever closer to the precipice that spells the end of our republic. By believing that only certain individuals and interests always have the public good in mind, and others never do, nor will, we close ourselves off to all the possibilities our forefathers created for us.

The revolutionary generation had found that citizens often formed, *"an attachment to different leaders ambitiously contending for pre-eminence and power; or to persons of other descriptions whose fortunes have been interesting to the human passions, have, in turn, divided mankind into parties, inflamed them with mutual animosity, and rendered them much more disposed to vex and oppress each other than to co-operate for their common good."*[14] Basically, the founders believed that the leaders of various interest groups and rival factions would rather incite the populace to rule over each other than to share the reins of the government. The actions of these interested people, supposedly striving for the general welfare, prove that their true intentions are not always merely for the public good. The need to analyze and understand the origins, motivations, and purposes of these interest groups is more important now for the continuation of our republic than ever.

Undue Influence- Greater Voices for "Greater" Citizens

> *"Of liberty I would say that, in the whole plentitude of its extent, it is unobstructed action according to our will. But rightful liberty is unobstructed action according to our will within limits drawn around us by the equal rights of others. I do not add 'within the limits of the law' because law is often but the tyrant's will, and always so when it violates the rights of the individual."*[15]
>
> *- Thomas Jefferson*

The entire notion of America, the true difference between it and all the governments of the Old World, has always been the fundamental belief that all citizens were created equal. Whatever success, wealth, or advantages that one American citizen might acquire in his life, in this country, it still does not permit him to force his opinions on his peers or to govern unilaterally over all other men. This is what has made America such an inspirational and powerful place for people who have immigrated here since its inception. The idea of a 'land of the free' is more than just words to most Americans; it is a way of existence. Equality founded by the laws and underneath the rule of law is the standard we strive for. And even when we fall short of such a lofty goal, we hold to it as the only basis for legitimate governance.

This is still what makes our republic, our American nation, different from the rest of the world; that there is nothing which inherently entitles any one particular citizen to govern over any other for any reason – not wealth, not noble birth, not even great brilliance or valor – the only laws that are valid are those that protect the rights and liberties of all individuals, equally. These beliefs are the reasons that the founding fathers worked so diligently to build a system that could protect the people and itself. They had seen the results of other societies before the great American experiment, which had tried to establish freedom and democratic rule, only to find themselves with a government still ruled by the few at the end of the day. Factions and interests became their greatest fear because of its ability to cause the undue influence of preeminent figures over all others. What they wanted least of all was a government, supposedly based on the consent of the governed, where "greater" citizens could arise and possess a greater voice on issues than everyone else – for how would that have been any different from what they were leaving behind under Britain's rule?

In creating our country, the founding generation established a government completely unlike any other ever in existence; one based on equality in law and an equal role in governance for every citizen. But it was never a perfect system, and even with all of its checks and balances, the founders still worried over the tendencies of men to want to assume supremacy over each other. It was an issue even in their own time, how to balance the will of the majority with those of all the minorities, how to incorporate everyone's interests even when they conflicted with one another, how to keep factions from taking over control of a popular-based government.

As we have aged as a nation, these problems have only increased as the need to galvanize a large and ever-growing citizenry intensifies. The real problem is that the interest groups of America and their leaders have forgotten their places and their duties to the rest of society. They have gotten so incredibly caught up in serving themselves and their supporters, they no longer try to serve in their capacity as regular, American citizens. Because in that role, they are supposed to set aside their own needs and wants, and consider the good and the will of our nation as a whole.

It is no easy thing to put aside what one firmly believes and respect the boundaries of others' beliefs, but it is what makes our form of government unique and our institutions' continuance viable. If we want to keep it this way instead of succumbing to the factionalism and internal divisions that destroyed the republics of old, perhaps we should recall an axiom of Thomas Jefferson's when we consider our responsibility to each other, *"What all agree upon is probably right; what no two agree in most probably is wrong."*[16] In seeking to impose our own will on others, we completely miss the point of having a republic for a government in the first place. It is only through a disinterested interest that we can hope to achieve the type of society envisioned by our founders and forefathers.

The danger of allowing the influential and the wealthy to manipulate our public society can never be underestimated. What separates us from a monarchy or an oligarchy than the very fact that everyone and not just certain special people rule over the whole in the first place? Our economic, social, and political leadership have begun to fail us; many of them have come to think that only they can decide for us how to best manage our government. They no longer merely try to convince us that their views are the rights ones for our whole society; instead they heavily rely on manipulating the people's feelings and our public systems of governance in order to accomplish whatever their ends might be. Factions take advantage of the freedoms of our society, and our personal feelings on the issues we face. Instead of trying to become part of a broader solution, they only further divide us, which conveniently allows them to gain more personal control and more freedom in the process.

Like George Washington, they know that *"Democratical States must always feel before they can see: it is this that makes their Governments slow but the people will be right at last."*[17] But without Washington's sense of duty and responsibility to the public, they end up betraying the will of the very people they are supposedly the agents of. When personal freedom becomes more important than the public freedom, and we allow our private feelings to corrupt the public trust placed in our hands and that of every single citizen, we pull the very foundation out from under our Constitutional government. In doing so, our society, despite its love of freedom, becomes part of the undoing of the very fabric that makes up our freedom in the first place.

BY POLITICS: BUYING OFFICE

> *"I know of no safe depository of the ultimate powers of the society but the people themselves; and if we think them not enlightened enough to exercise their control with wholesome discretion, the remedy is not to take it from them, but to inform their discretion."*[18]
>
> - *Thomas Jefferson*

At the heart of any government system lies politics – the give and take, the actual physical realities of day-to-day governance of a nation. There is absolutely no way to have a government without the political side to take care of the business of running society and enforcing the law. What makes America a republic is not that we call ourselves one or that our Constitution establishes us as one, but rather, that we maintain a political system where the people ultimately control their own governance via representation. The more our politics tend towards caring for the interests of the people, the truer our government stays to itself, and the less we as a people have to involve ourselves in the daily bureaucracy.

The reason for having the people as the final authority over the government in the first place comes not from the desire to bog the populace down in every political detail, but to enable them to maintain their own rights and equalities (or set them right if those elected to do so falter in their obligations). The true difference between a republic and a democracy is not popular control but how much of it is necessary to maintain government's daily functioning and the preservation of the people's liberties. The hope of a republican system is to give the people the power without imposing on them the burden of constantly having to utilize that power – hence the need and the reason for elected officials, whose job it is to act for the people in their stead.

Politics is what keeps our government going, and even if we want to consider it an evil, it is a necessary one. A government without politics can only be a dictatorship or a tyranny, because those are the only type of governments that function based on the will and dominance of a single person's or group's rule and beliefs. In understanding our own politics and their role in our governance, we are able to keep control over our country.

Keeping the people interested, informed, and enlightened about political affairs thus becomes of the utmost importance in a republic. If it is the people who are the ultimate authority, then they have the ability to decide the fates of politicians, laws, and the government itself, at their own discretion. This means that pleasing the most people possible will always be extremely vital to a politician's continued career and any political agenda he wishes to undertake. The reasons factions and interest groups have come about to begin with is their role in coalescing all these desires and ideas into a coherent political force.

An interested public is certainly not a bad thing in the sense that without popular participation, popular control is meaningless. And if the public opts not to play their part in the political process because they feel that either it does not mean very much or it is not important enough to spend time on, then the system is truly failing them somewhere. Shaping the structure of a sound government was only half the battle our founders faced; they also knew there had to be some way to maintain it.

The line between interest and over-interest plagued their development of a popular political system – they knew its faults, but they also knew they needed to keep the public participating in politics. Instead of relying on faction to express the will of the people, they created representatives who had to be accountable to the public for their political activities. They made elections frequent and mandatory for politicians who wanted to involve themselves in the leadership of a whole country. And they made the Presidency a position held to the highest standards of the public's will as a whole and not its individual interests and parts. In short, they constructed a system to counteract all the problems they knew had the ability to destroy popular politics, while trying to enable the country's continuance and capacity to self-correct.

But, no political system is perfect, not even ours. To expect it to be or to believe that the founding fathers could possibly have predicted every last political problem is unreasonable. Despite the likelihood of abuse and corruption, the founders felt the only safe haven of political power was in the people themselves. Even if the government did get off the right road from time to time, eventually the founders knew they would be forced back on it, by sheer threat of a revolution like the one that had separated America from Britain in the first place. Or as Thomas Jefferson aptly put it, *"Whenever the people are well informed, they can be trusted with their own government; that whenever things get so far wrong as to attract their notice, they may be relied on to set them to rights."*[19]

Our country has always had a firm basis and reliance in the ability of the people to stand up and change things if they go far enough astray. In a popular political system, this is a good thing because it adds yet another layer of accountability onto politicians, who certainly do not want to be removed from office through the loss of an election, let alone by force. John Adams pointed out, while advocating for the Constitution that: *"The right of a nation to kill a tyrant, in cases of necessity, can no more be doubted than to hang a robber, or kill a flea. But killing one tyrant only makes way for worse unless the people have sense, spirit, and honesty enough to establish and support a constitution guarded at all points against the tyranny of the one, the few, and the many."*[20]

Our popular system of government also means that manipulating public perception becomes one of the only real viable options to maintaining political power in this nation. Regardless of whether one is a full-blown faction, a rogue politician, or an entire political party, how the people see one becomes the key to a continued presence in our government. Without the backing of the majority of the people, the entire endeavor comes undone. Most Americans clearly have never had any real moral objection to defying any law or political opinion that overturns their liberties or violates their freedoms. Politics in the United States has always involved the art of balance – the mediation between competing ideals, interests, and needs is not just what our politics is, it is what holds our political system together. Ironic that what has the potential to divide us can also unite us in the pursuit of the common good.

The Price of a Vote
– Mouths and Means

"Every one sees what you appear to be, few really know what you are, and those few dare not oppose themselves to the opinion of the many, who have the majesty of the state to defend them."[1]

- Niccolo Machiavelli

Unfortunately, politics is not the means to a better end that it used to be during the days of the founders. The sense of obligation that once underlay the pursuit of political office in America has vanished with the belief that the most popular opinion must be the right one. Instead of striving to be the best elected official possible and to serve the needs of the public in the best way, politicians seek to be re-elected and to please as many people as possible in the short-term, ignoring the potential long-term consequences of their actions. And, despite the ability of the people to check a ruler or official back into his place, it does not necessarily make any difference when the entire political system becomes compromised by this type of behavior. Recognizing that political tyranny can come under many people, a few people, or just one person enables us to see politics for what is truly is – a means of control over others in business, society, and governance. Whether that control is benevolent or dominating in nature depends on how we perform our duty as citizens and serve in our capacity of balancing political power.

The role of politics in a republic is to serve the people, but often it enables factions and individuals to serve themselves, their friends, and their supporters. By ensuring the public's interest and participation on behalf of a certain person or group, interests keep the government going with their money and their ability to fuel the public's passion. Therefore, elected officials come to only need to rely on these factions to continue to be elected by the public. And, they cease to need the public in and of itself.

It is only natural that they begin to serve those who truly win them their political victories more than they serve the people to whom they supposedly owe their representational obligation. In America, our political system gives us our freedoms and asks only that we maintain them for our future generations. Our fore-fathers have fortunately already secured these freedoms for us, so we do not have to do it ourselves; we simply have to preserve them. When our political system becomes so engrossed in winning over the people, making them feel like their liberties are still intact, it stops actually trying to safeguard those same liberties. The danger in attaching a price to the means and mouths behind our political system turns our voice into just another number, instead of a true vote.

THE GREAT LOBBY – THE PERCEPTIONS OF THE PUBLIC

"Knowledge will forever govern ignorance: And a people who mean to be their own Governors, must arm themselves with the power which knowledge gives."[2]

- James Madison

Self-governance, or the duty required of a citizen in a republic to maintain that self-governance, is no easy task. In order to effectively function in this capacity, a citizen needs to know what they are voting for, who a candidate is, and what that official believes. Without this information, voting becomes just the practice of randomly selecting one person's name from a list of names. Similarly, not understanding the basis and function of one's government means that one loses one's effectiveness as a force in that government. Those armed with this knowledge will always possess power over those who lack it.

In our country, information is certainly abundant and accessible to the people, but it does not always serve the cause of increasing knowledge among the populace. Information in America is distilled and diluted by the sources that provide it, to accomplish or advocate for whatever ends they have in mind. Instead of giving power to the people through actual knowledge, information is used to mold public perceptions.

Basically, information is rarely given out for the sake of popular education, but rather, it is handed out for a reason. In doing this, the power the public could harness from knowledge is lost to those factions and great lobbies who dole out select tidbits, arranged just so, for national consumption. Politics and politicians have been only too happy to accept the help of these organizations in "spinning" their positions and actions. Political control becomes so much easier when the real source of government power accepts their own subjugation willingly, in the belief that others really are acting on their behalf. The great power of the lobby allows selective governance to take the place of self-governance.

"Ignorance is preferable to error; and he is less remote from the truth who believes nothing, than he who believes what is wrong."[3]

- Thomas Jefferson

The modern political process has essentially become about rallying the most people to one's side, regardless of how one has to go about procuring these votes. In using interest groups, factions, and lobbies to inform and ally the public, politicians and elected officials gain more power and popular control without actually having to do anything for it (as long as it *seems* like they are acting, they can maintain their place). Lobbies drum up support by playing to people's interests and attitudes, and by putting out a lot of misinformation (and in doing so, laying down a lot of dollars) towards their cause.

Nothing makes this practice more obvious than taking a quick look at all the studies funded by lobby groups, which shockingly, come to prove their point. The thing is for every study undertaken by a faction on one side; we can find a study run by the opposing faction showing how they are the right ones. So much for unbiased research and factual information helping the political process, the public barely has time to physically vote, much less wade through all of the conflicting and misleading information out there.

This is really what politics in America has come to rely on, literally overwhelming the public with perceptions and images, often of what they want to hear anyways. But, as Jefferson said, *"If a nation expects to be ignorant and free, in a state of civilization, it expects what never was and never will be."*[4] Interest groups have taken away the public's political power by catering to already-existing interests and manipulating them to fit any given situation that arises. Politicians, in turn, work with and use lobbies to keep the public informed and in acceptance of their actions. Our politics, therefore, become a self-fulfilling and unending circle where the social, economic, and political leadership play off each other and the public for their own ends, destroying any prospect of ever identifying the actual public will.

Though not just one person is to blame for these pressures and issues within our political system, few bother to try and change the way it works. Why rock the boat? Politicians require the financial and moral support of interest groups to fund their campaigns and gain supporters; interest groups need politicians to be their public personas and enact legislation positive to their goals; and the public needs information and a means of popular organization. Thus, all sides of this triangle become trapped within its own confines. After all, if a whole group or one single official did not engage the public, or even bother to try to do so at all (even if it was in a manipulative manner), then we clearly would have a bigger problem on our hands.

When politicians and lobbies stop caring about how the public perceives them, the opportunity to regain popular control without drastic measures has already been lost. As Washington himself explained it, *"If men are to be precluded from offering their sentiments on a matter which may involve the most serious and alarming consequences of mankind, reason is of no use to us; the freedom of speech may be taken away, and dumb and silent may we be led, like sheep to the slaughter."*[5] When we lose our ability to offer our values and voices effectively, then we have already lost our liberties and our votes before we can even cast them. When we expect politics to function as a constant clash between opposing interests, we allow our own interests to be over-shadowed in the process. The public often simultaneously expects too little from its officials and too much, placing them in a position from which they are unable to ever accomplish anything besides fighting over politics. Because the interests of lobbies and politicians so often coincide, they can control the populace by acting in concert, even though the public is often only semi-aware of the true depths of their inter-relationships.

Perhaps we would rather believe that our representatives, be they the government, interests groups, or even businesses, always place us as a people ahead of themselves. After all, the great hope of our American republic has always been in the ability of people to act with and for other people. What is a Medal of Honor, our nation's greatest military award, if not a physical symbol of our complete belief in the valor, necessity, and even requirement for self-sacrifice to further the good of the whole? What allows us to even trust in our representatives, senators, and governors, whom we elect, if not this same belief- that they can and will, at least some of the time, set aside their personal interests and act in the interest of their public? On a fundamental level, our nation firmly relies upon this principle; that there are things more important that one man's wants and needs, even though every man's needs should be protected.

All the national debate and discussion on sacrifice, service, and self is really about sympathy for one's fellows, and a commitment to the notion that what makes society better as a whole also makes it better for the individual. The Revolution itself was the ultimate expression of this idea. Giving up one's life so one's peers and posterity might enjoy freedom one might not live to possess oneself is the penultimate sacrifice of self-interest. We are lucky indeed that our political system and our politics come from these noble beliefs, and provide us with a standard to judge the interests and influences of individuals and groups over us. As Benjamin Franklin put it, *"I think opinions should be judged by their influences and effects; and if a man holds none that tend to make him less virtuous or more vicious, it may be concluded that he holds none that are dangerous."*[6] The great goal of politics, at least for the American populace, is ultimately to decide whose opinions help everyone the most and hurt everyone the least.

> *"Has it been found that bodies of men act with more rectitude or greater disinterestedness than individuals? The contrary of this has been inferred by all accurate observers of the conduct of mankind; and the influence is founded upon obvious reasons. Regard to reputation has a less active influence, when the infamy of a bad action is to be divided among a number than when it is to fall singly upon one. A spirit of faction, which is apt to mingle its poison in the deliberations of all bodies of men, will often hurry the persons of whom they are composed into improprieties and excesses, for which they would blush in a private capacity."*[7]
>
> *- Alexander Hamilton*

American politics is certainly not an occupation without its own perils, for a man's reputation, personal integrity, or even his family. Even though infamy and fame can be minimized in dividing them among a governing body, they can also completely conceal anything else a man has ever done, good or bad, in their shadows. One well-played action can secure a senator his seat until his retirement, despite any subsequent errors. And, one extreme mistake can cost the same man a shot at ever being elected again, despite any good he has done. The spirit of faction is strongest in its political role in this regard.

In pleasing or displeasing a particular interest or demographic, a politician can make or break an entire career, even if he never does anything else. Interest groups and lobbies will continue to fuel the perception that one person is better over another, even if that person has been found to serve their cause just once. They will even pull politician's public voting records, as if the sum of his interests, opinions, and activities, can be provided by a "yes or no" list. And in a spirit of success and support, our politicians will often rush into decisions that affect our national welfare long after the interest they are helping no longer exists or fades into the background. Faithful service to one's constituency is not the same as blindly following that constituency's passing whims.

Sadly, the problem is just as often the public itself as it is the politicians or lobbies. Interest groups might strive to manipulate our opinions, and politicians play to our perceptions, but we are the ones who permit it. And we fail to often appreciate those who serve us best, if they do not serve us the loudest. Telling the population what a good job one is doing for them often serves one better in politics than actually doing anything at all. Basically, if we do not see it or hear it or feel it (especially if it relates to our pocketbooks), then it does not exist for us as citizens. If we really wonder why politics in the United States is so wrapped up in image control, we have only to look to the people that those images are created for in the first place, us.

Money is poured into campaigns and causes just to tell the public, supposedly in control of the whole government, what is going on in that government. Politicians and factions spend the great majority of their time trying to remind the populace of their opinions and ideas so that they can actually ever have a hope of doing something about them. We cannot merely assign all the blame to self-interested parties, businesses, and politicians; we also have to accept that our own selfishness is at fault for the position we find ourselves in. In failing to give up our own interests for the consideration of the greater good, we fail in our duty as citizens, and actively allow politicians and interest groups an avenue towards greater control and power. In order to prevent ourselves from being used in the pursuit of political power by others, we have to stop pursuing government purely for ourselves and our own interests, and look to our nation as a whole.

Money is the Root of all Evil – Campaign Finance

> *"Lay down true principles and adhere to them inflexibly. Do not be frightened into their surrender by the alarms of the timid, or the croakings of wealth against the ascendancy of the people."*[8]
>
> - Thomas Jefferson

In the pursuit of power, money certainly plays its part. And in the pursuit of political gain, the amount of money that is laid out, for the purpose of producing public support, borders on the ludicrous. It is not a problem that we as Americans are completely unaware of either; in recent years, more and more questions, about where and how money is spent, as well as what are its origins, have arisen in the political realm. Yet little has been done to control this obvious source of influence and political corruption beyond acknowledging its existence as an issue.

Many justifications have been given for the continued state of campaign and political finance to remains as it is, citing anything from freedom of speech to the real need for money to run a campaign. It is not that some of these concerns have no basis; rather, the difficulty comes from the gray area between the right in this nation for every citizen to express and fund their political views, and permitting those with a great deal of wealth to manipulate the public and our political system (which would not be a "right" of any American).

Politicians, especially those in the process of campaigning really have to have funding to reach the people with their message and their opinions. Other citizens are certainly entitled to support them in their endeavors, because every person is permitted to have a voice in our electoral process. However, we run into a problem, once again, that certain voices can become greater, louder than others when backed with wealth and celebrity. It was certainly not the intention of our founding fathers, in creating a popular election system, to silence the voices of the average man without the resources to fund a politician on his own, anymore than it was their intent to silence the minorities of our nation just because the majority rules. Our political system is predicated on a belief in free speech, but that does not mean it provides any politicians or interest groups with the right to undue influence over the rest of society, let alone outright corruption.

To understand the issues and the real problems surrounding money in politics, and its major role in a great host of political evils, it is useful (though perhaps tedious) to go over our actual campaign finance laws and their effects. As of the 2008 general presidential election, the *Bipartisan Campaign Reform Act of 2002*[9] and the previous *Federal Election Campaign Act of 1972*[10] provide the governing regulations in these matters. These laws basically require disclosure of campaign contribution and spending habits, place donation limitations, and give the Federal Election Commission, or FEC, the power to monitor money given to and used by campaigning politicians. Both of these pieces of legislation were direct responses to actual corruption in the campaign process, and not just its possibility.

These laws specifically and directly regulate what is known as "hard" money contributions to campaigns, that is to say any physical monies donated directly to a certain candidate. It is also important to note that these rules do not govern any other sort of deals or contributions to a politician who is not actively engaged in the election process. The amount of dollars that individuals, Political Action Committees, Authorized Campaign Committees, and various levels of Party Committees can give to any candidate is supervised by the FEC, and most often, limited to a maximum dollar amount. These "hard" money contributions are not so much the problem, even though they too have incurred their share of abuses.[11] And the irony is that this side of campaign finance is actually fairly-well regulated and easier to identify when it does become abused for both the FEC and the regular citizen.

The real problem in campaign finance is "soft" money contributions, that is money which is not directly donated to a particular candidate, nor can it be used to specifically or "expressly advocate" for a single person's election. However, these dollars are the ones most used to influence election results. This money is typically spent by organizations and advocacy groups to support their candidate without actually saying they want him and only him to be elected. Before the passage of the *Bipartisan Campaign Reform Act*, these "soft" money campaign contributions were completely unlimited and entirely unregulated.

Due to this legislation, they do now face limitations, but it is mostly in how they must word their advertisements and perform their activities. Since a great deal of so-called "issue" advertising can stop short of actually, outright, supporting a certain candidate by name while still supporting that person in spirit, groups with "soft" money can effectively bypass these rules. The Act really only bans political parties from utilizing the influence of "soft" money in campaigns, and does not forbid its use by every organization which possesses it.

The most glaring and disappointing of these legal groups are *527 groups*,[12] which are not just simply in existence and business to influence elections – they are actually tax-exempt organizations as well. These groups raise and distribute funds, in support of certain causes but not certain candidates, (in theory at least), and they incur no regulation by the FEC or any other regulating body so long as they stick to issues and not specific people. They have no contribution limitations because they do not theoretically "contribute" to an actual, specific candidate.

In practice, "soft" money allows rife abuse in the electoral process. Under the guise of free political speech and issue advocacy, tax-exempt organizations like 527s take advantage of our civil liberties and loopholes in our campaign regulatory laws. In doing so, they effectively influence politicians and the public without any checks or balances at all on their activities. The problem with these types of politics is not merely their existence; it is their lack of a counter-balance in our government system.

Unfortunately, campaign finance during a candidate's actual, physical bid for election is not the only place where money can pose an unchecked, undue influence over our government. The exchange of money between hands, for selfish purposes, on the public's dime and rights, in no way stops just because the campaign ends and a victor is declared. Into the arena steps all the back-room deals, mutual kickbacks, and generally untraceable arrangements made for support and even just cash, that a politician agreed to so he could clinch the election.

When the candidate assumes his office, he is expected, and typically must, honor these deals. Because if he does not, he foregoes the mouths and means of his former compatriots forever, and even becomes a pariah among their opposition as someone who will not stick to an arrangement. Besides, since these groups are the ones who portray how successful a candidate is, he continues to need them to keep the public's perception and support on his side. Thus, these private deals are even more dangerous for our political system than any "soft" or "hard" money contributed during the campaign season can ever be.

These deals effectively exclude the public and the popular will from the equation of government. The people are never asked about and do not vote for or against any of these arrangements, and frequently they do not know about them, nor will they ever (unless the abuse becomes so painfully obvious that it can no longer be hidden). Government grants and contracts are given to lobbies and corporations for their support, non-elected positions are handed out to individual backers, and legislation is passed furthering mutually beneficial agendas – all of which rarely ever go towards anything inherently for the public or the national welfare.

The inability of politics to function without serious funding on all sides is fundamentally disturbing. In the 2004 general presidential race, the two main party candidates spent over $325 million dollars each.[13] According to the FEC, in the 2008 presidential race, the two main party candidates had more of a disparity in spending, with Barack Obama coming in at $513.5 million and John McCain at $346.6 million. If we include third party candidates, the total spending in 2008 was over $1.5 billion dollars. That is a great deal of money being spent just to persuade the public to vote for someone. And to what end do politicians truly spend this kind of money? Is it merely to be elected, to serve the public? Why raise this sort of revenue to convince the public to elect one if it is not worth anything (especially under an economic system like capitalism)?

As Thomas Jefferson noted, even in the days of the founders, we had developed *"a moneyed aristocracy in our country which has already set the government at defiance, and although forced at length to yield a little on this first essay of their strength, their principles are unyielded and unyielding. These have taken deep root in the hearts of that class from which our legislators are drawn, and the sop to Cerberus from fable has become history. Their principles lay hold of the good, their self of the bad, and thus those whom the Constitution has placed as guards to its portals, are sophisticated or suborned from their duties."*[14] Basically, political service has become yet another way for the already financially successful to gain more wealth through the exercise of power in government.

We can and do measure political accomplishments in terms of the dollars and cents that trickle back down to the rest of the populace. Those interest groups and politicians who ensure the greatest tax cuts and highest economic returns, the most money received in various social welfare programs, or the highest "humanitarian" payouts, are considered the "true" public servants, while those who do not so easily use the public's money are reproached. Even if these big-spending politicians fund their massive endeavors with the public's treasury, and then pay their friends and supporters to get these jobs done, they are still lauded and better appreciated than those who refuse to spend money for the sake of spending it on projects that do not contribute to national welfare in any way. Without enough dollars to spread around (or refusing to spend those dollars needlessly or loosely) in appearances and pet projects, a politician basically becomes meaningless.

The Next Election...and the Next

> *"Resolved... that it would be a dangerous delusion were a confidence in the men of our choice to silence our fears for the safety of our rights: that confidence is everywhere the parent of despotism – free government is founded in jealousy and not in confidence"*[15]

- Thomas Jefferson

As Jefferson so aptly put it over two centuries ago, having total faith in our elected officials to secure our liberties, without the public warily watching them is folly. Time has only proven this assessment more and more correct, even in America. Elected officials have found ways to corrupt the political process through wealth and influence, and divide society against itself into factions more concerned with the election of their favored politician than safeguarding the rights they ought to treasure most. Thus, our entire political system has embraced re-election as the real goal in government. If one is elected again, it "proves" the automatic acceptance of the American people of everything a politician ever did and whatever he continues to do (at least in his mind).

Re-election becomes the entire justification for and rationale behind pursuing the same policies, and maintaining the status quo, regardless of whether the public actually approved of those specific agendas or just might have preferred an incumbent to the other candidates, despite his previous political acts. Politicians can then show the rest of the public that they *must* be doing a good job because a majority re-voted them into office. And if an incumbent is overturned and defeated, his opponent assumes and desires that all of his predecessor's policies should go out the door with him, and whatever the opposite is should replace them. This is portrayed to the public as *their* will. Election results become the "mandate" of the public, even though it is highly doubtful that any one citizen can really cite one politician who has done everything they personally would have while in office.

Money only makes this problem worse. The dollars that are handed out to supporters, public or otherwise, before and afterwards, can make or break a candidacy. The election becomes more important than the politician's actual term or his policies. The public hears more on a politician's record during the few months when they are campaigning than they do for the many years in which that politician holds office. Wealth gains a heavy hand in the political process, being used to shape and alter public perception, dole out favors, and even elect candidates. After all, one cannot run without enough resources.

With the ascendancy of the election as the key to the public's will over how much a politician does during his actually term, those with the funding can completely dominate those without it. Image becomes more important than reality and special deals for critical votes more important than the public good. Our republic slowly starts the decline into an economic aristocracy where only those with the money to run an important and visible enough campaign, full of public promises and private arrangements, can come to political office.

When the election is more important than a politician's tangible tenure, those groups and interests involved in the electoral process become more important in the political process than everyone else. And this would be fine, if our government was not supposed to be a republic, where all are valued equally. How often do we hear of voter demographics and what appeals to them? How frequently do politicians try to appeal to certain groups, who vote in high numbers, with various plans and policies? Unlike the politics of our founding fathers, the "public good" is not mentioned nor the "general welfare," instead it is the "blue-collar worker" or the "senior citizen" or any other of the innumerable interests that make up our society that politicians play to. And of course, politicians are supposed to, and should consider all of these groups, but it is not their job to make certain that a particular one is happy while others are still not – elected officials are supposed to provide for the happiness of everyone.

Maybe this is the point where we have truly become the most lost as a nation, on what an elected official is really supposed to do and whom he is supposed to represent. He is not just the advocate for the people who get him into office, contrary to how politicians commonly behave today. An elected official is supposed to represent everyone, even those who did not financially support him or physically vote for him, and he still represents them even if they voted for his opponent. In forgetting this basic principle of our political system, the influence of those who actively contribute to campaigns becomes more important in our governance than those who do not (especially those who do not contribute money). This provides the access to government control that those who are able to corrupt always seek over those in power. The avenues in the electoral process, self-interest, and loose fiscal oversight in campaigns, make it easy for those who desire special favors or special influence in politics to get them.

> *"Our legislators are not sufficiently apprized of the rightful limits of their power; that their true office is to declare and enforce only our natural rights... and to take none of them from us. No man has a natural right to commit aggression on the equal rights of another; and this is all from which the laws ought to restrain him."*[16]
>
> - Thomas Jefferson

The question becomes who then do a people who want to self-govern in a republic such as ours trust to do their will in politics? Should only the wise or the very intelligent be allowed to rule? Except that even the most intelligent of men can have faults and self-interests that can supersede their best judgment. Should only the wealthy, who have an economic interest in the continued existence and strength of a society, make our laws? Except that they constantly will seek profit or economic gain from their positions, often to the determent of those presently without material wealth. Should one man or woman whose family has done great service to their country in centuries past judge what is best for all? Except that they often live in a world apart and forget about the needs and wants of those who rank beneath them and their great family honor.

The answer is obviously that none of these people should always rule anywhere or anything, or at least that is the American answer to the question; the answer which our Constitution gives. Our Constitution, our founding fathers, created a republic where every person – brilliant or not, wealthy or not, honored or not – gets to rule. The whole point of the American experiment was that no group of the few should ever rule the many. Every citizen is possessed of unalienable rights; natural rights that no government has the authority to take away or legislate upon. Only from the consent of the public as a whole does the government have any political power, and only from that and for that whole should decisions be made. It really is as simple as the *Declaration of*

Independence puts it, "*We hold these truths to be self-evident, that all men are created equal, that they are endowed by their Creator with certain unalienable Rights, that among these are Life, Liberty and the pursuit of Happiness. — That to secure these rights, Governments are instituted among Men, deriving their just powers from the consent of the governed.*"[17]

Who Can Yell the Loudest: The Two Party System

"Men by their constitutions are naturally divided into two parties: (1) Those that fear and distrust people, and wish to draw all powers from them into the hands of the higher classes. (2) Those who identify themselves with the people, have confidence in them, cherish and consider them safe, although not the most wise depository of the public interests. In every country these two parties exist; and in every one where they are free to think, speak, and write, they will declare themselves."[1]

- Thomas Jefferson

In our government, we constantly find our politics divided into two, often opposing camps. It is only natural that if there are citizens who want something one way, there are those who believe the exact opposite to be best. Among those citizens involved in our government as politicians and bureaucrats, it is typical to find many who do not think the vast majority of citizens are capable of handling the powers of self-governance (even though they might publicly claim otherwise). These people seek to draw more political control into their own hands and the hands of their active supporters, in the belief that they know better than, and know what is best for the average citizen. And sometimes it is true, some citizens can and do have better ideas than other citizens, but no one is always right.

The reason why every citizen gets a role in our government in the first place is so that all those whose ideas have some potential can be heard by everyone, and then everyone gets to decide what the general will is. Our government is predicated on the notion that, at the end of the day, the public is able to discover the best way to solve the problems and issues that confront them, and that they are the best source and defense of their own interests in politics. Thus, our republic strives to include every citizen and their opinions. There is nothing wrong with disagreement over how the government should operate; these kinds of divided opinions are what our government is built on after all. But to think that we can achieve a true republic of the people while caring only for what divides us, and having that which divides us represent us, is folly.

Both the official, national, political parties are guilty of a lack of confidence in the abilities of the people to govern. That is, after all, why they exist in the first place and maintain their existence now – they are citizens who think other members of the citizenry are not able to exercise the power of self-governance well enough. When any citizen sets up their own views on politics as the be all, end all, of the matter, they place themselves into the 'party' of people who believe only 'higher' classes should possess political power. The reason Jefferson stated it this way was because considering oneself, or, those who agree with one, the only 'right' people to make political decisions, is tantamount to believing that one belongs to a higher class (especially in a country without any form of hereditary aristocracy). Because our nation is founded on the right of everyone to have a say in their governance, those citizens who think themselves better governors because of status, wealth, or even great intelligence, set themselves above the public accordingly, effectively creating their own special class.

Political parties, especially in their most partisan activities, undermine our system because of this belief that their opinions and interests are the only right ones. Parties in a republic, besides being sources of combined interests, serve only to fuel the needs of the few, by their very nature. Despite the image they try to give to the people, political parties are not an original part of the American system, nor do they represent republican or democratic principles of popular government. Partisan politics merely creates another class of citizen; one composed of politicians and people who think they are the only ones capable of good governance. Parties merely indicate a lack of faith in the public will.

Partisanship

"I deem no government safe which is under the vassalage of any self-constituted authorities, or any authority other than that of the nation or its regular functionaries."[2]

- Thomas Jefferson

Political parties are, in fact, self-constituted authorities, at least in the United States of America. They do not derive their place in our political society from any portion of our Constitution, and any laws concerning them arose subsequent to their actual existence. Despite their lack of original Constitutional authority, parties did exist in the colonies and among the founders themselves. The Constitution itself was the origin of truly "American" political parties, separate from any of their British predecessors. But even then, founders and citizens on both sides greatly feared the establishment of permanent political parties in the new America.

Parties had been a big part of the colonial issues with the British Parliament in the first place. Endless bickering and highly partisan politics had plagued the Parliament of the Revolutionary generation, and many of the onerous Acts and ever-changing laws concerning colonial governance were the direct result of party changeovers back in Britain. The lack of colonial stability due to British party politics made even those highly passionate and partisan revolutionaries incredibly wary of the national institution of political parties. So despite their own participation in groups of essentially the same nature (at least at times), the founders deliberately excluded them from our Constitution and our original laws.

Our founders even generally refrained from the use of the word "party" in their own speeches and debates when describing the Federalist versus Anti-Federalist dispute, for fear of giving justification in the form of precedent. As Jefferson noted above, the power of any authorities not created by the legal government was considered dangerous. Britain had not provided safety for the rights of the colonists because of its own internal and partisan turmoil. Thus, the founders did not feel it prudent to rely on parties, who cannot be effectively regulated by the public, as the foundation of American political power.

> *"It is of great importance in a republic not only to guard against the oppression of its rulers, but to guard one part of the society against the injustice of the other part. Different interests necessarily exist in different classes of citizens. If a majority be united by a common interest, the rights of the minority will be insecure."*[3]

For our founding fathers, their main problem with parties stemmed from the insecurities partisanship causes – both to the rights of the citizenry and national policies. Any majority that only cares about its own interests to the detriment of any other interests in a republic will always seek to rule the minority opinion instead of coexisting with it. As a larger majority grouping, the political party is a particular cause for concern. In a republic like America, where popular opinion and the public will ultimately rule, political parties can too easily manipulate the line between general and self interest.

The founders knew that the leaders of political parties would gain too much power from their positions in the party; positions that would not be subject to the same laws or public pressures as those of regular government officials. Parties would create disproportion in a carefully planned and balanced political system, not to mention possessing an inherent interest in political power (a danger to any form of government). If a majority could claim most of the government's offices and install their supporters in many non-elected positions, the founders knew our republic would become more about which party currently had the power and forget about what the people want in the process.

They had even seen this with the last minute selection of the so-called "midnight judges", appointed by President John Adams on the eve of his departure from office. He deliberately appointed Federalist judges to the bench as Thomas Jefferson, an Anti-Federalist, was incoming to the Presidency, in order to leave a Federalist stronghold in the judiciary (despite the clear popular sentiment to the contrary). Partisanship helped to tear apart the once united founders and transformed many former friends into bitter political rivals (like Jefferson and Adams or even the ill-fated Hamilton and Burr). The founders intimately knew the dangers of party, and thus, gave no legitimate constitutional authority to them, knowing all to well their potential to destroy the good of the whole.

The state of the modern political system (with our two current parties) only shows how right the founders were about partisanship. Instead of individual politicians competing for election by the people, for the people's interests, our politics are full of party competition. In our Congress, it is not representing the will of the public that matters most, but how loyal one is to one's particular party. Many citizens have come to believe that it is more important to look at a candidate's party affiliation than his credentials and opinions to determine if that person should represent them. Instead of worrying about what the majority of the populace wants, our politicians worry over having a majority in the House of Representatives and the Senate (as well as taking the Presidency).

The key to our politics and our government is no longer the people then, but the parties themselves. Which party holds the most elected seats determines how the country will be run, the type of laws and legislation that will be passed, and who non-elected government officials will be. This obviously removes a great deal of power from the hands of the people, who in theory should be the ones in control of our government. The logic behind a politician deciding to follow party mandate instead of the people's will is obvious, especially once one considers the expanded size of our nation and the grouping of politicians together in one location. As *The Federalist Papers* put it, *"a distant prospect of public censure would be a very feeble restraint on power from those excesses to which it might be urged by the force of present motives...abuses would often have completed their mischievous effects before the remedial provision would be applied. And in the last place, when this might not be the case, they would be of long standing, would have taken deep root, and would not easily be extirpated."*[4] Basically, politicians have come to be most motivated by what is closest at the moment, regardless of the possibilities of the future.

The replacement of the popular will with the party will is what ultimately has a hand in nearly every fault that modern politics encounters within our system. Our nation is based on every citizen having a voice and a vote, on limitless interests and ideals. But when two political parties dominate our government, we find ourselves seeing who can yell the loudest, and our possibilities limited by whatever party happens to be in power. When parties become so important that a party needs their own Congressional majority to accomplish anything, it is the citizenry who loses their choices, and thus popular control. The founders knew that *"In a free government the security for civil rights must be the same as that for religious rights. It consists in the one case in the multiplicity of interests, and in the other in the multiplicity of sects. The degree of security in both cases will depend on the number of interests and sects."*[5]

In a popular government, it is not just choice that matters, but the amount of choice, because that is what keeps the majority from overturning the rights of the minority. When only two political parties can even have the option of presenting viable candidates, the public's voting power is usurped by the party system. How often does a citizen refuse to vote for a particular third-party candidate that they feel represents their views best, because then they will be *wasting* their vote since that third-party candidate cannot possibly win? For any citizen to feel they *have* to cast a vote for someone just because that person is the only one closest to their values who can actually win means that our republic is fundamentally failing in its goals. Two parties can clearly not represent the myriad of interests in America, they do not even represent a solid majority of the public will (otherwise there would only be a single party). Instead, they dominate the popular electoral system with their own designs and limit the citizens' choices of candidates and causes.

By undermining the ability of the public to choose, parties and partisan politics give undue influence and a greater voice to those involved in them. Obviously, that was not what the founding fathers intended when they created our Constitution (or even when they took part in their own partisan politics), and especially not when they specifically gave political power to the people. Parties and politicians who participate in parties are not inherently evil, nor do they cause problems for every type of political system. But in ours, they do. Our checks and balances, our combined federal and state system, our three separate branches of government, these were all designed to keep such factions from establishing permanent places in our politics. To quote the founders in this same vein, *"Each department should have a will of its own...the members of each should have as little agency as possible in the appointment of the members of the others...the members of each department should be as little dependent as possible on the others."*[6]

Our very system is based on the principle of not allowing those with similar interests to band together or use their combined power to force their interests on everyone else. Or as *The Federalist Papers* also state it, *"Ambition must be made to counteract ambition. The interest of the man must be connected with the constitutional rights of the place."*[7] When we allow political parties to dominate our government, unregulated by the Constitution as they are, we allow the ambitions, self-interests, and greed of those composing them to go unchecked. How can we possibly expect any more change or any less corruption when there is little motivation for politicians to cater to the citizenry and so much reason for them to serve their party? Without the public to control the political parties, even in the small ways available, do we really expect that they would serve the general will any more than any other special class of politicians has ever done in any other nation? In accepting their existence in our politics, we as citizens effectively condone their actions. If we want to maintain a government for the people, we must not rely on political parties, who can never represent all the people, to do it for us.

The Perks of Power: Gerrymandering

> *"Is it not natural that a man who is a candidate for the favor of the people, and who is dependent on the suffrages of his fellow-citizens for the continuance of his public honors...should be willing to allow them their proper degree of influence upon his conduct? This dependence and the necessity of being bound himself, and his posterity, by the laws to which he gives his assent, are the true, and they are the strong chords of sympathy between the representative and the constituent."*[8]
>
> *- Alexander Hamilton*

The benefits of political power have as much to do with the ability of the two-party system to maintain itself as self-interest does. Like many businesses, lobbies, and social interests, our parties play off the system and each other to accomplish their ends. Since our government is effectively vested in the party system, these extra-constitutional institutions have gained legal status and protections, as well as treasury dollars and federal support from the powers the party receives after elected.

Besides the influence over politics they now possess, parties actively influence the basic operations of our government – they are the ones to establish many of the rules involving the election process (especially the primaries), who use their elected positions to make the laws more manageable for the party (like the selection and assignment of district borders), and who dole out taxpayer dollars to supporting organizations, individuals, and areas in order to keep the votes of the people. Some of the most difficult governing and spending patterns for the public to keep track of and understand are the ones involving pet party projects that cater to one supporter or another. These are the perks of party power and political success, and parties in this country use them to fuel themselves indefinitely. So much so, that today, the public can no longer conceive of politics without parties.

While it was the intended design for a representative to be strongly bound to his constituents, the party system has effectively unbound many of these same cords. One of the privileges that come with election is the ability to change the rules for the next election. The assignment of voting districts and representational apportionments is controlled by those currently in power. And it is certainly much easier to change these rules to favor one's steadfast supporters and weaken one's opponents in the election process than it is to do so well at one's job that all one's constituents embrace one.

The method by which district lines are drawn up "creatively" in order to manipulate the election system is known as gerrymandering. The easiest way to understand what this entails is to envisage what it looks like on a map or in your own neighborhood (and in the most egregious cases, it becomes incredibly obvious if one simply views a map of where voting districts lie). Imagine that your normal voting district is composed of everyone living on Main Street; it makes sense that all the neighbors who live on this street should vote together because they share a neighborhood and so on. Now imagine that the representative you elected decides to change those district lines; so now your district includes your house, your neighbor behind you who does not live on Main Street, and then the line criss-crosses throughout the region, including only those who have red roofs.

Your district is now gerrymandered because it features a line that makes little sense for the region, but represents an enclosure of a certain group of voters (in this case, those with red roofs). Now substitute a political party affiliation or interest group membership as the way the lines are drawn instead of the arbitrary and relatively random apportionment of using people with red roofs. Now an elected official is not being selected *by* his constituents, he is choosing *them* to fit his own agenda. This is not popular representation.

Many American voting districts have circuitous routes and interesting lines that bring people together in the same district that do not really have any commonalities or sense of community. These districts are constantly being re-drawn to reflect the needs of whichever party happens to have power at the time, and few realize it. If you ever wondered why when you voted for something relating to a district, local matter that seemed to be fairly obvious and of interest to your general community and the referendum still failed; your district probably has been gerrymandered. A good, simple example being a referendum asking, "Do you want to spend taxpayer dollars on fences to enclose a playground near a busy street?" As a parent living in the community with small children, you might vote "yes", and since all your neighbors have small children and use that park, they might vote "yes" as well. Protecting children from traffic is an issue that most people, regardless of affiliation, tend to agree on when they have children.

Unfortunately, since your district has been gerrymandered to include a large retirement community ten miles down the road, the referendum fails because the older vote in that community does not live near the park, and does not have small children, so they all vote "no" because they want to see those dollars spent elsewhere. Now this might seem like a small matter, and whether or not a playground gets a fence is more likely than not an unintended result of the gerrymandering of your district. But your actual neighborhood and community just missed out on what was an issue of interest to them because a sub-community relatively far away has been arbitrarily grouped in with your actual community.

The real reason the lines were redrawn to include that retirement community is because older people tend to vote a certain way and tend to vote in large numbers, and whatever party came into office in your area needed to be sure the senior vote was there to balance out the more unpredictable parent vote (that might vote differently depending on the issues). The worst part of the situation is, your community probably initially elected the politician who changed these lines, entrusting him with your community's welfare. But it was more in his and his party's interest to shift them, so he did. Thus, gerrymandering undermines the community aspect of representation even at the most basic levels.

> *"There are others... which take their origins in private passions, in the attachments, enmities, interests, hopes, and fears of leading individuals in the communities of which they are members. Men of this class, whether the favorites of a king or of a people, have in too many instances abused the confidence they possessed; and assuming the pretext of some public*

motive, have not scrupled to sacrifice the national tranquility to personal advantage or personal gratification."[9]

When the election of a party majority can enable that party to hand itself victory in the subsequent election (and at the same time completely re-arrange district politics), it obviously undermines our self-representational system of governance. When individual citizens come together in their capacity as elected officials to deliberately alter the way their equal peers vote, a party can no longer claim to be acting in the public interest. Gerrymandering is a perfectly legal means (at least currently) of shifting around one's constituency, but that does not mean that as citizens we have to permit it.

The founders had to allow room in our Constitution and the law for the reapportionment of representatives. They did this because if all changes were illegal then the districts could not be adjusted for actual growth or reduction in physical size or population of a community. The problem is that political parties have used this legal leeway as a loophole to re-arrange districts at a whim so that those places where their support lies, can be better represented and balance out the places where they lack supporters. The manipulation of where district lines are placed in order for elected officials to bypass the will of the general public is quite possibly the greatest perk of political power (and also the biggest problem).

It enables politicians and political parties to only have to answer to their "bases" and to be able to ignore those dissenting voices by grouping them into small clusters surrounded by large groups of their own supporters. There is nothing "democratic" or "republican" about this exploitation of the laws governing our representational system. Using political power to maintain their control just makes political parties like every other dictatorship of the few that has ever existed. When parties, under the guise of the laws designed to accommodate population shifts, are permitted the perk of redesigning our voting system to suit their needs, we lose the very representation they are supposed to be providing to us as elected officials in the first place.

The Worth of Power: Pork-Barreling

> *"Happy it is when the interest which the government has in the preservation of its own power, coincides with a proper distribution of the public burdens, and tends to guard the least wealthy part of the community from oppression!"*[10]
>
> *- Alexander Hamilton*

Happy it would be indeed if the interest of our parties, in their governance of our financial obligations, was the fair apportionment and subsequent re-distribution of each citizen's taxes to meet our national financial obligations. And the founders had hoped that our system of government would allow this to happen, thus guarding both the rights of the wealthy and the average people. They had thought that the election process would be enough to keep politicians from going too far in government spending habits because the public could always elect a new official. However, with the advent of partisanship and extreme gerrymandering as the American political standard, politicians can keep their positions with much less effort and much less public oversight.

The value of power in dollars and cents helps parties and politicians to keep that power and to gain ever more. Through what has come to be known as "pork-barreling", politicians use their positions and their party majorities to pass special projects that cater to or reward specific interests with government funding and contracts, basically taxpayer money. Their power over this spending (once in office) allows them to reward campaign supporters with financial incentives and to show the public that they are receiving some sort of material gain from that candidate's election. Unfortunately, it also means that the way the government spends what is truly the money of the citizens becomes rife with abuse and corruption, and the great majority of the time is used to promote a politician's continued power and not the public will.

Because most spending bills are passed by legislatures as a whole, the party system becomes incredibly influential in the government spending process. It would be very difficult for a single politician to convince their peers to vote for a spending project that only helps their constituency without the support of a party to divvy out a little of that "pork" to everyone else. Parties exercise their political muscle at this point in the "pork-barreling" process by arranging for the necessary spending ventures to be tacked onto other bills that need to be passed or by ensuring that each politician gets a piece of the government pie from the overall budget. It also means that more money gets spent on projects with particular interests and voting blocks in mind than for the public good as a whole.

This occurs not just at the local levels, but more worryingly, at the state and federal levels as well. Spending general taxpayer money on one's constituency or advocating for the funds one's constituency requires is not necessarily a bad thing. After all, people elect their representatives to represent them, and obviously that includes the distribution of the general funds for projects the people require.

The problem is that when this practice becomes corrupted and fueled by party politics, it essentially amounts to buying one's constituency and supporters with government money. Those already in office can spend almost any amount of taxpayer money they want on their supporter's projects and in contracts to the companies of campaign contributors, as well as on earmarks specifically designed to only help their electorate (or at least that part of their electorate which actually votes for them). Besides being a potentially very corrupt exchange of cash, pork-barrel spending contributes to the huge amount of wasteful government spending on projects that do not benefit the general welfare.

The founders themselves were incredibly hesitant to undertake even the most charitable projects for fear of establishing a precedent by which the government could engage in this type of spending. Even in the face of the Great Depression, and having to help millions of jobless workers, Franklin D. Roosevelt, a President clearly not afraid to spend government money on public projects, feared merely bribing the public with work paid for by the government, purely for the purpose of creating work just to appease the jobless. As he put it when discussing the New Deal, *"All work undertaken should be useful — not just for a day, or a year, but useful in the sense that it affords permanent improvement in living conditions or that it creates future new wealth for the Nation.*"[11] And that truly expresses the standard that we need to apply to government spending and to understanding the difference between pork-barreling and legitimate funding for projects of the public good.

The federal legislature was given the Constitutional power and prerogative to control the purse strings of the federal treasury because it was thought that they would be held accountable by their voters. However, the party system has since realized that it can also use the federal pocketbook to buy off the citizenry by supplying not just their needs, but by actively using general taxpayer money to feed their desires as well. In a republic, the ability of a party to indefinitely maintain its own existence and political power through federal financing of supporting interests and citizens completely undermines our entire government. The entire situation becomes a catch-22, where everything begins to circle back onto itself and perpetuate its own abuses.

If there is anything close to a perpetual motion machine in existence, partisan spending habits in America would be it. Congress needs to control the finances because they are the ones directly accountable to the people. The people expect Congress to participate in projects that better their existences. Representatives in Congress want to please the people and want to stay in office. Politicians need a majority to pass these fiduciary measures, so they turn to their peers. They and their like-minded peers form a group to accomplish these ends, and thus turn into a party. The party enables these politicians to ensure that they meet their electorate's expectations, and thus the politicians stay with the party. The party's actions as a whole majority allow them to fund even more projects, and the party leadership can dole out more favors to individual politicians. Eventually, pleasing the party becomes more important than pleasing the public because the party controls the means by which a politician stays in favor with their public, and thus in power. So the purse strings, despite being in the hand of the people's representatives, come to be controlled by a political power other than the people.

> *"A government ought to contain in itself every power requisite to the full accomplishment of the objects committed to its care, and to the complete execution of the trusts for which it is responsible, free from every other control but a regard to the public good and to the sense of the people."*[12]

The government has to have the ability to spend money on the public good and people's projects, and to change voting apportionments to reflect the population of our nation. Part of the genius of our Constitution and the founding fathers' design was that they tried to account for these needs to the best of their knowledge and legal abilities. They had to allow the representatives to function as the advocates for their communities and constituencies so that everyone could have an equal voice in their own governance. But things have not gone exactly as the founders expected. They had hoped that competing political parties would not arise to overwhelm the delicate balance of the system. They counted on the candidates to have to do the will of their constituencies or not be able to be re-elected. What the founders failed to completely account for was the unbridled ambition and manipulative ability of those in power to want to maintain that power once they possessed it. They left the people to be their own guardians of their liberties and rights, and the rule of law to support them in it. But as citizens, we have often failed to safeguard them; we have allowed ourselves to be bought off.

Maintaining the Status Quo

"There is nothing which I dread so much as a division of the republic into two great parties, each arranged under its leader, and concerting measures in opposition to each other. This, in my humble apprehension, is to be dreaded as the greatest political evil under our Constitution."[1]

- John Adams

With the acceptance of the two-party system as the main force in American politics, our republic has become focused on good intentions instead of good government. For citizens, the media images and spinned portrayals of politicians and their parties have become more important than our government's actual activities. Through the power that this grants them, our two "great" parties and their members are able to maintain their private power even in the face of overwhelming public will. They have even found ways to manipulate our electoral system, the true source of the people's control, thus undermining the role of the citizenry in our republic.

With the matter of elections effectively under party control (even if a particular politician can still lose), the parties look to maintain the status quo in our politics and amongst our people. By promoting the idea that two parties constantly clashing and reversing one another's policies is the American norm, the political parties can keep the public in line and generally convince the citizenry that things are going alright with our government. When the most change that is required by the public is for the parties to switch whichever one is in the majority, it is easy for politicians to retain the powers they have already gained.

All the party's wealth and influence goes into ensuring that our government remains at a stand-still, constantly giving and returning ground that has already been fought over, without ever actually having to move forward. With the added ability of being able to spend the public's treasury dollars in the pursuit of political gain, the parties of our nation have been easily able to convince everyone that their ways are best.

But the truth is, our government cannot remain at an impasse, caught up in party politics forever. That is the reason why change has come with such violence throughout our brief history – it seems passion and the spirit of revolution are the only real guarantors that our system will not continue merely to feed us more of the same. Even Thomas Jefferson, one of the key architects of our government system, understood the part that these public passions played in politics. He once wrote that: *"God forbid we should ever be twenty years without such a rebellion. The people cannot be all, and always, well informed. The part which is wrong will be discontented, in proportion to the importance of the facts which they misconceive. If they remain quiet under such misconceptions, it is lethargy, the forerunner of death to the public liberty."*[2]

Silence in our republic has truly become acceptance, and our government seems to view the lack of armed rebellion as a signal that the status quo is thus satisfactory to the citizenry. Our political parties have seized the reins of public passion and channeled them into the partisan politics of oppositional policy positions, thus distracting the people from the real problems at hand. Without the citizens' involvement in the regular needs of self-governance, our republic will always fail to truly represent our people. What is the point of possessing the ultimate political power in a nation if we choose not to exercise it? When we allow two parties to control us as citizens and the choices we make for or against a cause, we forego the very rights that make our country different from any other despotism run by the few.

Party Rule

> *"The common and continual mischiefs of the spirit of party are sufficient to make it the interest and duty of a wise people to discourage and restrain it."*[3]

In permitting parties to rule our politics, we have given them a system they know that they can control. By combining the vast interests, politicians, and opinionated citizenry together, parties enable broad political organization. This allows them to create the necessary majorities to win Congressional votes, and to maintain their own existences, even though some of the very causes comprising the core of both parties are contradictory in the sides they represent. A very basic example of powerful issues that find homes in specific parties, despite these issues' lack of logical agreement is the fact that one party represents both the anti-gun control lobby and pro-life lobby simultaneously. While the other party represents the pro-gun control and pro-choice lobbies. That is, one party represents a weapon that kills and not killing, while the other desires to limit a killing weapon but still seeks to permit abortions.

If one were deciding these issues at their fundamental level, it would make infinitely more sense that one party be for pro-life and pro-gun control (essentially people concerned with the preservation of human life in all scenarios), and the other party be for anti-gun control and pro-choice (essentially people concerned with the capacity of human beings to choose in all scenarios). No matter what one's position on these issues, it is fairly obvious that they pair up more cohesively in this manner, despite being currently artificially under the same party umbrella. Every justification to the contrary, the same broad organization should not be representing both groups. That is not to say that some citizens do not hold these positions together for whatever reasons, because some certainly do, but rather, that such interests do not naturally belong under the same roof. When this happens, these interests lack true representation because the party can play them together.

Political parties have become such experts at controlling public perception that the citizenry actually believes the "spin" that is fed to them (for the most part). While one may choose a party or a cause, and most people know that politicians and interest groups lie and manipulate, people accept the fundamental flaw perpetuated by partisanship in America – that popular representation and the electoral process can only be managed through a two-party system. Though this has become tradition in American politics does not mean that this tradition is inherently correct just because it is old or even that it is actually constitutional just because it has been popularly permitted. In our passion over certain issues, we have allowed parties to take our rights and in some instances, even given them to them.

As Alexander Hamilton once wrote, *"The passions of a revolution are apt to hurry even good men into excess."*[4] Whether the revolution is social, political, or economic in nature, this has proven true in our nation. It has also hurried us into the waiting arms of those interested groups in our society who seek personal gain or to always win, no matter what our government or our laws dictate. Even the best and greatest of our citizens have been subject to the folly of partisanship, including our founding fathers. That is why they so feared and warned against factionalism because they had known its effects well. Despite that they actively sought to discourage their posterity from engaging in this type of partisan politics, their warning has gone unheeded. In the heat of contentious causes and political moments, where people desperately want to triumph in their views, they have turned to parties to secure the necessary majorities, despite the potential future consequences.

Partisanship, in the long term, only weakens the interests and the people it is supposed to be supporting. In constantly seeking to achieve their majorities, parties take the easy way in politics of lowering their standards in order to raise their averages. They cut deals among different interests and soften causes in order to suit as many of these groups as possible. Thus, they can create and pass lots of legislation that appears to be accomplishing something, but in reality, very little changes or gets done. The current conviction of most citizens that saying one supports a cause or group is the same as faithfully representing the same is promoted by the parties. Because of their ability to manipulate public perception, then they really do not have to alter the status quo. Parties can pass laws that are essentially just hollow words, without having to greatly upset anyone by really changing anything.

Why do we believe mere words constitute real change as citizens in this country? Why is it so easy for us to accept parties and legislators that do not really represent us? Benjamin Franklin once remarked that *"Mankind naturally and generally love to be flatter'd: Whatever sooths our Pride...we are pleas'd with and easily believe, when ungrateful Truths shall be with the utmost Indignation rejected."*[5] Basically, it is easier to believe that we are achieving greatness in our government than to face the truth that we might not be. It is not just simpler for the parties, who use this natural instinct to their own advantage in politics; it is also simpler for us as citizens to accept the "truths" and the list of "accomplishments" that the parties give us. It allows us to feel like we are nearing our goals and furthering our most fervent interests, as well as following in the steps of the illustrious and rebellious founders. But calling something "baby steps" when it is really stepping forward with one foot and back with the other does not change that we are really at a standstill.

Parties have built up their own value in the minds of the American citizenry, only further solidifying their role in our government. They use the feelings of the public in contentious causes, the core faith in the security of our representational government, and the ideals of the American dream to keep the public's expectations in line with their objectives. By building up the belief among the populace that the two-party system is an established American tradition, parties have placed themselves in a position of political dominance. When members of the general public, or even their own politicians, deviate from the party line, they are subject to the full force of that party's wealth and influence to bring them back into the fold. Those that enforce and advocate the party's positions are favored and given all the benefits of that party's political power. But, the ability of parties to punish and reward those who obey their dictates is not consistent with a government based on the rule of the people; rather it sounds more like a government ruled by the few (in this case, the few being the parties and their supporters).

George Washington once wrote that *"Arbitrary power is most easily established on the ruins of liberty abused to licentiousness."*[6] The self-created political power of parties in this country has developed through the slow erosion of the right of the people to representation. The parties have not just gained supremacy while the people still maintain their own. Government is not one of those things in which power can be shared, eventually someone seizes ultimate control. Even our founders realized that republics quickly turned into dictatorships when the people become dissatisfied under the authority of parties or their peers. When this happens, citizens tend to turn to the rule of one person versus the rule of the many or even the few in order to save themselves from the corruption and chaos caused by these systems. That is why interested parties, despite their claims to the contrary, are not an original part of the American system, nor can they ever ensure true representation or real stability in a republican government.

> *"Things cannot go on in the same train forever. It is much to be feared, as you observe, that the better kind of people being disgusted with the circumstances will have their minds prepared for any revolution whatever. We are apt to run from one extreme into another. To anticipate and prevent disastrous contingencies would be the part of wisdom and patriotism."*[7]

The American people, though a generally accepting citizenry, has a line on what it is prepared to tolerate from its politicians and parties, which is probably the only thing that has thus far staved off political and civil ruin. Maintaining the status quo has been the easy way for parties and our government to convince the majority of Americans that their country is still running according to design. It is the continuation of this belief that allows the few to remain in power while still satisfying the many who think that they remain in charge.

However, as Washington pointed out, the real danger lies in the potential of the people to completely throw our system out the window because they become so fed up with it. And if it takes too long for them to realize the abuses and corruption being perpetrated by their so-called representatives that may in fact be the only solution. By taking an honest look at our country and our government and how they are functioning, we can prevent such drastic circumstances from arising in the first place. While it may be fine for the political parties and the politicians who benefit from the status quo to maintain it, we as citizens will find a way to express our will once we are dissatisfied enough. We can either take Washington's advice by actively employing our power to make our government work for us now or we can wait until the parties have completely assumed all our political power before we require a change.

Political Stagnation

> *"There are men who could neither be distressed nor won into a sacrifice of their duty; but this stern virtue is the growth of few soils; and in the main it will be found that a power over a man's support is a power over his will."*[8]
>
> *- Alexander Hamilton*

The problem with party power in our government is that it leads to political stagnation. When the people are satisfied with more of the same, those in control will always have little incentive to change. Besides the fact that they already reap many benefits with the government operating as it does, with change comes risk. As Hamilton pointed out, few are those who cannot be convinced to give up on their obligations and objections when confronted with potentially negative consequences to those actions. Among parties, politicians are kept in line not just by the favors party membership confers, but mostly by the punishments and political difficulties parties cause for dissenters. This translates into greater power for parties, who can therefore control the actions of elected officials far more than their constituencies ever will.

This type of politics leads to an intense effort by said parties to combat any significant or meaningful change in government policies and legislation for two main reasons: firstly, with any adjustments to the status quo, the parties know that the potential increases that they might lose power (or expose the extent of the power they currently possess); secondly, change is rarely completely desired or completely opposed by the populace, so it brings great political risk for a party to seek change and possibly offend their core supporters. Change is a gamble for those trying to undertake it, and thus it can either pay off greatly or backfire miserably. This means that in politics, real change is very hard to enact, and for the parties, it is seldom to their advantage in any way to do so, particularly over the short term. Keeping power becomes much more important than possibly losing it by taking risks. That is why politics has become a zero-sum game; the parties would rather hold onto the power they have and have to exchange small portions of that power between each other rather than give that power up entirely.

This fear of loss is one of the largest motivating factors in the modern American political process. Even small defeats are made out to be major blows (likewise, tiny wins are portrayed as great victories) in the media and by a politician's opponents. So why are our parties and politicians so concerned with what are often very insignificant gains and losses? Besides the tendency of these issues to be blown out of proportion by the press or the oppositional faction, it is actually the political influence on the populace, of even the most minor misses. In a nation based on majority rule and the ideal of governance by the general will, the appearance of even a small lead for one side can alter the views of the undecided. Especially in matters where a citizen has none or very low interest, their opinions and votes are frequently swayed by what they perceive as their peers' desires on said matter. And even on major issues that one has a great deal of interest in, popular opinion will still often affect a citizen's ultimate judgment.

Since political parties, individual politicians, and interest groups all heavily rely on the people (at least some of them) for support socially, politically, and economically, maintaining the right public perceptions is key. When one side loses, even a little, the idea that a mandate has been established for the victorious side basically leads to political turnover. The majority (even if it is a small one) gains the ability to control the minority. For parties, their core power lies in the maintenance of their majority and the public acknowledgement of that majority. When they do not have to take political risks because they can keep up the status quo and still satisfy their part of the populace, parties can keep their own political control and the government in check without worrying over losing their influence or their elected seats.

> *"This is preeminently the time to speak the truth, the whole truth frankly and boldly. Nor need we shrink from honestly facing conditions in our country today. This great nation will endure as it has endured, will revive and prosper...the only thing we have to fear is fear itself – nameless, unreasoning, unjustified terror which paralyzes needed efforts to convert retreat into advance. In every dark hour of our national life a leadership of frankness and vigor has met with that understanding and support of the people themselves which is essential to victory."*[9]
>
> *- Franklin D. Roosevelt*

Because the parties fear to risk, maintaining relatively unchanging legislation and government becomes the objective of those in political power. Political success is no longer dependent on great leadership or governing ability, but rather, on whom can best manipulate the people and their support. Even preceding the time of Franklin D. Roosevelt, fear of change kept politicians from trying any truly big projects to save our economy from the Great Depression. Politicians, on both sides, were so concerned that they might worsen the situation, and then not be elected again (as happened to Herbert Hoover) that they ended up doing almost nothing to make the failing national economy better. Even with Roosevelt's brave guidance and acceptance of responsibility for the results of his legislation, he was often opposed by the parties purely out of fear of change.

Sometimes, these politicians' worries were justified; in enacting his plans, Roosevelt did create a great deal of power for the executive branch and the presidency that had not existed before. Some of Roosevelt's new laws and plans did indeed fail as well. This is in no way meant to suggest that politicians should rubber-stamp every proposal that they encounter, nor should they allow the balance of power between the executive and legislative branches to be undone. However, to not enact needed legislation or to even try something new in government only out of fear that if it does not work, one might lose his congressional seat and political power, completely ruins the entire idea of popular representation.

A true representative for the people, elected by the people, does not avoid momentarily angering the same people if an action might prove to help them in the future. Nor does he fear losing his seat if he fails, because he serves at the pleasure of his constituency. A true representative relies on the people's support and wisdom so that even if he does fail, he knows that they realize he was acting in their interests. If politicians and parties felt more concern for the people and respected them more, they would not feel such worry about the possibility of losing votes and support. Only when our system is allowed to function without being controlled by fear, will the people find real representation.

When a fear of change controls politics, our government comes to a standstill as parties and politicians gain and lose small pieces of the same ground. On the surface, this might not seem so problematic for the citizenry; after all, our government was designed for the people and it has performed well so far. Why change what we know works? Unfortunately, it is not that simple; representational government is based on change since it is supposed to represent the public will, which is never stagnant. If representatives fail to account for the general will, then they fail in their duties as elected officials of the people. Basically, standing still means one never moves forward. And though officials should not subject the government to every passing fancy of the majority, they are there to secure the people's long-term interests and future.

Or as Alexander Hamilton put it, *"When occasions present themselves, in which the interests of the people are at variance with their inclinations, it is the duty of the persons whom they have appointed to be guardians of their interests, to withstand temporary delusion, in order to give them time and opportunity for more cool and sedate reflection."*[10]

Representatives are supposed to maintain our government by distilling the general will into a coherent and lasting vision of governance. Merely maintaining the status quo, however, is not the same thing as maintaining our government. Without corrective changes, our system does not just stay the same as it has always been, it actually starts to stagnate and then degrade. Just like something as simple as a car, which needs oil changes and new tires routinely, but sometimes even new engine pieces or a battery to keep functioning properly, a government, too, *requires* adjustments to continue to operate as it should. We cannot simply expect our government to run forever without any actual maintenance (just as making an appointment for an oil change is not the same as physically having the oil changed). Saying that we are changing, writing words that claim we are changing, even enacting legislation for change, is all meaningless unless we actually make whatever the change is. As citizens, we must ensure our government performs these necessary repairs to our system when they are required instead of allowing our government to simply run itself down due to a lack of even basic maintenance.

Public Apathy

"If we can prevent the government from wasting the labors of the people, under the pretense of taking care of them, they must become happy."[11]

- Thomas Jefferson

As citizens, we are ultimately responsible for the actual maintenance of our government, and not merely the maintenance of the status quo. *"Here sir, the people govern; here they act by their immediate representatives."*[12] When politicians and parties seek to undo our system by doing nothing, they no longer serve as our representatives, and it becomes the public's responsibility to set them straight. Because the voting public has accepted parties as the conduit through which political power must flow, we have accepted the consequences that they have for our rights and the health of our government overall. Just as our representatives have a duty to us and the general will, and that duty comes with great responsibilities as well as power; so too does being a citizen of a free republic.

Our freedoms may be based on what we believe to be natural rights, but those rights have to be constantly defended. That we have allowed our political system to become so corrupted and our government so stagnated speaks to our failures in our duties as citizens. Parties would not be able to form in the first place or continue to exist if we as citizens did not permit their presence. As the ultimate power in the government of our nation, we decide, at the end of the day, what happens to its functioning.

If greedy party rule has caused our system to stagnate as it pursues only its own needs, public apathy to the situation is what allows politics to continue in this vein. The government can only be supported by the citizenry. As the founders knew, the best guarantor of the people's happiness under our government is the people themselves, and so they gave us the ability to control our political system. When we, as citizens, stop caring to exercise that control or to enact change, our country falls into decay.

Our government was based on the idea that correction, revolution, and change were all needed in order to maintain the happiness of its citizens (which is the very purpose of every government). Our founders and their war for independence did not just happen overnight, nor was it easy. It required a profound change in the people and their fundamental beliefs on how government operates. It also required the people's dedication to enacting the change they perceived as necessary in order to create a free society. As John Adams iterated on the topic:

> *"What do we mean by the American Revolution? Do we mean the America war? The Revolution was effected before the war commenced. The Revolution was in the minds and hearts of the people; a change in their religious sentiments, of their duties and obligations…This radical change in the principles, opinions, sentiments, and affections of the people was the real American Revolution."*[13]

Even though the results and the meaning of the Revolution had caused dispute and partisan activity, the nature of the Revolution itself had been indisputably about change. The founding fathers, as political leaders, guided the populace through a war and the formation of a new government, based on the people's will and their rights to freedom and representation in that government. But for our founding generation, the discussion and the changes did not just end with the war or even with the creation of the Constitution. Spirited debate over how the government should perform its duties characterized early American politics. The formation of parties came from this passionate and intense public participation in the political process.

The founders disliked even this mild partisan form, even though they engaged in it, and tried to build a union among the different interests composing the new America. Upon taking office, after winning the incredibly contentious 1800 Presidential election, which saw the popular overturning of the Federalist for the Anti-Federalists, Thomas Jefferson used his First Inaugural Address to remind the people of the duties and rights that being a citizen in a republic required. And he extended the olive branch to even his most bitter political rivals, who he strongly disagreed with, and even those who still did not want a republic, by promoting those principles of freedom of opinion and the right of the people to their own governance, *"We are all Republicans — we are all Federalists. If there be any among us who would wish to dissolve this Union or to change its republican form, let them stand undisturbed as monuments of the safety with which error of opinion may be tolerated where reason is left free to combat it."*[14] Jefferson knew that public participation in the government was more important than political ideology or being perfectly right all the time in every opinion one held. The core of the republic was its citizens, and as long as they remained concerned with their governance and changing it when things went awry, the American experiment would succeed.

The contributions of its citizens, in every aspect of the political process and governance, are what make America great. When the public decides not to take part or to embrace partisanship without thought, our country does not function as intended. It is the duty of the citizen to regulate our representatives, politicians, and parties. That is not just how we maintain our rights, but also how we ensure that our government is properly maintained. By being active in the political process, we guarantee that our representatives are doing what the title implies, representing us, all of us, – and not merely representing their parties, their own interests, businesses, or any other interest groups or political supporters. We are the only ones who can regulate our government because we, as citizens, are ultimately responsible for that government.

We are the power behind every action or inaction that occurs in this country. When the public becomes apathetic to the way the government behaves, or how the electoral process works, or who is elected and what they do in that capacity, we are permitting our government to destroy itself from within. We cannot allow anyone to control us or control our government simply because it is easier or because they seem powerful and important. John Adams once wrote that *"The rich, the well-born, and the able, acquire an influence among the people that will soon be too much for simple honesty and plain sense."*[15] Despite the warnings of our founders, we have allowed parties and personalities to dominate our politics. In doing so, we allow those who were not intended to be the supreme voices in our government, to have more of a voice than they should.

> *"Passion has helped us; but can do so no more. It will in the future be our enemy. Reason, cold, calculating, unimpassioned reason, must furnish all the materials for our future support and defence — Let those materials be moulded into general intelligence, sound morality, and in particular, a reverence for the constitution and laws."*[16]
>
> - Abraham Lincoln

Passionate politics has only led us into the waiting hands of the dominant few through the party system. And while we need the participation of all the people and their active faith in our nation and its laws, we also need our politicians and citizens alike to find the importance in exercising control and judgment in our governance. There is a difference between the fervor and ardent nature of believing in something and therefore seeking change, and a crazed rage that seeks to take those beliefs and that change and force them on everyone else. As citizens, we have to take charge of our government and ourselves, as the power behind that government.

It might be easy to maintain the status quo, and it might be very difficult to enact change; however, in doing so, our political system actually accomplishes something for us and our fellow citizens. We cannot merely go on in the same train forever and hope for things to turn out alright, we must take an active role as the ultimate power in our country. There is no reason to let the parties control our system or our future when we should be doing so ourselves. Washington once wrote that *"it is better to offer no excuse than a bad one."*[17] Even better is to do our duty as citizens and not need to offer anything to anyone for our failures. We are the current generation of American citizens and we have the obligation to make the changes needed to keep our country on the right path for all the generations to come.

By Us: Looking Towards the Future & Pursuing Permanence

> *"This government, the offspring of our own choice, uninfluenced and unawed, adopted upon full investigation and mature deliberation, completely free in its principles, in the distribution of its powers, uniting security with energy, and containing within itself a provision for its own amendment, has a just claim to your confidence and your support. Respect for its authority, compliance with its laws, acquiescence in its measures, are duties enjoined by the fundamental maxims of true liberty."*[18]
>
> - George Washington

Our nation was founded on ideals and rights meant to last for generations, if not hopefully forever. The founding fathers did not create our government and craft our Constitution merely for two or three centuries use; they built it to last. Yet some place along the way, we, as a country, have gone astray and wandered away from the path laid down for us. We have taken the strong foundation built by the founders and removed pieces from it as we have wanted or needed to. But more and more frequently we have failed to replace those supports, thus weakening the entire structure. With our very basis so destabilized, we face the question many generations of Americans have faced before us, how do we re-strengthen our system and put ourselves back on the road to a successful future instead of the one we can now see of future collapse?

It is our duty as citizens to ensure the continuation of our country for the next generation. If we do not correct the course we are now headed on, we will miss our opportunity to do so. Change is never easy, but it is necessary in order for us to keep our nation and our government moving forward. In looking towards the future, we should always be pursuing permanence for our rights, liberties, and way of life. In order to get back on the right track economically, socially, and politically (both for ourselves and for future generations), we have to take a hard look at where we are going (if we stay on the same path); what we must change; and why we need to change it.

As it stands now, our future as a nation looks more and more bleak as we continue down the same road without hesitation. Our government is plagued by corruption and decay, our businesses care only about end-line profits, and our people increasingly distance themselves from their duties as citizens. Like many of history's great powers, we are in danger of approaching the point of no return, where our decline and fall will become inevitable. In many books and even in the news, it is not uncommon to hear comparisons of the United States to old Rome, and the parallels between the historical paths of both. Many educated people predict the same end for us as the incredibly violent and chaotic one that befell the Roman Empire as it collapsed from the combined weight of internal discord and external force.

Even the founders worried that this might happen to America; when Benjamin Franklin lent his support to our Constitution he explained that: *"I agree to this Constitution with all its faults, if they are such; because I think a general Government necessary for us, and there is no form of Government but what may be a blessing to the people if well administered, and believe farther that this is likely to be well administered for a course of years, and can only end in Despotism, as other forms have done before it, when the people shall become so corrupted as to need despotic Government, being incapable of any other."*[19] The fear of the ease with which the republic would be abandoned in the face of chaos and corruption vexed the founding fathers even at the very birth of our nation. But because they had Rome's example, they firmly believed in our ability to not have to traverse the same road, and to be able to change paths before we ever came too close to the same end.

Our founders gave our system the ability to modify itself, even up to amending the Constitution itself, so that we would not be forced down the same path as so many of our ancient Greek and Roman predecessors. The founders' generation had looked to these early republics and democracies as an instructive example, but also with the understanding of where these models had failed, and how these nations had fallen. Their fear of parties, factionalism, monied interests, standing armies, strong Presidential power, and social immorality (and much more), all came from their studies of these ancient examples. In informing their generation and future ones about these evils, they studied and sought to understand the past in order to safeguard the future. The founding fathers hoped that history would be able to teach American citizens these ancient lessons so we would never be forced to repeat them.

In seeking to ensure our future and to safeguard our country against a failure through internal and external chaos, we must pursue long-term goals as a nation and a people. Without a coherent plan for our future as a whole, how can we ever hope to achieve a lasting permanency? When explaining the lengthy and contentious American transition from the war to the government under the Constitution, Thomas Jefferson once remarked that *"We are not to be expected to be transported from despotism to liberty in a featherbed."*[20] The path of revolution and the creation of a government that ensured the rights and liberties of the people was never an easy task, and it had required great thought and sacrifice from all of its participants. Similarly, we cannot expect that further change in our country will ever happen without its own share of difficulties.

Ironically, it is much easier to find oneself losing one's liberties than enhancing them. Citizens often take the road from liberty back to despotism because they find it quite comfortable and effortless. The ancient democracies and republics, as well as many modern ones, have fallen into dictatorships and despotisms because it was so easy, and at the time, seemed like such a better option than having to vigilantly preserve their rights and privileges. After all, having someone else make every decision for one, taking the duties and responsibilities off one's shoulders, looks so attractive when one's government is full of chaos and corruption, and when no matter how hard one tries to do one's duty, one's nation seems as if it is still in decay.

In a deteriorating political situation, when a charismatic and popular leader promises to give a failing nation everything while taking away nothing, citizens flock to give up the rights and duties they possess. Julius Caesar did not just take power and turn Rome into an empire by himself; it was the people who put him there, who offered him a crown, who beseeched him to become their ruler. Likewise, after the French Revolution and the subsequent Reign of Terror, the citizens of the First French Republic embraced Napoleon Bonaparte and gave him his powers as a dictator; he never even had to overthrow the people to gain the ultimate political power (once theirs). The citizens of these nations failed to hold sacred their liberties when times became difficult, and instead of attempting to rectify their situations the difficult way through political change and hard work, they chose to embrace dictators because that was the easy solution to all their woes.

Acquiring Economic Stability

"The commerce of the United States is essential, if not to their existence, at least to their comfort, their growth, prosperity, and happiness. The genius, character, and habits of the people are highly commercial. Their cities have been formed and exist upon commerce."[1]

- John Adams

If we want to maintain our government and our rights in the manner that they were given to us, we must first acquire economic stability. Since the colonial period, commerce has shaped the nature of our people and our government. Taxation and tariffs that adversely affected the revolutionary generation's commercial endeavors were one of the major factors that provoked them into the war for freedom against Britain.

The economy is both symptom and cause for much of what we use our government and laws to legislate upon, as well as what shapes our views on the condition of our rights. Without a sound economy, the happiness of the people, one of government's key purposes, can never fully be realized. A people in poverty or suffering under economic hardships cannot prosper. (And though some might believe that the importance of the standard of living reflects a materialist culture in America more than anything else, one can easily look to other cultures that pride themselves on the immaterial or even an ascetic lifestyle and still find that there is a standard of living which even they expect their government to maintain for them, like not starving to death despite desiring to live an abstemious existence.)

While Americans might be one of the world's wealthiest peoples, we are not exempt from many of the economic woes that are the markers of third world nations – growing disparities between the richest and poorest members of our nation, disproportionate taxation and government benefits among the citizenry, an incredibly high national debt as well as high individual debt among the people, unequal access to healthcare due to rising costs, growing unemployment, and rising inflation, just to name a few hallmarks. These are not the signs of a prospering people, but rather a decaying one. If we are to change our country's future, we must first embark on the path of economic change so desperately needed to reverse these trends. And we as a people must be diligent and resilient enough to make these corrections to our economy even when it makes our lives more difficult in the moment.

The changes required to repair our economy are immense, and needed at every level of commercial and financial activity in the country. The fluctuations in our economic condition throughout our nation's history, the sometimes incredible ups and downs, are not merely the workings of the natural cycles found in every economic system. Rather, in America, the intense magnitude of these shifts and their timing clearly demonstrate poor planning on the part of our government and our people. One obvious reason for this is the nature of republics – since our government is based on the will of the people and elected officials do not necessarily serve long enough in office to enact a complete plan, we generally only govern and plan for the short term. But the whims of the public and partisan attitudes on government finance that cause changeovers every time they trade places in a particular government office are no excuse for the lack of a moderate long-term vision for our country's economic future.

Up until the late 1800s, the vague, but sound goal of geographic expansion into the West fueled economic progress and provided great opportunities for growth and success at all levels of our society. During the first part of the 1900s, it was war that provided most of the new economic incentives and a goal of military superiority replaced expansionism. Yet as the latter part of the 1900s came to a close and we entered the 21st century, there has been no broad national economy-defining need or objective besides that of greed. And, while greed has indeed had its place in our previous economic activities, it has never before been the sole goal and purpose of our nation's economy as a whole. Without change to keep our country on the right path, to regulate the goal of private gain, and to establish a broad objective that defines our national economy and gives it a direction to head in, we will continue to flounder instead of achieving the economic prosperity we desire and the economic stability we need.

SLAVES TO THE DOLLAR

> *"When you witnessed our first struggles in the war of independence, you little calculated, more than we did, on the rapid growth and prosperity of this country; on the practical demonstration it was about to exhibit, of the happy truth that man is capable of self-government, and only rendered otherwise by the moral degradation designedly superinduced on him by the wicked acts of his tyrants."*[2]
>
> *- Thomas Jefferson*

The initial prosperity of the new American nation and our continued success has given a great example of what self-governance can achieve on a grand scale. However, simply stated, all of our triumphs have given us a great deal of over-confidence, hubris even, in the inherent strength and longevity of our government. Man is indeed perfectly capable of self-government, but man can also induce his own degradation and even be his own tyrant. In this country, our vital commerce has become so vital as to make many of our citizens slaves to the dollar.

We choose this slavery. For many different groups and types of people, from the very impoverished to the very wealthy, money for money's sake, is the driving force in their existence. A future where greed governs is not one that leads to more rights and freedoms for the people. The level of corporate corruption and control over the marketplace and our society are only growing. If we take this growth out to its only conclusion, corporations and their interests will eventually completely rule our government, without even bothering to answer to the people. Our government will truly become an economic oligarchy, one where only the wealthy are permitted to have a say. This is not an idle prophecy of doom, we have already seen a dramatic decline in the ability of those without great fortunes to pursue political positions and exercise social power.

There is no stability or security to be found, economically, socially or politically, in placing all the government's power into the hands of a wealthy elite. When we look at our economic future can we honestly say that it seems full of promise? Do we see our future as more prosperous than our past? Or do most of us experience problems with our financial situations and see only economic struggles in our future? Despite the overwhelming modern interest in the nation's economic situation, we cannot say that the future we see is a good one, in any way, for our government or for us as citizens. If we want to prosper once again and to find the successes self-government can bring, the only choice we have as citizens is to turn our country in a new direction.

Our founding fathers did not live in an America without economic inequality or its own financial woes. They struggled against a large national debt incurred by the states during the Revolutionary War. They had to create a brand new infrastructure for the American economy and establish American credit abroad, not to mention produce a sound currency for use at home. In doing so, they had to face down the numerous financial interests that had helped to fund and fight the Revolution.

The issue of banking and money-lending within American borders and under the auspices of the American government became an incredibly contentious issue among our founders and the citizens of that era. As the first Secretary of the Treasury, Alexander Hamilton faced the enormous task of developing the policies and institutions that would regulate, control, and finance the budding American economy. His advocacy for the establishment of a Federal Mint and the First Bank of the United States (which is no longer in existence) led to the first debate on the constitutionality of a federal proposal (he was strongly opposed by Thomas Jefferson and James Madison, especially on the matter of the Bank).

Without considering the constitutionality of the means, Hamilton's ends were in line with the needs of the new nation, particularly in his goal of establishing financial order in a country plagued by speculators, financial uncertainty (which speculators thrive on), and a lack of a sense of nation-hood. The Bank ended up meeting with Congressional approval, but for a limited term of 20 years, which could be renewed by the Congress at that time. When its term expired in 1811, it went unrenewed as the same constitutionality arguments surfaced, not to mention it was also roundly opposed by the founders then in power and many of the citizens. With the national economy on a firmer footing, the ends no longer justified the means, and the founders feared to set a dangerous precedent.

The founders had to work hard to establish order in a brand new economy and to regulate the new America's financial affairs. And yet, they managed to place the country in a good economic position without permanently establishing any systems that could damage that position in the future. They deliberately recognized the need to set the example to which later generations of Americans could look to when making their decisions and solving their own problems. Upon ascending to the Presidency, James Madison observed that *"It is my good fortune, moreover, to have the path in which I am to tread lighted by examples of illustrious services successfully rendered in the most trying difficulties by those who have marched before me."*[3] As Americans, we are fortunate in having the model provided by our founding fathers and previous generations of Americans who have successfully solved their own crises, especially the most severe economic ones that faced them.

Knowing our problems and understanding what our future will look like if we do not change, how then do we go about solving them? Our economy is intimately connected with our society and our government, and their jurisdictions and effects constantly overlap. This means that like the ultimate power over government, the ultimate power over the economy rests with us as citizens. In his first inaugural address, Madison also revealed that *"the source to which I look for, the aids which alone can supply my deficiencies, is in the well-tried intelligence and virtue of my fellow-citizens, and in the counsels of those representing them in the other departments associated in the care of the national interests."*[4] When we look to ourselves and our representatives to virtuously perform the duties required of us as citizens, we truly can solve the issues that present themselves. It is through our own choices that we have led our economy so far from its carefully planned days under the first American generation.

It is also through our own self-interest that personal gain has become the most important aspect of American economic life. If we want to change our system for everyone and to re-focus our government, we must first accept that sometimes that comes with personal sacrifice. We have to be willing to accept that a good like milk might be a dollar higher at the grocery store, but that means that dairy farmers are earning a wage more appropriate for their labors and that gives small or local dairy farmers a chance to compete. We have to be willing to accept that the good of the whole might negatively affect us personally in a small way, but it is for the best because it affects others in a much larger manner. We can either choose to place our country in the service of the few or in the service of all. If we believe as our founders did that a government for the whole will always be better on the individual over time than a government for the few, we can place our own individual interests on the back burner for a time in order to secure our nation's future.

Savings and Solutions

> *"Knowledge is in every country the surest basis of public happiness. In one, in which the measures of government receive their impression so immediately from the sense of the community, as in ours, it is proportionately essential. To the security of a free Constitution it contributes in various ways: By convincing those who are entrusted with the public administration, that every valuable end of government is best answered by the enlightened confidence of the people: And by teaching the people themselves to know, and to value their own rights; to discern and provide against invasions of them; to distinguish between oppression and the necessary exercise of lawful authority; between burdens proceeding from a disregard to their convenience, and those resulting from the inevitable exigencies of society; to discriminate the spirit of liberty from that of licentiousness, cherishing the first, avoiding the last, and uniting a speedy, but temperate vigilance against encroachments, with an inviolable respect to the laws."*[5]
>
> *- George Washington*

The old saying that "knowledge is power" has never more clearly applied to a situation than it does to our own. It could also be 'Knowledge is Wealth', at least in our society. From the days of the founding fathers to the present, knowledge has been the surest means the citizenry possesses of securing our Constitution, our laws, and most importantly, our rights. As George Washington explained above, knowledge is what maintains our government and allows the people to rightly judge what is necessary for the continuation of our country and our way of life. The very purpose of this book is to provide knowledge to the American people about what was, what is, and what will be should we not change; but also, what could be if we do.

The power that comes with knowledge, especially in a republic, is the reason image is so important to us (as a public) and to the people who seek to use image control when informing us. We form our perceptions and our opinions based on the information we receive, and the more of it we have and the more accurate it is, the better our judgment can become.

One of the national topics which Americans tend to have the least amount of knowledge on is economics and fiscal responsibility, especially as it relates to our government. This means that the ability of many Americans to properly determine how our government should be involved in our economy and even how to manage their own finances is seriously diminished. To re-gain the knowledge necessary to manage our economic future, the first step is understanding our past and our present, but the second step means seriously considering how change will affect our future. In proposing solutions for the problems that plague our economy and offering them for public consumption, the citizenry needs the ability to sift through their options, as well as have a starting point from which to develop a concrete plan for change.

> *"As a very important source of strength and security, cherish public credit. One method of preserving it is, to use it as sparingly as possible; avoiding occasions of expense by cultivating peace, but remembering also that timely disbursements to prepare for danger frequently prevent much greater disbursements to repel it; avoiding likewise the accumulation of debt, not only by shunning occasions of expense, but by vigorous exertions in time of peace to discharge the debts, which unavoidable wars may have occasioned, not ungenerously throwing upon posterity the burden, which we ourselves ought to bear."*[6]

The first major step in securing our economic future is addressing our debts, both as a nation and as individual citizens. For the founding fathers, the first economic priority for the new nation was the payment of the debts incurred during the Revolutionary War. After much debate (concerned more with states' rights than the nation's finances), the new federal government had assumed all the former colonies' debts and thereby created the first national debt. Under the first Secretary of the Treasury, Alexander Hamilton, the federal government worked diligently on plans to pay off these debts, thus re-establishing good credit for the American nation and placing the nation in a position of financial security.

For the time, the war debt was not insignificant; as of January 1791, it totaled almost $75.5 million. It took forty-five years, until January 1835 under President Andrew Jackson for the national debt to finally be paid off.[7] The importance of paying off debts that we had incurred was clear even at this early date. Our government in the modern era, however, has not decided to follow in the path of our founders. The debt we have taken on and continue to add to while pursuing various projects has become unacceptable, and so has our continual inability to pursue paying this debt off.

As of March 2011, the national debt was approximately $14.21 trillion (given our population that would make each citizen's personal share of the debt roughly $46,000). Far worse, the most disturbing aspect of our national debt is that it places our government at the mercy of private creditors who can turn their financial power over the United States government into political influence. Foreign powers currently hold roughly 25% of the national debt, including nations such as China, Saudi Arabia, and other OPEC countries. This is the aspect of our national debt that the founders had found most frightening- owing money to American creditors was bad enough, but even more so, owing money to foreign lenders placed our government in not just a bad economic position, but a bad political situation as well. That is why for our founding fathers, actually paying off the debt, and trying not to add to it (except in dire circumstances) was of the utmost importance.

Our high national debt is not dangerous only because it prevents our nation from securing credit during times of actual need, like an unplanned war or crisis, but also in the way it influences citizens to not pay their own personal debts. As the national debt has risen, so too has the amount of individual debt citizens are willing to take on. The past few decades have seen a marked rise in credit card debt, personal loans, and even unpaid or defaulted mortgages and automobile loans. The problem is not even that debt is inherently a bad thing; it enables our government and us to make purchases that we might need at the moment, like a house, and pay them off over time. As long as we actually are able to pay those loans off and then we proceed to do so, debt serves a useful function for our finances. However, we are not paying off our current national and personal debts, nor are we limiting their size to our means.

As a historical example, the national debt in 2007 was around $9.5 trillion. The United States government had a budget of $2.7 trillion during fiscal year 2007, and since that budget was unbalanced around $162 billion ended up being added to the national debt. Not to mention that the interest payments on the national debt alone during 2007 were approximately $237 billion, making it the fourth-largest part of the federal budget.[8] So not only did we not pay off any of the principal of our national debt, we actually added to it. This has been a continuing trend in American governance.

The even bigger issue than not paying our debt or even continuing to add to it is that our national debt is so much greater than our government's income. If we do not start to pay off this debt now, our children's children will have a government that cannot even afford to pay the balance on this debt, and they will barely be able to make the interest payments at that point. The first step towards economic stability is acknowledging the problems caused by this immense national debt, and making it government policy to devote at least a quarter of the amount each year as is paid in interest towards the balance itself.

> *"A little patience and we shall see the reign of witches pass over, their spells dissolve, and the people, recovering their true sight, restore their government to its true principles. It is true that in the meantime we are suffering deeply in spirit, and incurring the horrors of a war and long oppressions of enormous public debt. If the game runs sometimes against us at home we must have patience till luck turns, and then we shall have an opportunity of winning back the principles we have lost, for this is a game where principles are at stake."*[9]

The next major economic issue that we must face as a nation is the management of the money we do have, to include paying our debts (that is the money we already spent as a country). This process is known as budgeting. The purpose of a budget is not only to account for the money we have to spend each month, but also for what we take in, and what we set aside or save. A balanced budget is one in which the expenditures, debt payments, and savings are less than or equal to the amount received. Basically, it is a matter of making sure the plus column is greater than the minus column. Unfortunately, as the previously mentioned figures demonstrate, our government has done a very poor job of budgeting.

Like the national problem with debt, this trend of poor budgeting is also apparent in the citizen population. Many Americans find themselves in debt in the first place due to an inability to make and stick to a balanced household budget. Our first economic cornerstone as a nation should be the payment of debt, and then the use of this national debt only in emergencies such as unforeseen wars or crises. The second economic cornerstone is a balanced budget that accounts not only for expenditures, but also for savings and investments in America's future. If the American government could actually implement and follow a balanced budget, our reliance on debt could be significantly reduced because we would actually have savings and investments to draw on during times of unanticipated, but costly events. When the government's annual budget is in the trillions of dollars, there is absolutely no excuse for ever over-spending a budget, or drawing up one without allotments for debt payment, savings, and investments.

At the heart of this issue lies the fact that the money the government is spending is tax-payer money, it is from the citizens of this nation. The government's actions also greatly affect the same, and are supposed to serve them. That means that we, over any one else, should have a say in how our economic situation is governed. By demanding that the government produce a balanced budget every year, we are ensuring our own economic stability. The best way to guarantee that our Congress and President do in fact produce a balanced budget, without deficit spending and that includes debt payments, savings, and investments, is an amendment to our Constitution requiring a balanced budget under these conditions. If the amendment includes a clause for the emergency assumption of national debt after a congressional vote, there should never be an issue, even in worst-case scenarios.

Fiscal responsibility is not optional for a country as large and as desirous of prosperity as America. If our government is not prepared to provide a sound and stable economy for us under the current rule of law, then we must amend the law to ensure that they do, because our happiness is supposed to be their number one priority.

In the same line, we must understand that taxation goes both ways. It gives the government yet another responsibility and duty to us as citizens, but it also requires us to give up something for the whole. After our Constitution was amended to include income taxation, our government has earned more money than ever. The important part of the income tax is not how high that tax rate is or is not, but rather if it supports a balanced budget for the whole. Undeniably there need to be cuts to federal programs and contracts, as well as earmark spending, which does not serve the public. But even then, taxation will still be necessary, even if it goes to a lower rate. We will still have an immense national debt to pay off, so now is not the time to markedly decrease government revenues.

The only way to support repealing income taxation in general is to give our government, which works for the whole, another source of federal income. The founding fathers used tariffs and excise taxes[10] instead of income taxes, but that too, will still come from the pockets of citizens, and will have significant effects on the expense of foreign goods and the international aspect of our market economy. Likewise, cutting all government benefits does not serve the American people, especially when a majority still use them, as they are also members of the citizenry that pay (or have paid) into the national pot. But if we can achieve a balanced budget, both on paper and in reality, we can put our nation back on the right economic track, and on a track to impose less of a financial burden, no matter what type of taxation is in effect, on us as citizens.

> *"It is certain, that various objects in this country hold out advantages, which are with difficulty to be equaled elsewhere; and under the increasingly favorable impressions which are entertained of our government, the attractions will become more and more strong. These impressions will*

prove a rich mine of prosperity to the country, if they are confirmed and strengthened by the progress of our affairs. And, to secure this advantage, little more is now necessary than to foster industry, and cultivate order and tranquility at home and abroad."[11]

The third and final cornerstone of a sound economic policy is moderate, but enforced financial regulatory laws. The government's duty requires it to maintain a sound economic system that promotes success and prosperity for the American nation. To do so, the government must create and implement rules and regulations upon every person, business, and government authority that engages in any kind of commerce in America. Ironically, we no longer merely enact the laws just necessary to promote financial security and growth; instead, our economic regulations are a complex web of hard to understand and even harder to navigate rules that allow our government to enforce or not enforce our economic standards as they please.

Tax reform is not necessary because we need to necessarily do away with taxes (the government has to get the money to operate from somewhere), but because the tax system is incredibly complicated, and it is ridiculously difficult for the average citizen to file a tax return. Corporate codes are even worse, which lead to businesses hiring (and spending too much of their budgets on) accountants and lawyers, and having to add disclaimers and legal jargon to nearly everything they put out to the public. Government contracts, a major source of revenue for businesses and states in this country, and a major source of expenditures of our federal government, are awarded by Congress without a system, real regulation, or any actual enforcement of the contract's terms. This is what enables corruption and cronyism in our government, because the laws we do have are too numerous, and the ones we have that we need we do not enforce.

The regulating bodies we do have are either mired down in protocol, like the Internal Revenue Service, or are not true government agencies because of a semi-public (really part government, part private) nature, like the Federal Reserve Bank. This means that none of these groupings tend to operate in the interests of the citizenry, and in the case of the semi-public groups, permit the rise of a monied aristocracy in our economy and our government that seek personal gain from political power. Without policies and laws that are easy to comprehend and enforce by the appropriate federal authorities, our government fails to play its important regulatory role in our economy.

Our financial regulatory system needs to set a standard, with a minimum of confusing (and sometimes even contradictory) laws. So that instead, we can focus our economy on the greatest prosperity for the public with the least amount of private influence or interference from the government (except when needed to enforce its laws). We already know what happens when we do not hold corporations, businesses, and individuals accountable for their financial missteps and economic failures. Corruption becomes rampant, the law is only enforced at the whims of politicians, and failed economic endeavors are bailed out in a supposed effort to keep the nation from economic fallout. Unfortunately, all of this does nothing more than damage our economy over time.

It is truly ironic that we have so many laws and that still, so many of them are currently inadequate for the regulation of our economy. For example, outsourcing is a direct result of trade policies, tax legislation, and current legal restrictions that make it cheaper and easier for corporations to take their business abroad rather than do it here. Our foreign trade policies do not make it advantageous for a business to use more expensive American labor than to pay less per hour for labor overseas. Our tax legislation, besides being unnecessarily complicated, also contains loopholes that allow corporations to carry their business to other countries and still benefit tax-wise. The real irony is that the laws we do have do not make corporations more inclined to stay here and they still allow for a great deal of corruption to occur among those who do. But when our government provides real economic stability for this and other financial issues by minimizing the myriad of laws, (but taking action against those who break the ones we have) we have always prospered as a nation and will continue to do so.

These three bulwarks will steady our economy and bring us back to a prospering economic condition if we, as citizens, will take the time and effort to establish them and allow their effects to be seen. The economic stability and security that should be our ultimate goal is not always easy to achieve, but it is what we need in order to thrive as a nation. As citizens, we must act and take responsibility for our economic future; we must demand of our politicians and elected officials what our country needs in order to succeed. This is most true in matters pertaining to our economy, with the backing of the citizenry, we can turn our financial situation around, but without it, our government will merely continue on the path already laid before it. Economic stability is possible, if we can only set ourselves on the right path- despite its possible short-term difficulties, in order to secure a long-term financial future.

Real Social Security

"Lessons my dear Sir, are never wanting. Life and History are full. The Loss of Paradise, by eating a forbidden apple, has been many Thousand years a lesson to Mankind; but not much regarded. Moral Reflection, wise Maxims, religious Terrors, have little Effect upon Nations when they contradict a present Passion, Prejudice, Imagination, Enthusiasm, or Caprice."[1]

- John Adams

There can be no real change in our condition as citizens in this country without considering the role society at large plays in every aspect of our economic and political existences. And in this area, of all, is where people can prove the most intransigent. After all, it can be very difficult to concede victory to another's views; to place personal interests aside for the good of the whole; or even to agree to disagree on matters which invoke our highest passions. Yet, as citizens, we must be prepared to do all of this in order to protect and enhance society in our republic.

Society has seen much change since the early days of our nation, but these changes have typically pursued the direction started upon by our founders. We have seen an increase in equality, liberty, and the security of each and every citizen under the law. Today, however, our concerns have turned from social welfare to economic welfare, or at least we have so much equated the two as to treat them as one. A sense of entitlement has swept over society, fueling discord and disunity that is no longer about pursuing social rights and liberties, but rather about getting more things.

Unfortunately, economic change will not inherently stimulate social change. Typically in a nation like ours, social shifts are much more likely to spark economic corrections rather than the other way around. As citizens, we decide what the predominant beliefs, morals, and interests which govern our society will be and in turn, which will affect our business and our government. If we do not think about our culture as Americans, individuals, and our society as a whole, then how can we possibly discern where that society is headed?

Our economy may be incredibly important to our prosperity and our happiness, but it is certainly not the most important part of finding happiness as a nation. Nor should we limit ourselves by defining our society only in terms of finance and money. The American Dream is contingent upon so much more than a nice house and a nice car. What good are any of those things if in exchange one must remain silent and obedient to the will of an oppressive government? Real social security does not involve a government tax taken from each paycheck or a government check received each month in the mail. Real social security is built by the people of this country who pursue a society that seeks to help all and hinder none.

In order to maintain the type of society we envision ourselves as having, we must be ready to correct our own faults. In linking our economy to our society, we have created a culture focused on the material, on the short-term, and on instant gratification. A lack of attachment to the immaterial things that drive our nation forward over the long-term and into the future has led to social stagnation and cultural corruption that parallels our problems in the economic and political sectors. From the top down, our society has become devoted to mass consumerism, cultural conformity, and personal convenience. Instead of trying to find the solutions to the problems that plague our society, we have focused our energies on getting everything money can buy.

Pursuing prosperity is not in and of itself a detriment to our culture as a whole, but when it overshadows all of our other dilemmas and issues it becomes one. We cannot pretend that our society as Americans is so completely perfect that we do not need to pay any more attention to it. Abraham Lincoln once said that *"Understanding the spirit of our institutions to aim at the elevation of men, I am opposed to whatever tends to degrade them."*[2] Slavery might be gone, but we still have social institutions that do not advance our people and only seek to set up a different kind of social elite. If we want to put our nation back on the path we began on, (in the same spirit of always pursuing liberty and freedom) then we must also reform our society.

Putting the Pieces Together

> *"Your aristocrats are the most difficult animals to manage, of anything in the whole Theory and practice of Government. They will not suffer themselves to be governed. They not only exert all their own subtlety, industry, and courage, but they employ the Commonalty, to knock to pieces every Plan and Model that the most honest Architects in legislation can invent to keep them within bounds...Birth and Wealth together have prevailed over Virtue and Talents in all ages. The Many, will acknowledge no other aristocracy."*[3]
>
> -John Adams

Our social issues are not all the same as the ones that troubled our founder's generation, though their essence has remained relatively unchanged. For them, the most obvious issue, even at the time, was slavery. In a society that longed for freedom, as well as highly valued said freedom (enough to even rebel from their mother country), slavery was a clear contradiction to what they believed and fought Britain over. Then, just as now, those who wanted to maintain a social system, which was based on abusing part of society, tried to justify their actions and ideas with a highly manipulated take on the rights and rules of the nation. They attempted to turn the discussion of slavery from one of liberty and equality into one about property rights, in order to get around the issue. In the end, it would take almost a century and a bloody Civil War to resolve just that one social problem. And even then, it took another century to give the descendents of the formerly enslaved the same rights and privileges as other citizens in society.

Social inequalities have not just vanished overnight with the abolition of slavery or the success of the Civil Rights movement. Our nation still faces a social system where embedded groups and people try to keep others out. Just because we have gotten better and changed our position on race and gender over time does not mean that these and other forms of social inequality have just disappeared. In fact, the social aristocracy in our nation has seldom even been addressed by our government or society itself.

The founders had been conscious of the distinctions that separated men from one another in society, and they tried to use the law and the government to minimize them. In the Constitution, they made this very clear; it states that *"No Title of Nobility shall be granted by the United States: And no Person holding any Office of Profit or Trust under them, shall, without the Consent of the Congress, accept of any present Emolument, Office, or Title, of any kind whatever, from any King, Prince or foreign State."*[4] The revolutionary generation aimed our society towards a future where these artificial distinctions between men would be erased, and where only merit would ever qualify a man to be a leader among equals.

The electoral system was created not in order to help political machines or certain families maintain their own political power, but to allow the people to promote those among themselves who could best serve them. In turning away from our original direction to one where name and party matter more than ability, our society has returned to the traditional societal attitude that wealth and birth really do matter more than merit. Our society has chosen to give preference- something that the founding fathers never imagined would become a social bulwark in a democratic republic. For two and a half centuries, citizens in this country have fought to diminish the distinctions in society that divide us into interests, factions, and classes. Why then do we not often see this fight carried into our own time? Instead, social divisions have only been made worse under the guise of the term "equality."

Social differences are not always linked, at first, to family or fortune; societies often create these differences in order to elevate some groups and lower others. In America, the highest social classes often favor social divides among the rest of the populace in order to keep them from becoming unmanageable as a united whole. Returning to the example of American slavery and civil rights, it was not merely economic interests that drove the enslavement and persecution of African-Americans. A social desire for dominance and control in a structured society run by an elite (first the planter aristocracy and later the capital industrialists) also fueled the systematic oppression of one group of people by another, purely on the basis of skin coloring.

It is very difficult for people to find equality when everyone also wants to be and have the best, or when some find themselves more or less fortunate than others. It is even more difficult when an entrenched elite aggravates already existing differences and fears deliberately to keep a people distracted from the real issues in society and government. And it is very convenient for those who do not want to face harsh truths to accept false ones, and for everyone to use the government to support such societal claims. As Thomas Jefferson once wrote, *"It is error alone that needs the support of government. Truth can stand by itself."*[5]

The oppression of African-Americans (for just one example) allowed the rest of society to ignore actual social divisions in favor of manufactured ones, supported through our political system. Many of the most racist Caucasian farmers and laborers had far more in common with their African-American neighbors than their bosses and leaders who lived far off in their mansions, and who did not feel the same cares and concerns. Yet for a great deal of time in American history, the color of one's skin could make one a menace or a paragon without regard to one's actual actions or activities.

As modern society has eased former social restrictions based solely on race and gender (among other minority identifying traits), many citizens have started to notice some of the divisions that have not changed since the formation of American society. The divide between the social elite and the rest of society has been brushed by the more modern discussion of the vast gap between the very wealthy and the very poor in our society (and many others). We have used change in attempts to rectify some of our social ills, and the success of our society thus far can be attributed to the willingness of the America citizenry to address such concerns.

However, we must continue to face our problems and move on instead of ignoring them or becoming distracted and allowing them to continue. An increasingly powerful social elite in a supposedly democratic nation is just one part of a larger problem. The main issue we face, which encompasses many lesser ones in our society, is that social distinctions continue despite adjustments to our laws and our people's beliefs. The favors exchanged among the wealthy and among different interest groups that engage in the political process aptly illustrate our biggest woe – the preferment of different groups in government and society based on sets of highly specific criteria.

When we single out, in society or in politics, any one person for favor or disfavor based purely on their status as a member of a certain social group, we are not promoting equality. Ironically, oftentimes, in seeking to treat others fairly or to atone for sins of the past, we have actually failed to treat them equally, as required by our most basic laws and principles as a nation. Abraham Lincoln once explained that when a man *"governs himself, that is self-government; but when he governs himself and also governs another man, that is more than self-government — that is despotism... no man is good enough to govern another man without that other's consent."*[6]

Our founders created our country based on this same principle, that freedom and liberty were found only through equality. When the law and society place everyone on the same footing, every man finds the liberties necessary to govern themselves. Unfortunately, in order to maintain an increasingly equal place for everyone, we must always be ready to change our society and resolve its distinctions when they cause the few to seek to put themselves over the many. Besides, without change, where would our American society have found itself by this point in our history?

Saving a Society

> *"When I consider the weakness, the folly, the Pride, the Vanity, the Selfishness, the Artifice, the low craft and mean cunning, the want of Principle, the Avarice, the unbounded Ambition, the unfeeling Cruelty of a majority of those (in all Nations) who are allowed an aristocratical influence; and on the other hand, the Stupidity with which the more numerous multitude, not only become their Dupes, but even love to be Taken in by their Tricks: I feel a stronger disposition to weep at their destiny, than to laugh at their Folly."*[7]
>
> -John Adams

Social change, being the most difficult of all change, has never been quick to come to any society, even here in America. The founders formed our nation with a simple-sounding idea, equality. But that idea has taken much time and effort to actually develop into a basis for our nation. Our progress towards this ideal has been stagnated in the modern era by the perception that we have already completely accomplished this goal. But in actuality we have not, and the first step in fixing the problem is acknowledging that our society is not perfect.

The second step is realizing that there is more to the equality of the citizenry than just words. The principle that citizens in America are inherently equal goes well beyond gender, race, or faith (or anything else); it means that there are no greater citizens or lesser ones; rather, every person is the same under the law. What this means in the every day is that we should not place the value of any one person over that of anyone else. When we exalt individuals or groups above the rest of the people, we allow them to dominate a society that is supposed to be about equality.

The only way to change this trend is to actually put our knowledge into practice. We must think about our social interactions and the basis for them. We must strive to treat people in a manner that corresponds to the fundamental American belief that each person is created equal. In a society based on this ideal, the exaltation of people is just as bad as the degradation of them. When we allow ourselves to be influenced on the basis of another person's wealth, power, or connections, we often ignore the advice of other citizens with wisdom, talent, or intellect or even those average citizens with a strong sense of what is right and wrong for our nation.

In evaluating the best course for our society, we must be prepared to take into account all sides of an argument, all the beliefs of the citizenry, and not merely act because some well-recognized person told us to do something or to vote in a certain way. Celebrities, politicians, and mouthpieces for various causes do not inherently possess the best or most correct opinions, and what they say should not always mean more to us than the voice of the average citizen. Why bother with a republic at all if only the views of the illustrious few mean anything to our political process?

The core of our nation is, and has always been, the common man, the average citizen. The founders devoted themselves to the creation of a constitution that would support and protect these people, the portion of society that had never before had a voice in government. By basing our nation on a government ruled by the majority, they hoped to enable the previously unrepresented to find representation.

As the leaders of the new American nation, the founders had both idealized and worried over this new hub of political power. Because most of the nation was heavily agricultural at this time, the majority of people were engaged in farming as a profession. The virtue and courage of the yeoman farmer had already been tested by the rigors of the Revolution itself. During this time, it became very common for politicians and political writers to sign their pamphlets as this or that "farmer" to demonstrate their union with the most numerous part of the population. However, the founders were just as unsure about the people's wisdom and ability to properly use power as they were sure that the people needed a part in the new government.

Instead of excluding them or curtailing their influence over the new government, the founders chose to focus on ensuring the education of the common people as a way to give them good and stable judgment. As Thomas Jefferson wrote to a colleague, *"Preach, my dear Sir, a crusade against ignorance; establish & improve the law for educating the common people. Let our countrymen know that the people alone can protect us against these evils."*[8] They realized that education and knowledge were the keys that would ensure the common people's prominent place in the new America. By placing the trust and hope of our nation in the average citizen, the founders sought to protect the people from the woes of government based on inequalities.

An educated public is just as important to our political process as any elected official or celebrity. When we realize this, we can focus our attention on ensuring our society's continuance and continual improvement through both education and equality. In conjunction with disengaging ourselves from a society of icons (as is currently the norm) we must begin to once again place the life of the average or simple citizen on par with the most celebrated of the citizenry. Even the founding fathers realized that their unadorned existence imparted to the people the great virtue they possessed.

We do not need someone to tell us how wonderful they are or how right they are to know that they are or are not these things. So why allow some citizens with loud voices and high profile television appearances to influence our most important political decisions simply because they are telling us what to do? In American society, one's importance is not supposed to be determined by the size of one's pocketbook, one's affiliations, or how many times one appears on television. But to escape from the grasp of this type of societal aristocracy, we must embrace the same vision that our founders held- that of an educated, equal citizenry where every man was also a common man. To change our society to one where equality really does hold sway, we must first change our attitudes as to what is truly important in a citizen of this nation.

"What spectacle can be more edifying or more seasonable than that of

> *liberty and learning, each leaning on the other for their mutual and surest support?"*[9]
>
> -James Madison

Liberty and learning are the keys to building up our government and our ideal society. With them, we are able to evaluate the interests and social factions that seek to influence us as citizens. Without them, we allow our personal passions to dictate our choices instead of using our informed judgment. Interest groups play off of our societal and cultural ideas and our desire to belong to a community of citizens. And since interested factions often appear to promote and further social unity, it is easy to see why they are so pervasive and popular. Unfortunately, social unity is not the same thing as cultural conformity. When we are governed politically, financially, and socially by the opinions of others, without regard to the facts, we cannot function with any semblance of cohesiveness. When the interest groups in our society seek to promote their causes and their beliefs to the detriment of all others; this means that they actually weaken unity as well as the equality advocated by our Constitution.

While we have a society that seeks to embrace all differences, our unity comes from respecting and understanding those differences, and that every citizen has a fundamental right to their personal interests, opinions, and beliefs. Our equality is based in the unity provided by the freedoms we all possess as members of the American nation. As interest groups and factions have eroded our liberties, our equality and our unity have also ebbed away. The only way to prevent ignorance and discord from ruining our society and our government is to direct ourselves away from our current heading, that we only started down at the urging of those who believe only themselves and their supporters are right.

Change means starting now in a renewed effort to ensure that liberty and learning triumph over factionalism and divisive attitudes. It has often been remarked by our founders and many of our forefathers that keeping our freedoms means that we must also be prepared to defend them. This maxim does not merely apply to politics or government, it also concerns the way we live our lives in our national community. If we do not protect the spirit behind the freedoms and equalities we possess under the law, then how can we ever expect our government to believe in and protect the same?

> *"How can any one who abhors the oppression of negroes, be in favor of degrading classes of white people? Our progress in degeneracy appears to me to be pretty rapid. As a nation, we began by declaring that 'all men are created equal.' We now practically read it 'all men are created equal, except negroes.' When the Know-Nothings[10] get control, it will read 'all men are created equal, except negroes, and foreigners, and catholics.' When it comes to this I should prefer emigrating to some country where they make no pretence of loving liberty — to Russia, for instance, where despotism can be taken pure, and without the base alloy of hypocrisy."*[11]
>
> - Abraham Lincoln

The solutions that we have come up with in the time that our nation has attempted to solve social and political inequalities have been drastic and subtle, right and wrong. Our differences have, in the long run, not ruined our society as many at one time thought they would, but rather, have empowered it. The ideal America for most citizens is no longer a place of homogeneity; it is one where those of diverse backgrounds and varied interests and beliefs can unite under one flag in respect of the equality of everyone else. It is a high standard that we still do not always live up to in word or in practice.

Our society still has its difficulties with racial relations and cultural divides, and we have still not completely risen above the petty baiting or simple misunderstandings that could easily be resolved by an educated and level-headed outlook. It is the relationships between citizens that shape the society we live in, and when those relationships are based in inequality and bad information then our ideal society becomes corrupted. Inequality does not just come in one form, and as Abraham Lincoln's quote points out, it has been directed at more people in American society than just African-Americans.

Ignoring the past will not make it go away, to pretend as if America has not been a place of bigotry or intolerance is to doom ourselves to repeat the same mistakes. But to try and solve the past by reversing old inequalities in the present is equally foolish; any advantages given to any group merely perpetuates the problems of the past. We have already taken the first needed steps by establishing equality under the law for everyone, making everyone in society equal in the eyes of the government. However, to place all people on equal footing in society, education is the only real solution. Accurate information and knowledge is the only way for society to function and maintain itself in a truly equal fashion.

Freedom of the press is what maintains the public's perceptions, not just in our political views, but also in our social ones. Without an independent and candid source of news in our nation, the people cannot possibly maintain an equal society. Instead of spending their time, efforts, and resources playing different interest groups and social factions off of one another, the press should be providing the people with unbiased information. De-biasing the press in America will no longer be an easy task. The pursuit of profit by the mass media and the desire to play a role in shaping public perception now dominates the news sources in this country.

Because of the important role of the free press in our country, it is easy for the media to confuse the citizenry and change the truth to meet their own agenda. As Samuel Adams once pointed out, *"How strangely will the Tools of a Tyrant pervert the plain Meaning of Words!"*[12] This means that the ability of the powerful to manipulate society to their own ends and standards only grows when they can control the media that interprets our actions as a people and a nation. The only way to change these behaviors is to hold these organizations accountable. At this point, the only way to do that is for the citizenry, who acts as the consumer of the material the media sells, to refuse to read or watch press publications that do not hold themselves to a high journalistic standard. In order for our society to acquire the knowledge it needs, those who broker information need to be held to an ethical standard by the public that demands that the information be accurate.

Like the freedom of the press, the freedom of religion is also paramount to our security and solidarity as a society. Morality and virtue have always been a part of the American experience, but one "true" faith has never been our standard. When we take personal faith from the private to the public arena, we undermine the equality and liberty that our founders strived to achieve. For the revolutionary generation, with their high passion in matters of faith, religion was just as important and valuable to society as it is now.

When a society begins to fall prey to commercial and factional interests, virtue helps to bolster the citizenry against attacks on their rights. However, when religion becomes just another tool of corporations and interest groups, its ability to perform its vital part in maintaining our liberties is lost. The few have never been above using faith to manipulate the many. That is why leaders and citizens, like founding father Thomas Jefferson, refused to limitlessly accept everything espoused by one group or person. As Jefferson explained, *"I never submitted the whole system of my opinions to the creed of any party of men whatever in religion, in philosophy, in politics, or in anything else where I was capable of thinking for myself. Such an addiction is the last degradation of a free and moral agent."*[13] Like Jefferson, in order to change our society and maintain a good government, we must be willing to evaluate each claim made by powerful groups and individuals for its truth.

> *"The liberties of our Country, the freedom of our civil constitution are worth defending at all hazards: And it is our duty to defend them against all attacks. Let us contemplate our forefathers and posterity; and resolve to maintain the rights bequeath'd to us from the former, for the sake of the latter. — Instead of sitting down satisfied with the efforts we have already made, which is the wish of our enemies, the necessity of the times, more than ever, calls for our utmost circumspection, deliberation, fortitude, and perseverance."*[14]
>
> - Samuel Adams

There is no magic cure for the many problems we face in our society. While greater education and freedom of information will certainly bring change, these two remedies take a great deal of time to become effective. They also require a commitment from the present generation to their future posterity if they are ever going to properly work. Unfortunately, modern society is focused on the quick fix, on finding the easiest and fastest solution for a problem instead of the right one. The process of changing our society is not going to be a fast one; it has taken over two centuries to reach our current state of what is still probably more aptly referred to as toleration instead of true equality. It had taken another two centuries before that for colonial Americans to decide that liberty and freedom were important enough to break with their mother nation of Great Britain.

Societies change their attitudes and habits very slowly, but what they can accomplish when they are willing to allow this change to progress has clearly been amazing. As we seek to educate our society as a whole, we cannot simply continue to make education just a formality or merely cursory in nature. The most important thing is for that education to be focused and clear; providing future American citizens, from youth on, with the solid basis they will need to make judgments on our political system. Education should not be equated with the possession of a degree or higher academics as something only for the brilliant few. Rather, it should be the bulwark of every American citizen in society and politics against the perversion of our freedoms and the removal of our liberties.

The real solution that education provides is that it allows every free person the ability to think for themselves. In a society based on liberty with free information at its side, education always allows the citizenry to make the best choices from what their governors present them with. Without this ability, we are not a people but merely a mass, only capable of being moved by the strongest forces among us. This is what the founders feared most about democracy and the average under-educated citizens of their day (hence the motivation behind the creation of the Electoral College); they dreaded that demagogues and powerful personages would become the only citizens able to orchestrate and control the masses.

When we can truly think for ourselves, because the information we receive is accurate and the education we possess prevalent over our passions, we, as citizens in our society, can never be so manipulated. Until our society chooses to return to our origins as a people with a free-thinking nature, we will always find ourselves locked in the same tired patterns. Leadership and guidance by competent and qualified citizens is not the same as domination by the powerful and wealthy among us. Education and information will return America to what it truly stands for – freedom of thought for every individual, expressible in speech, print, act, and even creed.

Perfecting Politics

"Tyranny of all kinds is to be abhorred, whether it be in the hands of one, or of the few, or of the many."[1]

- James Otis, revolutionary pamphleteer

The political process has never been perfect; it undoubtedly never will be. But just because we cannot necessarily achieve utter perfection does not mean that we should stop trying. Our government began on the basis of freedom from tyranny of any kind. As our politics have evolved, the struggle against any chains that would attempt to bind our freedoms has been a constant effort. And for over two centuries, this effort has been mostly successful in securing the rights and liberties of the citizens of this country. Our country's commitment to this continual struggle and the ideals of the founders and the revolutionary generation has never been in vain. But it is a commitment, and not an easy one. Good government under a republic requires a firm and permanent resistance by the people to any encroachments of their rights, as well as the conviction among the citizenry that both maintaining and expanding freedoms is worth the fight.

In the modern era, we have become more apathetic about our government and less vigilant against attacks on its origins from within and without. Our political process is no longer an attempt at perfection or a struggle for freedom, but rather, a study in the pitfalls presented by popular government. Modern politics makes a mockery of the things that our predecessors valued most in a popular political system. When did politics for politics' sake become so important that it was worth allowing popular liberties to be eroded? The great irony of the modern political game is that the people are more generally dissatisfied with their governance than ever before. The national opinion of all three branches of government has reached record lows, and still, little has changed. Throughout our nation, we all have become so wrapped up in our individual situations and issues that despite overwhelming dissatisfaction with our government, we have done nothing.

The key to political transformation is as simple and as difficult as actually doing something. If every member of the citizenry would stand up and struggle for what they believed was right in our government instead of relying on other people to do it for them, we would right now be inching closer to that political perfection we should always be trying to achieve. If our government, founded for us and by us, was more important to us, then there would not be the current, massive and national dissatisfaction with the political process. The citizenry still holds the real, substantiated power in politics, but nothing changes because we choose to do nothing. We have given over our power to intermediaries who do not always act in our interest or anyone else's interest but their own. To be an integral part of a popular government, we as citizens much actually participate in that government. It is our own involvement in politics that is the most needed part to continue fueling the fires of freedom.

Becoming an Eminent Citizen

> *"All see, and most admire, the glare which hovers round the external trappings of elevated office. To me there is nothing in it, beyond the lustre*

> *which may be reflected from its connection with a power of promoting human felicity.*"[2]
>
> *- George Washington*

Engaging ourselves in the political process is not just a minor role in our government; it is everything that our government is about. Our most eminent citizens did not become great because they wanted political power or to be President. Our greatest citizens, some of whom have been our greatest Presidents, were committed members of the community first. Men like George Washington or Abraham Lincoln, two of the greatest Presidents in all American history, were bound by obligation and a sense of duty as members of our country.

Washington and Lincoln were not men who pursued the Presidency for the sake of power or fame, nor did they consider themselves better or inherently more worthy than their countrymen to occupy that position. Instead they devoted themselves to their country and their people, not politics. And they firmly believed that their actions and example were an important part of the duty that was required of them as citizens. As Washington put it, *"Example, whether it be good or bad, has a powerful influence."*[3] They recognized that for our government to work, being a good citizen was the most important job of all.

Of all the Presidents in history, Washington is definitively the most beloved and admired. But why? Washington was a very mediocre general: he suffered many losses on the field; and the Continental Congress even considered downgrading him from Commander-in-Chief on multiple occasions. Among the founding fathers, Washington was not the most intelligent, nor was he the wisest, nor even the most popular. In fact, in contrast to the other founders, Washington was well below average. As President, his tenure was marked by the same amount of successes and mistakes as any other. Most of his Presidency had little long-term impact beyond the tradition (and eventual law) of the two term limit. Really, in most ways, George Washington was a very average man.

On the postponement of his initial ascension to the Presidency, he wrote to General Henry Knox and confided that: *"For myself the delay may be compared with a reprieve...so unwilling am I, in the evening of a life nearly consumed in public cares, to quit a peaceful abode for an Ocean of difficulties, without that competency of political skill, abilities and inclination which is necessary to manage the helm."*[4] Washington, above all others, knew his own lack of great abilities, and readily admitted as much numerous times, publicly and privately. And yet, both then and now, Washington has been considered the most respected and esteemed American to ever live. What makes an otherwise ordinary man the very person which an entire nation aspires to become more like?

Duty – if there was one trait that George Washington personified above all others it was that. His sense of obligation and responsibility made him the greatest and most respected citizen of his generation, not to mention a general, founding father, and President. Though he might have been an average man, his life and his contributions to our country have created for every generation, including his own, the model of the perfect citizen. When the nation called him, George Washington always answered, and it was this that made him a great leader of men as well as a great citizen. No task was ever too great or too small if it was done in service of his country.

Washington was a man with a sense of deep and abiding responsibility, of obligation to the country that had given him everything despite his own weaknesses. As a younger man, he once wrote that *"Nothing is a greater stranger to my breast, or a sin that my soul more abhors, than that black and detestable one, ingratitude."*[5] And as long as Washington lived, he expressed his gratitude in continuing to do his duty as a citizen, for his nation, regardless of his own personal desires and wants. He longed for his home and a quiet life on his plantation. After the Revolutionary War, he resigned his commission in 1783, and tried to withdraw from public life, only to be recalled to duty as the first President in 1789. Even after his retirement from the Presidency in 1797, Washington was called back to serve as a general by John Adams. When he died in 1799, he had still not managed to retire from public life. In devoting himself to his role as an American citizen, George Washington became the greatest citizen we have ever had, not bad for an average, simple man.

> *"First in war, first in peace, and first in the hearts of his countrymen, he was second to none in humble and enduring scenes of private life. Pious, just, humane, temperate, and sincere; uniform, dignified, and commanding; his example was as edifying to all around him as were the effects of that example lasting...Correct throughout, vice shuddered in his presence and virtue always felt his fostering hand. The purity of his private character gave effulgence to his public virtues...Such was the man for whom our nation mourns."[6]*
>
> *- Henry Lee's Eulogy for George Washington*

Abraham Lincoln, like George Washington, also commands the admiration of the American public, past and present. And yet, he too was a surprisingly simple, and frequently unsuccessful man. As a businessman and a politician, Abraham Lincoln had been an abject failure: his stint as a storeowner was decidedly not prosperous, and forced Lincoln into the militia service for income. And as a politician, he was recurrently and resoundingly defeated during numerous elections. Though an intelligent man, Lincoln had little formal education, and no claims to any learning through higher schooling, even as a lawyer. During his actual Presidency, Lincoln was neither popular nor particularly good as an administrator; in fact, there were assassination attempts on him before he even took office.

The opening portion of the Civil War was marred by grave error, confusion, and failures on Lincoln's part. Lincoln failed to see that the Union would break apart as severely as it did, and withheld action against the Southern States until after they fired the first shot. This left the North woefully unprepared and caused many setbacks during the opening phases of the war. His inexperience led to a poor selection of generals and aides. His policies stood in sharp contrast to his proclaimed devotion to the Constitution (like the revocation of habeas corpus and other violations of civil liberties) and they damaged his reputation as President.

As Lincoln himself put it, *"I claim not to have controlled events, but confess plainly that events have controlled me. Now, at the end of three years struggle the nation's condition is not what either party, or any man devised, or expected."*[7] He knew that his actions had been as much a response to events as a part of any great plan to control them. He held no illusions about his own perfection or the reasons behind even his most ill-calculated actions. But like Washington, despite his many missteps, Abraham Lincoln eventually became one of the most admired and respected Americans or Presidents to ever live. How did Abraham Lincoln ever rise above these problems to become so loved by the American public?

Simply put – morality – Abraham Lincoln always obeyed the dictates of his conscience. It was this trait that led him into his greatest mistakes, but also earned him his greatest triumphs. He was a man who embodied the very model of a virtuous citizen in a moral republic, as first envisioned by the Founding Fathers. Lincoln firmly believed that principles rather than mere self-interest should guide his own actions, and he trusted that if they guided the people's efforts as well, then the nation would never fail. During his *First Inaugural Address*, in an attempt to quell discord in the country over his election, as well as lay out his intentions for his administration, he reminded his listeners that *"While the people retain their virtue and vigilance, no administration, by any extreme of wickedness or folly, can very seriously injure the government in the short space of four years... Intelligence, patriotism, Christianity, and a firm reliance on Him, who has never yet forsaken this favored land, are still competent to adjust, in the best way, all our present difficulty."*[8]

For Lincoln, morality or virtue, present in himself and the American population, could solve even the most complex of issues, like slavery and states' rights or the identification of the true purpose of the Union. His sense of morality was the true revolutionary kind of republican virtue, one that was not necessarily dependent on his own opinions, but rather on the dictates of conscience, a communal conscience. Lincoln truly did oppose slavery, but when he was elected President, he tried to hold the Union together rather than tear it apart over the issue. It was his moral sense that led him to the conclusion that what was best for the country, and its people, was to try every alternative before war instead of causing more pain and suffering by aggravating an issue he believed the people would eventually right anyway. For his uncompromising virtue, Lincoln was rewarded with numerous political failures, and eventually assassination, but he never stopped trying. Abraham Lincoln's moral fortitude would later transform even his worst failures into triumphs, especially when seen through the lenses of history, and he has become one of our most beloved American icons.

> *"Abraham Lincoln had a moral elevation most rare in a statesman, or indeed in any man."*[9]
>
> – *William Gladstone, British Prime Minister*

George Washington and Abraham Lincoln are two of the greatest figures among both American Presidents and citizens. The sacrifices they made for their country, and the immeasurable good that they did for us as well have become things of legend in American culture. But why are they so important to us as icons and examples? Why have they earned a permanent place in our pantheon of truly great Americans? Because both of these men placed the responsibility of being a good citizen as a top priority. They helped to change and shape our country and to lead it through some of its most difficult periods by first and foremost understanding that role and what it required of them.

By embracing duty and morality and cultivating these traits, Washington and Lincoln became leaders of their fellow citizens by being good citizens, not superior ones. John Adams once wrote that *"A whole government of our own choice, managed by persons whom we love, revere, and can confide in, has charms in it for which men will fight."*[10] Washington and Lincoln both inspired generations of Americans to fight literally and metaphorically for the things they believed our government should stand for. And above all, they demonstrated for the future citizens of America the true nature of civic responsibility. Both of these men participated in our government during periods of intense transformation, and if we truly wish to change our own circumstances as citizens and to rediscover an America worth fighting for, then it is examples like these that we must follow. They showed their fellow citizens and all future ones that America truly is a country that functions greatly when it is run by the people and for the people. And they showed us that, though true citizenship can be both extremely difficult and intensely rewarding, it is always necessary.

Speak Loudly...

> *"What occurs to me is that the great principle 'that man cannot be justly bound by laws in making which they have no share,' consecrated as it is by our Revolution and the Bill of Rights, and sanctioned by examples around us is so engraven on the public mind here that it ought to have a preponderating influence in all questions involved..."*[11]
>
> - James Madison

The right to be involved in the creation of the law and the functioning of the government is an inherent part of the American experiment. As great as individual citizens like Washington and Lincoln have been, it is the collective community of citizens that truly shapes the nature of our government. Men on par with the truly remarkable Washington and Lincoln can only arise in a political system where there is a place for them. America has been one of the few places in the entire world throughout history where a man can and will be esteemed purely for his attachment and love for his country, and his devotion to its progress and its people. The right to a voice in our government has given each citizen the ability to excel, to achieve, and to triumph equally in service to and service from our country. By possessing the fundamental basis of power in the American government, the citizenry has the ultimate control over every facet of our society, including the ability to change that society.

Yet as time has elapsed, the citizens of this nation have seemed less and less inclined to utilize the power they have. Our founding fathers and the rest of the revolutionary generation fought and gave their lives for the right to representation in their own government. The Civil War was the ultimate expression of the American belief that every voice should be heard and that the character and spirit of our government are important enough to die over. But, in the modern era, these things have not just become taken for granted, they have become forgotten. The American people have been split into many factions while their dissatisfaction with their own governance has only grown, and still nothing has changed.

Despite the example of our forbearers, the right to a voice, to have a say in how our government acts, is not the privilege it once was. Citizens will gladly argue or complain or wonder at our government, but when the time comes, they will not vote, they will not exercise the very ability that allows them to make all the difference in our country. Or much worse, they will not deeply consider or concern themselves with who or what they are voting for, instead using their voice to merely echo those of a favored party or political faction without due consideration to the matter at hand. Our trivialization of the importance of the right to vote is a far cry from the immense value that our founders and forefathers placed on it. And without understanding or cherishing our right to self-governance, our country has floundered, unable to find the path we need to be on to continue to prosper.

> *"...let it always be remembered to your praise, and as an instructive example in our annals, that under circumstances in which the passions, agitated in every direction, were liable to mislead, amidst appearances sometimes dubious, vicissitudes of fortune often discouraging, in situations in which not unfrequently want of success has countenanced the spirit of criticism, the constancy of your support was the essential prop of the efforts, and a guarantee of the plans by which they effected."*[12]

Without the people as a backbone, our politicians, our leaders, our very government, all become meaningless. With the power to control the government, we must also accept the responsibility for the character and direction that government takes. Without the voice of the citizenry to regulate and guide it, our government will never properly function because its very design is based in the utter supremacy of that voice. The right to vote is the ultimate expression of the faith our founders had in the will of the people, and the exercise of that right is what marks us as free citizens instead of slaves to our government's will. When used as a tool by the people, the vote confers upon them the ability to alter any situation that may arise and to judge who and what best serves their interests in government.

Perhaps the greatest irony of that greatest achievement in representation, the popular vote, is that in becoming so broad, it has become unpopular, in every sense of the word. Despite numerous previously disenfranchised groups gaining the right to vote (through a series of amendments, no less), much of the American population still does not actually utilize this privilege. If any single thing is truly responsible for a lack of movement in our government's progress, it is this. How can we, as citizens of this nation, seriously expect our government to function when we cannot even perform the bare minimum of citizenly obligation, (not to mention the prospect of going above and beyond the minimum like national heroes George Washington and Abraham Lincoln)?

If a citizen cannot answer the call to vote on representatives and measures for his own community and country, there is no means of correcting the government's activities that will work. Our ability to vote is what can change everything. When we do not use it, nothing is within our control. But there is still hope, since it truly seems that the lack of voting is due to a belief that 'one vote does not count' more than the total disinterest of the people. It is those who desire to gain greater power over our political system and undermine the power of the population that attempt to keep up this appearance. In fact, they do everything that they can to make it a reality. However, if the citizenry truly desires to use the vote and to use it well, then there are other tools at our disposal as Americans to amplify the sound of our collective voice.

> *"I do not mean, fellow citizens, to arrogate to myself the merit of the measures; that is due, in the first place, to the reflecting character of our citizens at large, who, by the weight of public opinion, influence and*

> *strengthen the public measures; it is due to the sound discretion with which they select from among themselves those to whom they confide the legislative duties; it is due to the zeal and wisdom of the characters thus selected, who lay the foundations of public happiness in wholesome laws, the execution of which alone remains for others; and it is due to the able and faithful auxiliaries, whose patriotism has associated with me in the executive functions."*[13]

In combination with the power of the vote, our rights of petition and assembly permit the popular vote to speak loudly into the ears of our representative government. Problems in our society are not solved by hoping that our elected officials will inherently understand and carry out our wishes, but rather in ensuring that there cannot be any mistaking the will of the people. Since the days of our founding generation, public opinion has always had the ability to express itself through both word and deed. The very first amendment to the Constitution guarantees the *"right of the people peaceably to assemble, and to petition the government for a redress of grievances."*[14]

These rights were not just arbitrarily given; they were a direct reflection of the struggles between the British and the Colonists that had preceded the Revolutionary War. The American colonials had tried on numerous occasions, through numerous venues, to send word to both the British Parliament and the King that they believed the British government was violating their right to representation. On more than one occasion, the British responded by declaring all petitioners to be traitors and forced them to re-declare loyalty to King George III. The colonists held multiple assemblies (both peaceable and not) to debate or protest British actions, and many times British soldiers shut such assemblies of the people down. As time wore on, the lack of civil rights combined with the lack of representation really left the colonists with no other recourse to their political dissatisfaction besides armed conflict. Further armed with this knowledge during the formative years of our government, our founders ensured that there would be other ways to correct the new American government alongside the basic representation secured by the Constitution.

In the modern era, the rights to assembly and petition are frequently unused or used ineffectively. However, as with everything in our government, if the citizenry desires to put the effort into these rights, they have been proven incredibly powerful. The best example of the power of these tools is demonstrated by the Civil Rights movement of the mid-twentieth century. Mass demonstrations and addresses directed at the government aimed to cure the inequities still lingering between people of different races in America. The movement broadly employed the rights to assembly and petition to create peaceful civil disobedience and change after the repeated failures of litigation and legislation to actually create any progress on the issue.

The most glaring example of these failures was the inability of many African-Americans to actually vote despite the ratification of the fifteenth amendment in 1870, which explicitly stated that *"The right of citizens of the United States to vote shall not be denied or abridged by the United States or by any State on account of race, color, or previous condition of servitude,"*[15] and gave Congress the power to enforce this right. The Civil Rights Movement therefore began to utilize the power of assembly and petition to get the government to actually enforce the laws it had created a century previously. Sit-ins, freedom rides, voter registration organization, boycotts, and marches all became part of the American catalog of petition and assembly practices. These tactics not only focused the nation on the cause of civil rights, they actually worked in accomplishing the movement's agenda. It has not been so long that we, as citizens, cannot do something by utilizing these same tools in old ways or in creating new methods. Between the power to vote and the power to assemble and petition, we as citizens always have the ability to act for or against the actions of our government.

...And Carry a Big Stick

> *"Government implies the power of making laws. It is essential to the idea of a law, that it be attended with a sanction; or, in other words, a penalty or punishment for disobedience. If there be no penalty annexed to disobe-*

> *dience, the resolutions or commands which pretend to be laws will, in fact, amount to nothing more than advice or recommendation."*[16]

- Alexander Hamilton

The combination of our rights allows us to act to carry out our will in government. The final step in returning the control of our government to the citizenry is to ensure that there is punishment for those who do not govern according to the general will of the people. Oftentimes, we fail as citizens to punish elected officials by spurning them in the next election for simple fear of the other candidate, or because they spend great deals of money campaigning to convince us that they will change their ways. We do not want to be the advisors to our representatives; they are to be our advisors and the actors of our desires in government. And the penalty for disobedience should be the ability to remonstrate or remove any elected official from his office.

That is not to say that politicians will and should always express their views in exactly the same way or that the people will always agree on what their elected officials will do. But there are times, especially in recent years, when politicians blatantly disregard the need or want of the people in order to serve themselves and their allies, and then try to hide the fact from those who elect them. A combination of visibility, memory, and disciplinary activity will infinitely better serve the citizenry of this country in their handling of elected officials (who are supposed to be representing their districts and their nation). Through our rights and these principles, we, as the people of this nation, will be able to understand and monitor the political figures who seek to lead us and rule, in our stead, as our representatives.

> *"Government is a trust, and the officers of the government are trustees; and both the trust and the trustees are created for the benefit of the people."*[17]

Our government is a trust, and in order for that trust to work, we must be able to rely upon our trustees to act according to our will and for our benefit. Acting according to the people's benefit does not mean submitting to the people's momentary whims, but rather, standing above the fray and judging the people's true interests and will steadily. This requires a great deal from a representative in our form of government; it requires a willingness to become largely unpopular (and even lose one's seat), perhaps only becoming vindicated in later days.

Staying above the tide often requires great sacrifice by those individuals who serve in our government. And there will never truly be recompense for the times when they are called to do so, earning many of the population's unjust wraths for the moment. Perhaps that is why so many representatives follow the people's every whim or try to manufacture that whim among the people so that they can serve themselves in their government capacities. So how will we know then if an elected official is merely acting according to self-interests when he goes against our immediate will or if that official is trying to hold our long-term will in mind? Simply stated, it is visibility and memory pertaining to our government and to our elected officials' actions and activities that allows us to make this determination, as well as any others related to the votes and actions of our officials.

Visibility and a long memory are the best safeguards the people can require of the government in order to monitor how our representatives serve us. The American people have a right to information on and from their government and its officers. This is why roll call vote counts in our Congress are always 'yay' or 'nay', and publicly recorded for every individual member. However, only a small number of bills are actually subject to roll call votes, and the process by which a bill makes its way from committee through debate to actual voting is extraordinarily complex. And that is what makes it so hard to determine a member of Congress' actual views and complete record. It is also why it is so easy for parties and interest groups to manipulate the public's opinions on a member's positions, because they can merely present a partial view of a politician through the few bills that actually had roll calls.

The legislative system is at best, overly complicated, and at worst, easily manipulated. In the short term, every vote in Congress should require a public roll call simply because it allows the public to see what their representatives are doing, to ensure that they are keeping the public trust. Legislative reforms to make the process itself simpler and more visible are more long term solutions to these issues. Accurate record keeping, our written memories of Congressional history, allow visibility to be maintained over time, keeping the government consistently in sync with the will of the people. By forcing our representatives to keep their records public, the public always benefits.

> *"All obstructions to the execution of the laws, all combinations and associations, under whatever plausible character...are destructive of this fundamental principle, and of fatal tendency. They serve to organize faction, to give it an artificial and extraordinary force; to put, in the place of the delegated will of the nation the will of a party, often a small but artful and enterprising minority of the community...to make the public administration the mirror of the ill-concerted and incongruous projects of faction, rather than the organ of consistent and wholesome plans digested by common counsels and modified by mutual interests."*[18]

The government of the American nation, and those who seek to govern our nation should have no problem with the public persevering in understanding and changing their own government. Without discipline, the rules controlling our representatives lose their meaning. With it, the citizenry can ensure that their elected officials both represent them and receive appropriate punishment when they fail to do so. The vote and petition are not inherently punitive tools. However, there are three basic levels of punishment that can utilize these tools to achieve a disciplinary end.

The first is censure. Censure is when the rest of an elected body formally reprimands one of its members for behaving inappropriately. Clearly, the petition can easily be used to convince members of Congress to vote to censure their own.

The second is impeachment. Impeachment is when a legislative body votes to impeach and then convicts one of their own members, thus forcibly removing that member from office. Again, the vote and the petition are powerful tools to convince other members of Congress to undertake such a step.

The final and most drastic of all tools to punish an elected official is a recall election; in a recall election, the citizens petition and vote to remove an official from office for failing to do their will. Recalls are currently only permitted in some of the states, and banned at the federal level in America (despite being proposed as an electoral reform at various points in American history). Of any electoral reform proposed in this country, the right to recall possesses the most serious implications for elected officials, which is why it is such a hard change to get passed. Recall returns the power of the petition and the vote to the citizenry if a representative fails them, without having to wait for that official's term to be up or convincing the rest of their peers to censure or impeach them. Since the entire purpose of representational government is for the people to be represented, it is not a far cry to expect that the people should not need to wait for a crime to occur or a Congress to act to remove an official who is not representing them.

As with any protection of, or use of, our rights, it is up to us as citizens to carry the big stick – to compel those who we elect to always keep the trust they were given. Our founding fathers and predecessors have given us both examples of great citizenship and the tools we need to be productive and worthy citizens. When we follow in their footsteps and always seek to take action to maintain and correct our government, then our country and system of governance never fail us.

Every one of the problems, issues, and dilemmas we face as a nation and as a people has models from our past that we can utilize to create solutions for our future. The ultimate political achievement in this country is to be a good citizen, one who does their civic duty by carefully using their rights and their vote to take action in our society – regardless of whether one is the President or just a regular voting member of the public. It is upon us whether or not this nation will remain a "city on the hill" or fall into decay, and our actions are what will decide this for ourselves and our posterity. We are the people of this nation, the people for whom this nation was created and designed for, and we deserve every right and every freedom our founders constructed into our Constitution and that our predecessors fought to establish. The only freedoms better than the ones we have are the ones we make for our future and to create a more perfect union.

> *"Citizens, by birth or choice, of a common country, that country has a right to concentrate your affections. The name of American, which belongs to you in your national capacity, must always exalt the just pride of patriotism...the independence and liberty you possess are the work of joint counsels, and joint efforts of common dangers, sufferings, and successes."*[19]
>
> - George Washington

Endnotes

Preface

1. Preamble, *United States Constitution*

Introduction

1. Jean-Jacques Rousseau *The Social Contract* p. 88
2. George Washington, *Farewell Address* 1796.
3. Thomas Jefferson, letter to Judge William Johnson, form Monticello, June 12, 1823
4. Thomas Jefferson, letter to Judge William Johnson, form Monticello, June 12, 1823

1. The Founding Fathers: The Goodly Gentlemen

1. 56th of the Rules of Civility and Decency
2. Act 2 Scene 4 of Addison's *Cato*
3. 9 July 1789 message from George Washington to Congress
4. Francois-Rene de Chateaubriand in *Memories d'outre-tombe* (1848-1850) Book VI, Ch.8: Comparison of Washington and Bonaparte
5. 1775 letter from George Washington to Benedict Arnold
6. First Newburgh Address
7. 1791 letter from Thomas Jefferson to Archibald Stuart
8. Benjamin Rush on Thomas Jefferson
9. the epitaph on Jefferson's tomb, which he left both drawings for its design and the exact wording now seen on it
10. April 29, 1962 dinner honoring 49 Nobel Laureates (*Simpson's Contemporary Quotations*, 1988, from *Public Papers of the Presidents of the United States*: John F. Kennedy, 1962, p. 347).
11. John Adams letter to Jonathan Sewall October 1759
12. Thomas Jefferson on John Adams letter to James Madison 1789
13. Adams at the 1770 Boston Massacre Trials in defense of the British soldiers
14. 04 March 1813 2nd Inaugural Address
15. Jefferson on Madison in *Autobiography* 06 January 1821
16. Federalist No 51 06 February 1788
17. Alexander Hamilton letter 16 April 1802
18. George Washington letter to John Sullivan 04 February 1781
19. Alexander Hamilton, speech in New York, 21 July 1788
20. Statement by Franklin at the signing of the Declaration of Independence on 04 July 1776 as quoted in *The Record of the Celebration of the Two Hundredth Anniversary of the Birth of Benjamin Franklin* (1906) by Isaac Minis Hays, p. 90

21. French economist Anne Robert Jacques Turgot, Baron de Laune on Benjamin Franklin as quoted in *Benjamin Franklin: An American Life* (2004) by Walter Isaacson, p. 145
22. a soap and candle maker
23. Benjamin Franklin in *The Pennsylvania Gazette*, August 8, 1751 article titled "Appeal for the Hospital"
24. George Washington's General Orders as Commander and Chief of the Continental Army, 18 April 1783
25. Thomas Jefferson, letter to Richard Price, 8 January 1789

2. Radical Theories & Major Debates

1. John Locke *Second Treatise Chapter 4 Line 21*
2. Abraham Lincoln Statement to Indiana Regiment passing through Washington DC, 17 March 1865
3. *American Declaration of Independence* 04 July 1776
4. "Three Virginia Counties Defend Slavery" – political tract sent to the Virginia legislature, 1785 - *Major Problems in the Era of the American Revolution p. 260*
5. Thomas Jefferson, *Summary View of the Rights of British America*, 1774
6. George Washington, *General Orders*, 02 May 1778
7. John Adams, *The Novanglus Papers*, Boston Gazette 1774-1775 No. 2
8. Daniel Webster, 17 July 1850, Address to the Senate
9. Samuel Adams, essay published in *The Advertiser* in 1748, reported in *The Life and Public Service of Samuel Adams*, Volume 1 by William Vincent Well published Little, Brown and Co. Boston, 1865
10. George Washington *Farewell Address* 17 September 1796
11. That is the highest percentage of electorate turnout since 1968. However, given that a good portion of the eligible electorate was not actually able to vote (though legally allowed to) until the late 1980s (specifically African-Americans and women in many communities), the figures are skewed. Also, this percentage is up only 6.4% from that of the 2000 election, which was not particularly full of conflict. Most reports indicate that at least 78 million eligible Americans failed to show up on Election Day 2004. More people can cast a vote now than ever, and little more than half the people who could bothered to show.
12. Thomas Jefferson, letter to William Hunter, 11 March 1790
13. All one really needs to see to prove this in the modern era is the questions raised during the presidential election of 2000.
14. John Adams, letter to John Taylor, 15 April 1814
15. George Washington's 1st Inaugural Address, 30 April 1789
16. John Adams *A Defence of the Constitutions of Government of the United States of America* vol 1 letter XXVI 1787
17. Thomas Jefferson, *Opinion on Creating a National Bank*, 1791, quoted in *Writings of Thomas Jefferson Memorial Edition* ed. Andrew A Lipscomb and Albert E. Bergh, Vol. 3, p. 146. 1904
18. Alexander Hamilton, *Opinion on the Constitutionality of the Bank* 23 February 1791
19. James Madison, *Annals of Congress*, House of Representatives, 3rd Congress, 1st Session, p. 170 10 January 1794

20. Benjamin Franklin, title page motto of the book *An Historical Review of the Constitution and Government Of Pennsylvania (1760)*, which Franklin did not author but did publish, and he is considered to be the originator of the statement

3. Our Foundation – The Constitution

1. Thomas Jefferson, 16 January 1787, letter to Edward Carrington
2. John Adams, *The Novanglus Papers*, Boston Gazette, No 7, 1774-5
3. Opening Paragraph of the United States Constitution
4. US Constitution Article One, Section 2
5. US Constitution Article One, Section 8
6. US Constitution, Article One, Section 7
7. ibid
8. habeas corpus is basically a petition for another judicial authority to review the authority by which a person is kept in prison
9. bills of attainder are laws passed by Congress declaring a person guilty without the benefit of a trial, ex post facto laws are retroactive laws-basically it keeps laws from being retroactively applied to find a person guilty of a crime
10. US Constitution, Article VI
11. Alexander Hamilton, Federalist Paper Number 1
12. James Madison, Federalist Paper Number 10
13. Alexander Hamilton, Federalist Paper Number 9
14. Abraham Lincoln, First Inaugural Address, 04 March 1861
15. John Marshall, fourth Supreme Court Justice of the United States from 1801-1835. From the case *McCulloch v. Maryland* (1819) in 4 Wheaton 316, 421
16. George Washington, *Farewell Address*, 17 September 1796
17. John Adams, letter to Thomas Jefferson, August 25, 1787, *The Works of John Adams*
18. Though of course, there will always be various schools of thought among historians as to what truly "drives" history be it economics, great men, war, etc.
19. Thomas Jefferson, First Inaugural Address, 04 March 1801

4. Capitalism and the American Dream

1. Benjamin Franklin, letter to Jean-Baptist Leroy, 13 November 1789
2. Thomas Jefferson, letter to John Taylor, 28 May 1816
3. James Madison, "Political Observations" 20 April 1795
4. Franklin D. Roosevelt, "State of the Union Message to Congress", 11 January 1944
5. Abraham Lincoln, First Debate with Stephen Douglas during the Lincoln-Douglas Debates for 1858 US Senate Campaign, 21 August 1858 at Ottawa, Illinois
6. Benjamin Franklin, *On the Price of Corn and Management of the Poor*, 29 November 1766
7. Abraham Lincoln, Reply to New York Workingmen's Democratic Republican Association, 21 March 1864
8. Declaration of Independence
9. Franklin D. Roosevelt, *The Four Freedoms Speech*, 6 January 1941
10. Franklin D. Roosevelt, *State of the Union Address*, 4 January 1935
11. ibid

12. Franklin D. Roosevelt, *Second Inaugural Address*, 20 January 1937
13. John Adams, letter to Thomas Jefferson, 02 February 1816. *"de très bon foi"* is French for "very sincerely," literally read as "in very good faith;" French was both a popular and common language among the educated colonial class at the time. Both Adams and Jefferson had served turns in France as diplomats for the colonies.
14. The 16th Amendment of the United States Constitution. Some people still argue that this Amendment is illegal in nature because it violates the original Constitution, however, given that the original Constitution makes itself modifiable, this argument is flawed.
15. Plato, *The Republic*, Book I
16. Alexander Hamilton, letter to Robert Morris, 30 April 1781
17. Thomas Jefferson, letter to John Taylor, 28 May 1816
18. Thomas Jefferson, letter to William Plumer, 21 July 1816
19. James Madison, letter to James Robertson, 20 April 1831
20. George Washington, Letter to the Hebrew Congregation of Newport, Rhode Island, 1790
21. Alexander Hamilton, Essay in the *American Daily Advertiser*, August 28, 1794

5. The Big Business Boom and Bust

1. Abraham Lincoln, Speech to Illinois Legislature, January 1837 from "Lincoln's First Reported Speech" in *Sangamo Journal* 28 January 1837, according to *McClure's Magazine* March 1896, also in *Lincoln's Complete Works* (1905) ed. Nicolay and Hay, Vol. 1, p. 24
2. Franklin D. Roosevelt, letter to Col. Edward Mandell House, 21 November 1933, as quoted in *F.D.R.: His Personal Letters, 1928-1945*, ed. Elliot Roosevelt, New York: Duell, Sloan, and Pearce, 1950, p. 373
3. Thomas Jefferson, letter to William C. Rives, 1819 in *The Writings of Thomas Jefferson, Memorial Edition*, ed. Lipscomb and Bergh, Washington DC, 1903-04, Vol. 15, p. 232
4. Thomas Jefferson, letter to Horatio G. Spafford, 17 March 1814
5. 1886 Santa Clara County v. Southern Pacific Railroad
6. Franklin D. Roosevelt, Second State of the Union Address, 04 January 1935
7. Franklin D. Roosevelt, Statement on the National Industrial Recovery Act, 16 June 1933
8. Franklin D. Roosevelt, Speech to the Democratic National Convention in Philadelphia, PA, 27 June 1936
9. Thomas Jefferson, Nos. 3 & 4 from "A Decalogue of Canons for Observation in Practical Life", 21 February 1825
10. Franklin D. Roosevelt, First Inaugural Address, 04 March 1933
11. as of 24 July 2007
12. assuming a 40 hour work week for 52 straight weeks
13. "What the Boss Makes" by Scott DeCarlo, *Forbes Magazine*, 20 April 2006
14. This runs the gamut from a low of $624,000 to a high of $249.3 million (some CEOs do in fact reportedly make only $1 in wages, however, with exercised stock options, bonuses, and perks they usually earn within the same range as their officially salaried fellows)

15. as of 2011
16. John Adams, notes for an oration at Braintree, Spring 1772
17. James Madison, statement on 26 June 1787 as quoted in *Notes of the Secret Debates of the Federal Convention of 1787*, edited by Robert Yates
18. Andrew Jackson, veto message regarding the Bank of the United States, 10 July 1832
19. Franklin D. Roosevelt, Second State of the Union Address, 04 January 1935

6. In Pursuit of Happiness – American Financial Life

1. IBID
2. John Quincy Adams, "Society and Civilization," *The American Whig Review*. New York: Wiley and Putnam, etc., Vol.2 Issue 1, July 1845
3. James Madison, *The Federalist Papers*, No. 10, 22 November 1787
4. Franklin D. Roosevelt, Speech of the Democratic National Convention in Philadelphia, Pennsylvania. 27 June 1936
5. Franklin D. Roosevelt, Second Inaugural Address, 20 January 1937
6. Franklin D. Roosevelt, Second State of the Union Address, 04 January 1935
7. Alexander Hamilton, *The Federalist Papers*, No. 6
8. Alexander Hamilton, *The Federalist Papers*, No. 30
9. Samuel Adams, letter to James Warren, 04 November 1775, reprinted in *The Writings of Samuel Adams*, ed. Harry Alonzo Cushing, G.P. Putnam's Sons, 1907. Vol. III, p. 236
10. Benjamin Franklin, *Autobiography*, 1817
11. Franklin D. Roosevelt, Oglethorpe University Commencement Address 22 May 1932
12. George Washington, Farewell Address, 17 September 1796
13. Theodore Roosevelt, State of the Union Address, December 2, 1902
14. Theodore Roosevelt, Speech at New York, 11 November 1902
15. John Adams, letter to the Officers of the First Brigade of the Third Division of the Militia of Massachusetts, 11 October 1798
16. Abraham Lincoln, First Debate with Stephen Douglas, Ottawa Illinois, 21 August 1858

7. The Press or the Business of Informing America

1. James Madison, report on the Virginia Resolutions, "House of Representatives: Report of the Committee to whom were referred the Communications of the various states, relative to the Resolutions of the Last General Assembly of the state, concerning the Alien and Sedition Laws", 20 January 1800
2. Benjamin Franklin, *Apology for Printers*, in *The Pennsylvania Gazette*, 27 May 1731
3. George Washington, response to news criticism of his Presidency as quoted in *The Alumni Register of the University of Pennsylvania* (1925) p. 473
4. The Sedition Act or *The Act for the Punishment of Certain Crimes against the United States* enacted 14 July 1798 (expired 03 March 1801 and was never renewed or reenacted)

5. Thomas Jefferson, letter to Colonel Edward Carrington, 16 January 1787
6. Abraham Lincoln, Speech at Bloomington, 29 May 1856
7. John Jay, *The Federalist Papers*, No.2
8. The tale of the *USS Maine* actually carries even greater irony. The day after the incident, then Assistant Secretary of the Navy, Theodore Roosevelt, remarked that *"we shall never find out definitely"* what caused the destruction of the ship. Thus far, he has been proven right. Four investigations into the matter later, three of which were conducted by the United States Navy (two of which were official Courts of Inquiry), the exact cause and scenario are still uncertain. Conducted in 1898, 1911, 1976, and 1999, none of these groups came to the exact same conclusions on the matter either, and among Naval historians, the question is still considered to not be answered conclusively.
9. The publisher of the *New York World*, Joseph Pulitzer, would later express deep remorse over his "yellow sins", and would go on to re-shape the *World* as a highly investigative publication, but much less of a salacious one than it had previously been. Upon his death, he would leave money to Columbia University that helped to establish its school of Journalism and the now famous Pulitzer Prizes.
10. Thomas Jefferson, letter to John Norvell, 14 June 1807
11. Thomas Jefferson, ibid
12. Abraham Lincoln, letter to Allen N. Ford, 11 August 1846
13. Thomas Jefferson, letter to John Norvell, 14 June 1807
14. Thomas Jefferson, letter to John Norvell, 14 June 1807
15. Thomas Jefferson, letter to John Norvell, 14 June 1807
16. Thomas Jefferson, ibid

8. The Preacher- Finding the God of Freedom

1. John Adams, letter to Thomas Jefferson, 19 April 1817
2. George Washington, Farewell Address, 17 September 1796
3. John Adams, letter to Zabdiel Adams, 21 June 1776
4. Jonathan Edwards, "Sinners in the Hands of an Angry God", famously preached 18 July 1741 in Enfield, Connecticut
5. Thomas Paine, *Common Sense*, originally published 14 February 1776
6. Nathaniel Whitaker, "An Antidote Against Toryism", preached originally in Salem, MA and printed in 1777 as printed in *Faith and Free Government*, ed. Daniel C. Palm, Lanham, MD: Rowman and Littlefield Publishers, 2001, p. 160
7. Oliver Noble, March 1775 Sermon, as quoted in Dale S. Kuehne, *Massachusetts Congregationalist Political Thought 1760-1790: The Design of Heaven*, Columbia: University of Missouri Press, 1996, p. 117
8. John Adams, letter to Abigail Adams, 03 July 1776
9. George Washington, *The Farewell Address*, 17 September 1796
10. Thomas Jefferson, *The Virginia Statute for Religious Liberty*, 1786, in William Waller Hening, ed. *Statutes at Large of Virginia*. Richmond: AMS Press, 1823. Vol. 12, p.84-86
11. John Adams, letter to Abigail Adams, 15 April 1776

12. Thomas Jefferson, *Notes on Religion,* October 1776, published in *The Works of Thomas Jefferson in 12 Volumes,* Federal Edition, Paul Ford, ed. New York: Putnam and Sons, 1904. Vol. 2, p. 256
13. Thomas Jefferson, letter to Danbury Baptist Association in Connecticut, 01 January 1802. This letter, and elaboration by Jefferson, not the Constitution itself, is the origin of the statement "separation between church and State."
14. Thomas Jefferson, letter to Mrs. Harrison Smith, 06 August 1816
15. James Madison, letter to Edward Livingston, 10 July 1822
16. George Washington, letter to Edward Newenham, 20 October 1792
17. Thomas Jefferson, letter to Edward Dose, 19 April 1803
18. Thomas Jefferson, letter to John Adams, 11 April 1823
19. Thomas Jefferson, letter to N.G. Dufief, a Philadelphia bookseller, 1814. Sent upon learning that said bookseller had been prosecuted for selling the book, *Sur la Creation du Monde, un Systeme d'Organisation Primitive* (by M. de Becourt), which Jefferson had purchased prior to the incident.
20. Thomas Jefferson, letter to P. H. Wendover, 1815
21. James Madison, "Monopolies, Perpetuities, Corporations, Ecclesiastical Endowments", 1832
22. Thomas Jefferson, *Notes on Religion,* 1776
23. Alexander Hamilton, *The Federalist Papers,* No. 1

9. Cultural Conformity: Wealth and Power in America

1. Jean-Jacques Rousseau, *The Social Contract,* 1763
2. Jean-Jacques Rousseau, *The Social Contract,* 1763
3. James Madison, *The Federalist Papers,* No. 10, originally published 23 November 1787
4. Presumably James Madison, *The Federalist Papers,* No. 57, 19 February 1788. The authorship of this particular paper is disputed, and it could have been either Hamilton or Madison, but it is modernly historically considered to have been Madison.
5. James Madison, *The Federalist Papers,* No. 10, originally published 23 November 1787
6. George Washington, *The Farewell Address,* 17 September 1796
7. James Madison, *The Federalist Papers,* No. 10, originally published 23 November 1787
8. James Madison, letter to Thomas Jefferson, 17 October 1788
9. John Adams, Diary entry, 19 February 1756
10. Thomas Jefferson, *First Inaugural Address,* 04 March 1801
11. James Madison, *The Federalist Papers,* No. 10, originally published 23 November 1787
12. John Adams, "Discourses on Davila: A Series of Paper on Political History," No. 15, *Gazette of the United States,* 1791
13. John Adams, *A Dissertation on the Canon and Feudal Law,* 1765
14. James Madison, *The Federalist Papers,* No. 10, originally published 23 November 1787

15. Thomas Jefferson, letter to Isaac H. Tiffany, 1819
16. Thomas Jefferson, letter to John Adams, 11 January 1817. This statement as frequently been known as Jefferson's Axiom.
17. George Washington, letter to the Marquis de Lafayette, 25 July 1785
18. Thomas Jefferson, letter to William Charles Jarvis, 28 September 1820
19. Thomas Jefferson, letter to Richard Price, 08 January 1789
20. John Adams, *A Defence of the Constitutions of Government*, 1787

10. THE PRICE OF A VOTE – MOUTHS AND MEANS

1. Niccolo Machiavelli, *The Prince*, 1513, Ch. 18
2. James Madison, letter to W.T. Barry, 04 August 1822
3. Thomas Jefferson, *Notes on the State of Virginia*, 1785, Query 6
4. Thomas Jefferson, letter to Colonel Charles Yancey, 06 January 1816
5. George Washington, Address to the Officers of the Army, 15 March 1783
6. Benjamin Franklin, letter to his parents, c. 1728, as quoted in *Benjamin Franklin: An American Life* (2003) by Walter Isaacson
7. Alexander Hamilton, *The Federalist Papers*, No. 15, originally published 01 December 1787
8. Thomas Jefferson, letter to Samuel Keneval, 1816
9. Enacted 27 March 2002, Pub.L.107-155, also known as the McCain-Feingold Act
10. Enacted 07 February 1972, Pub.L.92-225, 86 Stat.3, 2 U.S.C. § 431 et seq.
11. Most recently, the issue of "bundling" has been brought up. This is where, due to individual contribution limits, people who combine many of these smaller donations together for a single campaign become highly influential in the election process.
12. So-called for their section in United States Tax Code, 26 U.S.C. § 527
13. G.W. Bush (R) spent $367,227,801 and John Kerry (D) spent $326,236,288 according to the FEC
14. Thomas Jefferson, letter to Josephus B. Stuart, 1817
15. Thomas Jefferson, *The Kentucky Resolution, 16 November 1798*
16. Thomas Jefferson, letter to Francis W. Gilmer, 27 June 1816
17. *The Declaration of Independence*, enacted by the Continental Congress of the United States of America, 04 July 1776

11. WHO CAN YELL THE LOUDEST: THE TWO PARTY SYSTEM

1. Thomas Jefferson, letter to Henry Lee, 10 August 1824
2. Thomas Jefferson, letter to Albert Gallatin, 13 December 1803
3. Presumably James Madison, *The Federalist Papers*, No. 51, originally published 08 February 1788
4. James Madison (possibly Alexander Hamilton), *The Federalist Papers*, No. 50, originally published 05 February 1788
5. James Madison (possibly Alexander Hamilton), *The Federalist Papers*, No. 51, originally published 08 February 1788

6. James Madison (possibly Alexander Hamilton), *The Federalist Papers*, No. 51, originally published 08 February 1788
7. Ibid
8. Alexander Hamilton, *The Federalist Papers*, No. 35, originally published January 1788
9. Alexander Hamilton, *The Federalist Papers*, No. 6, 1787
10. Alexander Hamilton, *The Federalist Papers*, No. 36, originally published 08 January 1788
11. Franklin D. Roosevelt, *Second State of the Union Address*, 04 January 1935
12. Alexander Hamilton, *The Federalist Papers*, No. 31, originally published 01 January 1788

12. Maintaining the Status Quo

1. John Adams, letter to Jonathan Jackson, 02 October 1789
2. Thomas Jefferson, letter to William Stevens Smith, 13 November 1787
3. George Washington, *The Farewell Address*, 17 September 1796
4. Alexander Hamilton, essay, 12 August 1795
5. Benjamin Franklin, *A Dissertation on Liberty and Necessity, Pleasure and Pain*, 1725
6. George Washington, *Circular to the States*, 09 May 1753
7. George Washington, letter to John Jay, 15 August 1786
8. Alexander Hamilton, *The Federalist Papers*, No. 73, 21 March 1788
9. Franklin D. Roosevelt, *First Inaugural Address*, 04 March 1933
10. Alexander Hamilton, *The Federalist Papers*, No. 71, originally published 18 March 1788
11. Thomas Jefferson, letter to Thomas Cooper, 29 November 1802
12. Alexander Hamilton, remarks on the United States House of Representatives at New York state convention on the adoption of the US Federal Constitution, Poughkeepsie, New York, 27 July 1788
13. John Adams, letter to H. Niles, 13 February 1818
14. Thomas Jefferson, First Inaugural Address, 04 March 1801
15. John Adams, *A Defence of the Constitutions of Government of the United States of America*, 1787, Vol. I, Preface, p. xi
16. Abraham Lincoln, *The Lyceum Address*, entitled *The Perpetuation of Our Political Institutions*, given to the Young Men's Lyceum of Springfield, Illinois, 27 January 1838
17. George Washington, letter to Harriet Washington (his niece), 30 October 1791
18. George Washington, *The Farewell Address*, 1796
19. Benjamin Franklin, speech before the Constitutional Convention in Philadelphia, Pennsylvania on its closing day as recorded by James Madison in *The Debates in the Federal Convention of 1787, which framed the Constitution of the United States of America, reported by James Madison, a delegate from the state of Virginia*, 17 September 1787
20. Thomas Jefferson, letter to the Marquis de Lafayette, 02 April 1790

13. Acquiring Economic Stability

1. John Adams, First Annual Message to Congress, 22 November 1797
2. Thomas Jefferson, letter to Francois de Marbois, 14 June 1817
3. James Madison, First Inaugural Address, 04 March 1809
4. James Madison, First Inaugural Address, 04 March 1809
5. George Washington, First Annual Message, 08 January 1790
6. George Washington, The Farewell Address, 17 September 1796
7. It did not stay that way for long; especially following the Civil War, the United States had incurred a great deal of new national debt. However, it has only been in the modern era that the amount of national debt has reached ridiculous figures, particularly following World War II and the Cold War, and we have been constantly adding to that debt instead of paying it.
8. Fourth after Defense, Social Security, and Medicare, see p. 26 of the Budget of the United States Government, Fiscal Year 2009, Summary Tables, which contains the projected fiscal years 2009 interest as well as figures for fiscal years 2007 and 2008
9. Thomas Jefferson, letter 1798, after the passage of the Alien and Sedition Acts
10. The most famous of which was the Whiskey tax which resulted in the Whiskey Rebellion.
11. Alexander Hamilton, *Report on Manufactures*, communicated to the House of Representatives, 05 December 1791

14. Real Social Security

1. John Adams, letter to Thomas Jefferson, 09 October 1787
2. Abraham Lincoln, letter to Dr. Theodore Canisius, 17 May 1859
3. John Adams, letter to Thomas Jefferson, 09 July 1813
4. *The Constitution of the United States of America*, Article I, Section 10
5. Thomas Jefferson, *Notes on the State of Virginia*, 1787
6. Abraham Lincoln, Speech at Peoria, Illinois, in response to Senator Stephen Douglas, 16 October 1854
7. John Adams, letter to Thomas Jefferson, 15 November 1813
8. Thomas Jefferson, letter to George Wythe, 13 August 1786, referring to the evils of monarchy and aristocracy
9. James Madison, letter to W. T. Barry, 04 August 1822
10. a social and political movement during the mid-1800s that believed in American nativism that started with its basis in the social fears and prejudices about the large influx of Irish and German Catholic immigrants to America
11. Abraham Lincoln, letter to Joshua F. Speed, 24 August 1855, Russia at the time was still under control of the Tsars and serfdom there had yet to be abolished
12. Samuel Adams, letter to John Pitts, 21 January 1776
13. Thomas Jefferson, letter to Francis Hopkinson, 13 March 1789
14. Samuel Adams, essay published in *The Boston Gazette*, 14 October 1771, under the pseudonym Candidus

15. Perfecting Politics

1. James Otis, *The Rights of the British Colonies Asserted and Proved*, 1764
2. George Washington, letter to Catherine Macaulay Graham, 09 January 1790
3. George Washington, letter to Lord Stirling, 30 September 1779
4. George Washington, letter to General Henry Knox, March 1789
5. George Washington, letter to Governor Dinwiddie, 29 May 1754
6. Congressman Henry Lee III, father of General Robert E. Lee, "Eulogy on Washington", 26 December 1799
7. Abraham Lincoln, letter to Albert G. Hodges, "If Slavery is Not Wrong, Nothing is Wrong," 4 April 1864
8. Abraham Lincoln, *First Inaugural Address*, 04 March 1861
9. William Gladstone, British Prime Minister upon hearing of Lincoln's *First Inaugural Address*
10. John Adams, letter to Abigail Adams, 17 May 1776
11. James Madison, letter to Joseph C. Cabell, 05 January 1829
12. George Washington, *The Farwell Address*, 19 September 1796
13. Thomas Jefferson, *Second Inaugural Address*, 04 March 1805
14. *The United States Constitution*, Amendment 1
15. *The United States Constitution*, Amendment Fifteen, Article 1
16. Alexander Hamilton, *The Federalist Papers*, No. 15, 01 December 1787
17. Henry Clay, speech in Ashland, Kentucky, March 1829
18. George Washington, *The Farwell Address*, 19 September 1796
19. George Washington, *The Farewell Address*, 19 September 1796

Acknowledgments

I would be remiss if I did not thank and acknowledge my husband, Jeremy. He has always believed in me and has always given me his unwavering support. Thank you, my heart, for the gift of your constant faith in my efforts. With you beside me, anything and everything becomes possible.

About the Author

A.M.N. Goldman is a historian and a retired U.S. Naval Officer. In addition to contributing numerous articles, reviews, and essays for a wide array of academic publications, Ms. Goldman has also taught history for several universities, and serves as an editor and evangelist for compendiums of classic literature and prose. She lives in St. Augustine, Florida, the oldest city in the United States.

Her latest work can be found at AngelicaGoldman.com

 facebook.com/AngelicaGoldman
 x.com/goldmanangelic1
 instagram.com/goldmanangelica

Other Tomes from Our Hoard
Discover More from La Lune Literary

Speculative Fiction

Horsemen of the Apocalypse by Angel Goldman

Strings of Gravity by Angel Goldman

Fantasy

Blood is Thicker by Angel Goldman

The Other Hans by Rebecca Jordan

Cozy Fantasy

A Tale of Mistletoe & Magic by Jacques de Bombelles

Thrillers

Blue Lines by Marie Goldman

Compromised by Benjamin Baker

Classical Poetry

Songs of the Sea by Angelica Goldman

Poems for the Holidays by Angelica Goldman

Children's Books

Mr. Morin's Musicians by Angelica Goldman

The Magic Violin by Angelica Goldman

Non-Fiction

A More Perfect Union by A.M.N. Goldman

Foundations of Freedom by A.M.N.Goldman

The story doesn't end here! Sign up for La Lune Literary's newsletter and you'll be first to hear about upcoming books, magical extras, and secret glimpses into worlds still waiting to be written.

https://www.laluneliterary.com/newsletter

www.ingramcontent.com/pod-product-compliance
Lightning Source LLC
LaVergne TN
LVHW041539070426
835507LV00011B/830